ADVANCE PRAISE FOR *A BETTER PLACE ON EARTH*

"Fighting inequality is integral to my passionate heart . . . *A Better Place on Earth* lit me on fire and made me want to run in the streets, banging pots and pans, echoing the sentiments and words."

—BIF NAKED, MUSICIAN AND ACTIVIST

"Our province is growing more unequal by the day, with increasing numbers of people living in poverty. MacLeod's book is an important insight into the effects of income inequality on people, communities and our economy, and points to what can be done to reverse this disturbing trend."

—IRENE LANZINGER, BC FEDERATION OF LABOUR PRESIDENT

"Poverty and income inequality sometimes resemble that hoary joke about the weather—everybody talks about it but nobody ever does anything. Andrew MacLeod, the legislative bureau chief for the online magazine *The Tyee*, has done something. *A Better Place on Earth*, examining the growing income gap between rich and poor and contemplating the moral, ethical, social and political choices it creates, frames one of the most important discussions that will challenge British Columbians in coming decades. MacLeod's book is a significant work of investigative journalism. It deserves a wide audience."

—STEPHEN HUME, JOURNALIST AND AUTHOR

"In our wealthy province it's outrageous that many people are struggling to pay for food. As MacLeod argues, this is a problem that together we can—and must—solve. In our 1 percent society, 100 percent of people need to hear the compassionate message of this book."

—ALISA SMITH, CO-AUTHOR OF *THE 100-MILE DIET: A YEAR OF LOCAL EATING*

"MacLeod's frank and investigative conversations with British Columbia's rich and poor, policy analysts and political elite are lucid, probing and deeply troubling. If relentless poverty, inequality and social injustice seem never-ending, read, mark, learn and inwardly digest this essential reading for changing BC's worn out neo-liberal political landscape in the 2017 provincial election. Policies for change are clearly documented."

—GRAHAM RICHES, UBC EMERITUS PROFESSOR OF SOCIAL WORK AND CO-EDITOR OF *FIRST WORLD HUNGER REVISITED: FOOD CHARITY OR THE RIGHT TO FOOD?*

"Inequality is a critical issue around the world, and in British Columbia it is no accident—inequality is a deliberate policy of the provincial government. That BC is Canada's most unequal province despite its abundant natural wealth is a travesty uncovered by Andrew MacLeod's important book."

—BILL TIELEMAN, *24 HOURS VANCOUVER* AND *THE TYEE* COLUMNIST, POLITICAL COMMENTATOR

"As the rich in BC continue to amass far too much wealth and the poor are disregarded, Andrew MacLeod's book is a must-read for anyone interested in constructing a more just and prosperous society."

—SARAH KHAN, STAFF LAWYER, BC PUBLIC INTEREST ADVOCACY CENTRE

A BETTER
PLACE
ON EARTH

A BETTER
PLACE
ON EARTH

THE SEARCH FOR FAIRNESS
IN SUPER UNEQUAL BRITISH COLUMBIA

ANDREW MACLEOD

**HARBOUR
PUBLISHING**
www.harbourpublishing.com

Harbour Publishing Co. Ltd.
P.O. Box 219, Madeira Park, BC, VON 2HO
www.harbourpublishing.com

Edited by Cheryl Cohen
Indexed by Nicola Goshulak
Cover and text design by Diane Robertson
Cover illustration by Teresa Wojcicka

PRINTED AND BOUND IN CANADA

BRITISH COLUMBIA
ARTS COUNCIL
An agency of the Province of British Columbia

Canada Council   Conseil des Arts
for the Arts   du Canada

Harbour Publishing acknowledges the support of the
Canada Council for the Arts, which last year invested
$157 million to bring the arts to Canadians throughout
the country. We also gratefully acknowledge financial
support from the Government of Canada through the
Canada Book Fund and from the Province of British
Columbia through the BC Arts Council and the Book
Publishing Tax Credit.

Cataloguing data available from Library and
Archives Canada

ISBN 978-1-55017-704-6 (paper)
ISBN 978-1-55017-705-3 (ebook)

TO SUZANNE:
*May our daughters, and everyone's children,
inherit the world we desire for them.*

CONTENTS

INTRODUCTION

"The rising tide lifts all boats, unless you're living in the trailer park, in which case you're flooded out."

—Mary Ellen Turpel-Lafond, BC Representative
for Children and Youth (interview)

O N WEEKENDS I OFTEN BICYCLE for a few hours around British Columbia's Capital Regional District. The ride inevitably takes me past the gates of waterfront mansions, through First Nations communities marked by rundown homes, alongside marinas harbouring yachts worth millions and past a line of people waiting to get into a downtown shelter for a meal or a place to sleep.

To say that there is inequality in British Columbia, a wealthy province that the government has at times promoted as The Best Place on Earth, is to state the obvious. Like me on my weekend ride, you can see massive wealth alongside dire poverty for yourself pretty much anywhere in the province, often within a few blocks of each other. More than one person I spoke to for this book described following Hastings Street in Vancouver eastward until both buildings and people became distinctly shabbier. Within a block, you go from high-end jewelry stores to payday loan businesses and shops with bars over their windows. In Prince George it's a short drive from the hardscrabble downtown to a bustling mall, then out half an hour to homes by the Mud River that list for more than a million dollars each. Kelowna, which boasts winery tourism and swish lakefront properties, also features people living in some 2,400 mobile homes. A childhood friend living in Kamloops tells me the north side of town is best avoided.

Inequality is certainly to be found, in differing ways, in other parts of Canada too. In British Columbia, like elsewhere, the wealth of the richest 1 percent has grown exponentially in recent decades while the majority have found their incomes stagnant at best or even declining. As seems to have become normal in North America, many in the middle feel they are working harder without getting ahead. While the wealth and celebrity of our richest is the stuff of fawning headlines, the stories run beside others about the persistence of child poverty and the continued reliance of many on food banks. Our richest have wealth that is counted in the billions, while others sleep in downtown doorways.

Statistics also tell the story (see Appendix 1: "Inequality by the Numbers"). British Columbia has in recent years often ranked as either the most or second-most unequal province in the country, behind only Alberta at times, when income is measured. This while the gap has widened in the nation as a whole—not yet on the level of countries like Brazil, Nigeria or the United States, but headed in that direction. If we look at accumulated wealth, British Columbia is easily the most unequal province in Canada. As this book was going to press, the most affluent 10 percent in the province held 56.2 percent of the wealth, a greater share than their counterparts were enjoying anywhere else in the country (see Chapter 3). By comparison, the bottom half of the population held 3.1 percent of the wealth, an amount that masked the fact that people in the bottom 10 percent had negative wealth—they owed more than they owned.

The disparity raises many questions: How did we get this way? How much does it matter? If unequal outcomes are necessary in a competitive economy, how much of a divide is optimal? Are we doing enough to make sure everyone has an equal opportunity to succeed? And can we rely on jobs and development, as incumbent Premier Christy Clark has promoted, to provide for everyone?

Examining the dynamics of inequality in British Columbia—what we've gotten wrong and right in the province—will, I hope, be useful to people everywhere. There are clearly lessons for British Columbians, but also for people outside the province assessing the fairness of political and economic systems in their own jurisdictions.

Reducing inequality is one of the defining challenges of our time. While the political left has long focused on the issue, today calling for action on it puts me in company that stretches far across the political spectrum. In recent years Bank of England Governor Mark Carney, US Federal Reserve System chair Janet Yellen, American billionaire Warren Buffett, the Organization for Economic Co-operation and Development (OECD), and the Business Council of British Columbia (BCBC) have all touted inequality as a subject that needs closer attention. There are questions about what can be done, and what stands in the way of doing those things. If incomes become more equal, how do you balance that with the limits of the environment? If the planet is strained already, can we all hope to live with ecological footprints that match those of the 1-percenters?

Writing a book on income and wealth inequality seems to demand some self-reflection. Like many Canadians, I think of myself as middle class, though the details of anyone's life tend to add up to a more complicated picture than the label suggests. My father, a medical doctor and academic, has been in the top tier of earners for much of his career. I was raised in a home where there was always money for vacations, recreation, books and other nice things, not to mention food and shelter. My mother has a university degree, but stayed home while my sister and I were young. My parents separated when I was ten years old. I went to public schools, some in working-class neighbourhoods, but attended a summer camp where the instructors and other campers included children of the country's political and business elite.

I would also say that as an adult I'm downwardly mobile, thanks mainly to having been drawn to a modestly paying profession in what some see as a sunset industry. Income figures are most often quoted as a median, the number where there are an equal number of people who earn higher and lower. Medians are different from averages, which can skew things. BC magnate Jim Pattison and I averaged something like $600 million in 2013, but that doesn't tell you much about how either of us actually did. I make an income significantly above the 2011 BC median for individuals of $28,930, but for several years while my wife, Suzanne, stayed home raising our young children we were well below the household median of $69,150. A social worker, she has since returned to full-time work, bumping us up a couple of notches. We live with our two children in a comfortable house that we bought before the real estate market skyrocketed. We try to limit our consumerism. We both come from family backgrounds that valued and helped pay for post-secondary education, and there's been help in saving money for our kids to go to college or university. Which is all to say that thanks largely to lucky real estate timing, family help and general thriftiness, our household net worth is above average. In general, our life is not a struggle.

The point is that we each come to these issues from our own perspective. I recognize my own has been coloured by privilege. But finances don't tell the whole story. I believe that the security I want for myself and my family, and that we've had, should be available to all. By and large the system has benefited me and my extended family. At the same time, I don't have to look far in my everyday life to find people who have ended up on the losing end of the economy.

In 2004, the first pieces I ever wrote for *The Tyee*—an independent online BC magazine—formed a four-part series on the welfare system and the challenges people living in poverty face. Over the years I have covered child poverty rates, welfare cutbacks and the rise in homelessness and food bank use as if they were somehow separate from the province's obvious wealth. Stepping back and looking at those issues now through the wider lens of inequality, bringing both poor and rich into view, makes it clear that we all have a place in the picture. There are still people who see poverty as someone else's problem, but inequality really does involve everyone in British Columbia—and everyone around the planet, for that matter. Increasingly inequality is breaking into public consciousness with demonstrations like those of the Occupy movement or Idle No More, or a surprise bestselling book like *Capital in the Twenty-First Century* (2014), by French economist Thomas Piketty. In mid-2014 the OECD warned that, in the words of The Canadian Press, "inequality is rising in Canada and…it is increasingly becoming a two-speed economy." People from many facets of life—business and politics included—are starting to recognize the importance of the issue, even if there's little agreement on the solutions.

The good news is there's nothing natural about the current distribution of incomes and wealth. As Piketty expressed it, "The history of inequality has not been a long, tranquil river. There have been many twists and turns and certainly no irrepressible, regular tendency toward a 'natural' equilibrium." We've gotten where we are through public policies that led to one set of results, and we can achieve a different result by either adjusting those policies or replacing them with others that are fairer. Our trend in recent decades has been towards greater inequality, but there is a growing global consensus and concern that the current distribution is damaging to individuals, societies and economies.

Many of the policies that would make a difference can be set at the national and provincial levels. With sustained attention we can make sure everyone's basic needs are met, pull back stratospheric incomes and create a fairer society with a stronger economy. If we're careful about it, we can do this in a way that doesn't increase the burden on the environment. We can build an economy that's more resilient and that allows individuals room to take chances, make mistakes or experience bad luck without condemning them to a life of poverty. In British Columbia, with ample natural resources and a diverse population, we are particularly well placed to lead in

SUFFERING IN PARADISE: INEVITABLE OR A "ONE-WAY STREET TO THE FRENCH REVOLUTION"?

IT WAS A SUNNY DAY in British Columbia's capital when I met Jessica Sothcott and her fourteen-year-old daughter, Rosalie, on the front steps of the provincial parliament building. In one of the wealthiest provinces in one of the richest countries in the world, where signs of affluence are everywhere, the mother and daughter were suffering.

They were at the legislature in May 2014 as guests of the official Opposition, which for months had been pushing the government to reverse a policy under which every dollar that parents like Sothcott were getting in child support was being clawed back from the disability or welfare payments they received from the province.

"I was shocked," said Sothcott, a mother of two, her dark hair pulled into a ponytail, a brace on one wrist. She could go to a job and earn as much as $9,600 a year without it affecting the amount she received in disability payments, but had discovered what she was receiving in child support from her daughter's father was deducted in full from what the government would provide.

Sothcott said she raised the matter with the office that administers the province's Persons With Disabilities benefits. "When I finally got on PWD, I went there and I said, 'Why are you taking my child support off my cheque still, because I'm allowed to earn $800 a month?' And they said, 'Oh, you don't *earn* that money.'

"I walked away," she said. "I didn't know what to say. I'm like, well, I'm pretty sure I do."

Sitting on a wall outside the legislature, Sothcott outlined her family's budget. Disability payments from the government covered her rent in subsidized housing in downtown Victoria, leaving $500 a month for everything else, including nearly $200 for medication to treat what she described as a workplace injury. The child support payments that the government was taking back amounted to $187 a month, a significant amount in their tight budget, she said.

"Having that money would mean a lot for both of us," Sothcott said. "It would mean more food. It would mean maybe being able to go out to a beach somewhere, pay for gas. It would mean her having pocket money to spend time with her friends, go to movies, do normal teenager stuff and not have to worry about what we're eating for dinner."

Besides Rosalie, Sothcott had a twenty-one-year-old son who had been having difficulty finding work. He was eating with his mom and Rosalie, but sleeping at his stepfather's house. "We don't skip meals, just my mom does," Rosalie said. "She has to sometimes not eat so we can have enough food." A Grade 8 student at Colquitz Middle School in Victoria, she found the government's policy made little sense. "I think the clawback—that whole thing—is ridiculous," she said. "Why are you taking a fourteen-year-old girl's money? I just think it's so dumb."

The provincial New Democratic Party spent much of early 2014 going after the BC Liberal government in the legislature on the child support clawback decision, making the point that many people, mainly single women and their children living in poverty, were in the same situation. "There are many children who are impacted by this policy who can't share their story, they're too young," Michelle Mungall, the NDP critic for social development, said in an interview. "For as long as their parent is on income assistance—and for many it will be for their life because their parents have disabilities that prevent them from working—those children will not be able to access their child support," she said, noting it was courageous of Sothcott's daughter to come to the legislature and have her story shared with the public.

Sothcott said she wasn't interested in politics and had never voted, but she found seeing the NDP fight to end the clawback of child support inspiring. "I'm seeing it in a different light now," she said. "I think it's time people stand up and start fighting...That's hopeful because the current government is wrong on so many levels."

Later that day, with the Sothcotts watching from the public gallery, provincial NDP leader John Horgan raised the issue during Question Period. Premier Christy Clark began her response on a note of empathy. Her son Hamish was then twelve years old, and since around 2009 she'd been separated from his father whom she had since divorced. "Being a single parent is difficult," said Clark. "Any of us who experience that on a day-to-day basis know how hard it is, but for some parents it is a lot more difficult than it is for others." At the same time, the government needs to be fair both to people who are dependent on the system and to people who pay taxes, said Clark, who as premier was making around $180,000 a year—enough to put her just shy of being in the top 1 percent of earners in Canada. "The reason that the government asks for that money back is because it's income," she said. While some parents might receive quite a bit of child support, others were receiving little, she said. "We want to make sure we're fair across the system." Rather than supporting people directly, the main help the government could provide was to assist parents getting back into the workforce, she said. "We believe on this side of the House that the best and the only way to lift people out of poverty, to lift families out of poverty, is to grow the economy."

NDP leader Horgan derided the premier's response. If the government has acknowledged someone has a disability and needs support, it's ludicrous to tell that person to find a job, he said. "I thought it was impossible, but somehow the premier just said liquefied natural gas is going to help people on disability income assistance feed their children," he said. "I don't know how that's going to happen, but apparently in the world the premier lives in, that's the case."

Clark later told reporters she favours raising assistance rates, particularly for people with disabilities, once the provincial economy and government budget can sustain the increase. "We need to do it when we can afford it, and it needs to be done across the board," she said. "When it comes to child support payments, some are quite small, some are quite large. I don't think taxpayers across the province would say that in the case of every child support payment, they would like to add on their support for people who may or may not need it."

Don McRae, BC's social development minister, said in an interview that while he was sympathetic, the government couldn't afford the roughly $17 million it would cost to allow parents receiving government benefits to keep child support payments. The needed amount is tiny compared to the provincial budget, which was in the order of $45 billion in 2014. The NDP pointed out repeatedly that the figure was similar to the amount the government spent on advertising ahead of the 2013 election. "You know what, I would like to continue to reform income assistance opportunities or programs in the province," McRae said. "One of the things I'd like to do is grow the economy so we can make these choices. There's lots of good ideas out there, by all means." Asked why child support payments are clawed back while money from earned income is not, McRae said, "That was a policy decision based before my time." He added, "Income assistance is income of last resort. The first responsibility is for the parents to pay for the children's needs. That's what we want to happen in British Columbia." McRae left the door open to making the change, which the government did eventually announce as part of the February 2015 budget. "I can't say today we're making a change tomorrow, because every time you make a change, it comes at an expense."

Later that day I found Sothcott outside the parliament building as she and Rosalie were leaving. "It's clear to me they don't care," she said, reflecting on what she had heard in the legislature and finding it insulting. "They do not care about the children of BC, they do not care about my child. They don't care." She questioned how much Clark understood about the realities people like her face. "I'd love to be a single mom in her position," she said. "Guess how much I made last year. Less than $10,000. I'd like her to take my place and talk about being a single mom." Sothcott, who supported herself and her children by working until she was injured in 2012, did not find Clark's get-a-job line of advice helpful either. "I should get a job, right," she said. "It's unbelievable to me. She has zero idea, she has no idea what real life is like." Sothcott did, however, say she hoped her daughter would learn it's important to fight for what's right and to not get discouraged. "I'm happy we came," she said. "That woman needs to change the policy. It's wrong."

Sothcott was near one end of the income spectrum, with Clark at the other, though of course there are a considerable number of top earners in the province who make a lot more money than the BC premier does. As a career reporter, I have talked with many people who, like Sothcott, were articulate on questions about wealth, poverty, fairness and inequality. One of the most memorable was Dave Nash, an activist who showed up at my office one day in 2003 bemused that a local shelter was giving out soon-to-expire emergency rations—the kind of food intended for people who have been in a disaster like an earthquake or a shipwreck. He was known for carrying a ladder in a protest with a sign that said, "When I look up the corporate ladder, all I see is assholes." Nash, who lived many years in poverty, died at the relatively young age of fifty-five.

I have also had occasional opportunities to talk with a wide range of business leaders, including corporate big shots like Chip Wilson, founder of the Lululemon yoga clothing label, and Don Lindsay, who as chief executive officer of the Teck Resources mining company was paid just under $10 million in 2013. And I've had access to the municipal, provincial and federal politicians who make decisions, or push positions, that have outsized impacts on the lives of people like Nash and Sothcott. Political choices about such matters as what taxes to implement, who gets access to land and resources, what the minimum wage will be and which programs will exist to help people in need all make a difference.

Awareness that there's a problem has gotten to the point where even the province's elites have been ruminating about what can be done. At a gathering of business people in Vancouver in mid-November 2013, Carole Taylor—the BC Liberal finance minister from 2005 to 2008—described the fears many people have about the provincial economy. Despite economic growth in the province, she said, "a growing number of the middle class and those who are trying to achieve that status really feel they are not sharing or participating in that prosperity."

The facts (to be revisited in later chapters) confirm those feelings are well based. By some measures British Columbia is the worst province for inequality in Canada. Take, for example, the average after-tax income for the top-earning 20 percent and the bottom 20 percent, and calculate the ratio using 2011 statistics, as did the Canadian Centre for Policy Alternatives think tank in 2014: British Columbia was the most unequal province in Canada, with a ratio of $6 to $1 (see Figure 1.1). That followed decades of diverging fortunes for the rich and the rest of the province's residents. Since 1982, after-tax income for the top 1 percent of British Columbians had grown by 60 percent. For pretty much everyone else, the bottom 90 percent, that measure had remained essentially flat. However the income numbers are crunched, and there are many

FIGURE 1.1: RATIO OF AVERAGE AFTER-TAX INCOMES OF TOP 20% TO BOTTOM 20%, 2011

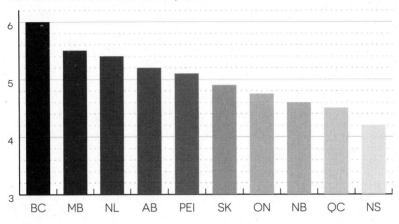

Source: BC office of the Canadian Centre for Policy Alternatives

ways to measure inequality, BC families had the highest after-tax income inequality in Canada for the six years from 2005 to 2010, slipping marginally behind only Alberta in 2011, the most recent year for which statistics were available as of this writing. By 2012 the top 10 percent in British Columbia held 56.2 percent of the wealth, a greater concentration than anywhere else in Canada.

While the strain on people at the bottom is obvious, the winners in this equation should also be worried, argued Taylor, who was named the chancellor of Simon Fraser University in 2010 (a position she held from mid-2011 to mid-2014) and is or has been a director for some major Canadian corporations, including Bell Canada Enterprises, Toronto-Dominion Bank, Canadian Pacific Railway, Canfor Corporation and Fairmont Hotels. "There's a growing disconnect," she said. "'Why should I care about business doing well, why should I care about a strong economy, if I'm not feeling any of the effects?'" Without that feeling of connection and benefit from economic growth, the business people in the room would fail to win the social licence they need for their projects to move ahead, she said. "There has to be a solid line between the two things." Despite lower taxes and "modest gains" in disposable income, Canadians are carrying high debt loads, the cost of living is rising, job insecurity is rife and many are uncertain about retirement, she said. "You've got this sense of dis-ease."

Taylor made the comments as she introduced the findings of the *BC Agenda for Shared Prosperity*, a joint report from the Business Council of British Columbia and the BC Chamber of Commerce. That many people are convinced today's economy is rigged against them should be unsurprising. The fact that a tiny minority has grown staggeringly rich while the wages for most people have stagnated or shrunk is well documented and widely accepted. *Canadian Business* magazine's list of the richest people in Canada for 2014 included the news that Jim Pattison, the wealthiest person in British Columbia, had accumulated some $7.39 billion—enough money to buy a new Prius for nearly 260,000 households. The second-richest British Columbian, Lululemon Athletica founder Chip Wilson, was a relative pauper with a net worth of $3.73 billion. That would still be enough to buy eight pairs of $100 yoga pants for every British Columbian, male or female, adult or child.

In contrast, when First Call—the BC child and youth advocacy group—released their *2013 BC Child Poverty Report Card*, they found the province once again had the highest child poverty rate in Canada. Based on 2011 statistics, one out of five children in British Columbia lived in poverty—some 153,000 kids. This was up significantly from a year earlier. For children living in families headed by single mothers, the poverty rate was 50 percent. The authors of the report noted:

> *British Columbia continued to have the most unequal distribution of income among rich and poor families with children, primarily due to the very low incomes for the poorest families. The ratio of the average incomes of the richest 10 per cent compared to the poorest 10 per cent was 12.6 to one.*

Within Canada, the two most western provinces have for at least a decade been the most unequal when comparing after-tax household income. And among Organization for Economic Co-operation and Development countries, Canada is one of the more unequal, as of late 2014 not yet on the level of the United States or Chile, but significantly worse than Denmark, Norway, France, Slovenia and many other countries. British Columbia and Canada were also doing poorly when compared to their past selves, with inequality measures up significantly from lows through the 1970s and '80s.

Much has been done to bring the issue to public attention. In recent years we've had Idle No More in Canada drawing attention to First Nations poverty. The Occupy movement, sparked from Vancouver, made common knowledge of the division between the top 1 percent and everyone else in North America. In Toronto-Centre, Chrystia Freeland, author of the 2012 book *Plutocrats: The Rise of the New Global Super-Rich and the Fall of Everyone Else*, faced off in a by-election against Linda McQuaig, co-author of the 2010 book *The Trouble with Billionaires: How the Super-Rich Hijacked the World and How We Can Take It Back*.

When Ed Clark retired as the president and CEO of TD Bank Group in 2014, he said Canadians have become complacent about inequality. "We have to deal with the fact that technological change, combined with globalization, increases inequality," a *Toronto Star* article by Madhavi Acharya-Tom Yew quoted him as saying. "I believe that growing inequality is a very corrosive thing in society…The risk is that Canadians are too complacent because we did so well [during the global financial crisis] that they don't really see that these problems are going to come." Clark, retiring at sixty-seven years of age, noted that financial industry salaries had contributed to the growth in inequality, though his own pay had been relatively small considering TD's profits. "I say that I should do the right thing with [the money] and give it to people who need it more than me and my kids need it," he said. The *Star* article noted that Clark's retirement pension would give him $2.49 million annually and payments would continue to his spouse for as long as she survived after his death.

There is a growing international consensus that the current distribution is unjust and unsustainable.

South of the border, prominent books like Nobel Prize winner Joseph Stiglitz's *The Price of Inequality* (2012) and Robert Reich's *Beyond Outrage* (2012) have examined the problem. Overseas, Richard Wilkinson and Kate Pickett make a convincing argument about the harms of inequality in *The Spirit Level: Why More Equal Societies Almost Always Do Better* (2010). And French economist Thomas Piketty's *Capital in the Twenty-First Century* (2014) became a surprise bestseller. US President Barack Obama in a 2013 speech called income inequality the "defining challenge of our time," though he later backed off on the issue amid accusations of engaging in class warfare. New York elected Bill de Blasio as mayor in 2013 on a platform that promised to make fighting inequality his top priority.

When the Business Council of British Columbia and the BC Chamber of Commerce examined inequality for their September 2013 report *The BC Agenda for Shared Prosperity*, they too found reason to worry. The twelve people on the advisory council examining inequality for the report included business owners like Gerry Martin, but also Kim Baird from the Tsawwassen First Nation; SFU president Andrew Petter, formerly an NDP cabinet minister; and Reid Johnson, who in September 2013 resigned as the Health Sciences Association of BC union president.

"While BC's economy as a whole has performed moderately well in recent times, the reality is that not all British Columbians are sharing in its success," the report found. It continued:

> *This is clearly not just an issue in BC. Many countries are faced with a situation where moderate and low-income earners are not enjoying the benefits of the economic recovery. And certain people in BC—notably young workers, First Nations and some parents with young children—are facing especially tough obstacles.*

Later, the report added that inequality can, "if unchecked, lead to dysfunction and unacceptable social stresses."

As the report turned to look for causes and solutions, however, it appeared to lose some of that sense of urgency. The report described the causes of inequality as "complex and not all amenable to policy interventions—particularly for small sub-national jurisdictions such as BC." Nor did it say the process that led to the report found much support for the most obvious solutions: increasing taxes and spending more on social programs that help people in need. There was much disagreement on how to address the issue, the report acknowledged, throughout the advisory council's community consultations, a process that a footnote in the report said failed to include First Nations and "specific immigrant communities." Taylor in her November 2013 speech described the process as akin to "herding lions."

In the end, the authors offered little more than a pitch for the status quo: "What BC needs today is a more concerted focus on tackling challenges and realizing opportunities; a focus that recognizes that in order to improve the distributional side of prosperity, we first need to create a more prosperous economy." As Taylor put it in her speech, "obviously we can't get to the point of talking about sharing prosperity unless we really nurture that growth and prosperity."

That's in line with the direction of an eighty-two-page report a House of Commons committee released in Ottawa on income inequality in December 2013. The Conservative-dominated committee found income inequality had risen in Canada, and had done so for a variety of reasons. However, in recommendations that a headline on a Carol Goar column described as a "lump of coal" for the poor, it argued for continuing to fight inequality by promoting job growth and keeping taxes low. The late Canadian finance minister Jim Flaherty had made a similar argument in responding to provincial governments that wanted the Canada Pension Plan expanded. He supported the idea, he said, but not until the economy was stronger. And Premier Christy Clark has said the same thing, that there will be more money to support people in need once the economy grows, though it's never clear just how much economic growth there will have to be before the needs of the poor become a priority. When I asked her in Kelowna one day how much growth was needed before single parents on welfare could keep child support payments, Clark responded by saying there were many competing priorities.

It's a promise of future comfort that many Canadians are becoming more skeptical about. In 2014 the federal government was promoting a new trade agreement with the European Union by saying the boost to economic activity would be the equivalent of "increasing the average Canadian family's annual income by $1,000." But as I asked people in interviews if and when they expected to see that extra money, most laughed. Bill Hopwood, an organizer in Vancouver of the Raise the Rates Coalition—which advocates for higher welfare payments—said we don't have trickle-down economics, we have flow-up economics. "It's almost unimaginable how rich the rich are," he said. "We don't even begin to comprehend the level of affluence of some of the super rich...The majority of us are standing still. Society as a whole is better off, but most of the gain has gone to the rich."

As with Premier Clark, it was unclear from Taylor's remarks how much prosperity is needed before it can be shared, exactly how many billions the super rich should have first. And Taylor, a former journalist who criticized reporters in her speech for focusing on extremes and ignoring people in the middle, was unavailable for an interview. A couple of days after my interview request, a spokesperson said Taylor had left the country. (Whether Taylor's unavailability had anything to do with The Tyee's 2009 coverage of her taking a lucrative position on a bank board after using her role as finance minister to eliminate a tax on banks, I don't know.)

Speaking in the legislature in 2014, Clark described jobs and equality as closely linked. "We have an obligation as a generation to ensure that everyone across the province has an equal opportunity to take part in the economic growth that is coming in our province," Clark said (see Appendix 2: "State of the Debate"). "We believe that the best way out of poverty is to make sure that people are participating in the economic growth and that they have the skills that they need to take those jobs."

Once economic growth leads to larger government revenues, the *BC Agenda for Shared Prosperity* authors suggested, priority should be given to education and investments in infrastructure such as public transit. To improve outcomes for low- and modest-income working families, they had just three suggestions. The first was a Working Income Tax Credit they hoped would give individuals with low incomes a greater incentive to work. They also suggested "regular, predictable, modest increases in BC's statutory minimum wage that are tied to inflation" and considering pension reform, including "simplified pooled pension plans," to encourage people to save for retirement. The few suggestions seemed meagre when compared to the ten they had for improving public discourse, which appeared to be aimed at convincing people that economic growth will benefit them.

The report is a start, said Iglika Ivanova—an economist with the BC office of the Canadian Centre for Policy Alternatives—in an interview. "I'm encouraged to see they're talking about it," she said. "If we don't share prosperity, bad things happen eventually. It's a one-way street to the French Revolution."

Sometimes change can be won without erecting guillotines in town squares. In February, 2015, Finance Minister Mike de Jong announced BC would stop clawing back child support payments from single parents like Sothcott who receive welfare or disability benefits. The change would help some 5,400 children living in 3,200 families that on average would keep another $300 a month. Ivanova welcomed the news as positive, but said the policy would affect a relatively small number of families and much more was needed to properly invest in the province's people.

CHAPTER 2

ADDRESSING INEQUALITY: WHAT'S FAIR IN A LAND OF PLENTY?

WITH ACCEPTANCE GROWING IN RECENT years—across the ideological spectrum—that inequality is unhealthy for both people and economies, there is even support for the idea among the world's business elite. There is vigorous disagreement, though, on how to tackle the issue.

As noted in Chapter 1, the Business Council of British Columbia—which represents some 250 companies that employ about one out of every four working British Columbians—helped produce a 2013 report that found inequality is a serious issue for the province but argued for addressing it only after growing the economy. "We're starting from a pretty good place," said Greg D'Avignon, BCBC president and CEO, when I asked him in a phone interview about the conclusion of the report, which was called *The BC Agenda for Shared Prosperity*. D'Avignon is a middle-aged man with hair greying at the temples. In photographs available on the internet he is always in a suit jacket, though I did find one where he was without a tie, his dress shirt open at the collar. The province does have challenges and could do much better, he acknowledged, but he also argued that BC and Canada continue to have stronger social supports and better social mobility than do many other jurisdictions. "We don't have an appreciation of how good we've got it," D'Avignon said.

Many people's perception of inequality is driven by the much more stark reality in the neighbouring United States and they forget what Canada has got right, D'Avignon said. He has a point. On a 2014 road trip that included stops in Portland and Seattle, my family found the poverty obvious. There were people showing the effects of drugs and alcohol, or sleeping on the streets, like in British Columbia but in greater numbers. Perhaps the biggest surprise for us came at a highway rest area, where an elementary-school-aged boy stood in front of a black truck holding a sign that said his family needed money for gas; I can't recall ever seeing a child begging in BC, though it may well happen. Elsewhere on the trip we noticed the many fancy cars zipping by on the freeway and the surprising number of people lined up to splurge on gourmet doughnuts in Portland for as much as $4 each. In recent years, among thirty-four Organization for Economic Co-operation and Development countries, the only ones measuring worse than the United States for inequality after taxes and transfers have been Turkey, Mexico and Chile. Canada has consistently done better than the United States, but nonetheless has featured in the bottom quarter within the OECD.

There are stronger supports and much better social mobility in British Columbia and Canada as a whole than in the United States, D'Avignon said. "We've got a very diversified and open economy which allows for people to seek out opportunities," he said. In this province, the education and health care systems are better than the Canadian average, which in turn is better than in most of the world, D'Avignon said. For health outcomes like life expectancy, if British Columbia were a country it would be among the top ten in the world. BC does well on early childhood education compared to other provinces, but not as well as Belgium and some other countries, he said.

Not long after we spoke, the OECD released its report on education. While slippage on math scores was the stuff of hand-wringing in Canada, the BC government found much to like in the results compared to the other sixty-four countries and economies included in the report. "Only one jurisdiction statistically performed above BC's range in reading, only two jurisdictions in science, and nine jurisdictions in mathematics," a December 2013 government press release said. "On a straight numerical rank basis, BC is sixth in both reading and science and twelfth in mathematics." And the results weren't a matter of a few good schools pulling up the average, the release said. "BC also demonstrated high equity in student performance, which is the gap between the highest- and lowest-performing students, showing the system is delivering high student achievement in an equitable manner," it said.

Similarly, Canada tends to do well on international measures of well-being, such as the United Nations' Human Development Index, which takes into account life expectancy, education and income. For several years during the 1990s Canada came out on top, though the country dropped several positions when the index adjusted for gender and race. As this book was being written, Canada sat in eighth place. Norway was at the top and other countries ahead of Canada included nations as diverse as the United States, Australia and Germany. And within Canada, British Columbia tends to score well on life expectancy, low cancer risk and other quality-of-life indicators. Other commentators have pointed out that despite growing inequality, even the relatively poor enjoy material comforts like cheap food, big-screen televisions and cellphone service that past generations could only dream about. Better to be middle class or even poor in a developed country today than a rich person in the eighteenth century, the argument goes.

D'Avignon said despite British Columbia's successes, the status quo could be better. "We've got some challenges in the Lower Mainland particularly," he said. Median incomes in Metro Vancouver were in the lower third for municipalities in Canada, he noted. Debt in the region was the highest per capita. The cost of living was relatively high, and driven mainly by the high price of housing. Many immigrants were attracted to the Lower Mainland, but it was taking them longer to integrate into the Canadian economy than it did a decade ago, he said. The middle class was stretched by the cost of both housing and transportation. Across the province, child poverty rates were the highest in the country.

"It's difficult," D'Avignon said when asked how to make housing more affordable. "Everyone says we should have more affordable housing, but nobody's prepared to do anything about it." The City of Vancouver, for example, said it supported affordable housing but it also charged higher development fees than other cities did, he noted. Prices are driven higher by a combination of factors, including the limited supply of land in a city nestled between mountains, ocean and the agricultural land reserve, D'Avignon noted. One could also add to the list cheap interest rates, which have made it possible in recent years for more people to borrow more money and drive up prices. A December 14, 2013 article in *The Globe and Mail* suggested foreign speculators looking for investment properties could also be pushing up prices.

In general, on the question of inequality, D'Avignon said the Business Council of British Columbia recognized the problem but didn't have all the answers. Of the 391,000 businesses in the province, 98.4 percent had fewer than fifty employees, he said. In recent years they had been hit, he said, by a reversal on the harmonized sales tax, the introduction of a carbon tax, a 5-percent increase to WorkSafeBC (the Workers' Compensation Board of BC) fees and higher ferry prices. It's a version of history that ignores that much of what was raised in the carbon tax has been returned to businesses as lower corporate taxes, but his point is that all the expenses the government has layered together have an impact and that businesses are not generally in a position to give more back.

And there has been help for those at the bottom, D'Avignon said. Under former Liberal premier Gordon Campbell, for whom D'Avignon worked in 2009 as a campaign manager, the government eliminated provincial income tax for people earning up to $30,000, he said, arguing that disposable incomes went up even if wages did not. When I pointed out that tax cuts don't help people who aren't working, D'Avignon acknowledged it's a problem. "There are people you know aren't going to be able to participate in the economy," he said. There are others who are starting out behind and we need to find ways to help them find a role that brings a paycheque, he said. "When economic growth takes place, we've invested in supports that make sense." That's meant more money for Kindergarten to Grade 12, and steady increases to health care spending, he said. The building of the new Evergreen Line in Vancouver—the 10.9-kilometre extension to the SkyTrain rapid transit system—is a direct result of the government being able to afford it, he said.

Meanwhile it's impossible to find enough people to work in the north of the province, D'Avignon said. "We've got a labour mobility issue in the province as well." Many people don't want to leave Metro Vancouver, even young people who can't find traction in their career path. D'Avignon also said British Columbia needed to increase its productivity per hour worked, which had been growing more slowly than the national average.*

"Our position is the business community isn't going to solve all those problems, but we should be talking about them," he said. "We don't have all the answers, but we wanted to start the conversation and be part of the solution."

I asked D'Avignon about the most obvious way to address the problem: raising taxes and spending the new revenue on social

---

*   When Phil Hochstein, president of the Independent Contractors and Businesses Association of BC, was making a similar argument that young people should leave the Lower Mainland for a few years and build some wealth, he admitted to me he'd never himself lived in the north of the province. "I have a job," he said.

programs that benefit people at the lower end of the income scale. He responded, "The research shows it doesn't work."

The University of Calgary is Canada's home to neo-liberal economics, and when researchers there looked into the issue in 2013 they too found that inequality has grown in Canada, but argued fixing it would pose an even greater risk to the economy. It's a theme picked up by conservative commentators who either argue inequality is not so serious in Canada or that the obvious fixes wouldn't work.

Former investment banker Paul Summerville disagrees. He argues that an economy that delivers unequal outcomes is desirable, but that we should also protect the things that ensure everyone has equal opportunities. Summerville, who lives in Victoria, has run for office in provincial and federal elections as a New Democratic and Liberal candidate. Based on personal experience, he argues that successful citizens are made, not born. He described his roots as lower middle class, coming from Scarborough, a blue-collar part of Toronto. He worked hard and by the age of thirty-one finished a PhD without student debt, he said, noting the education was in those days cheap considering its quality. A couple of times when he had health issues, the Canadian health care system was there for him. He went on to an international banking career at institutions such as the Lehman Brothers global financial services firm, which declared bankruptcy in 2008, and the Royal Bank. During his career, Summerville spent two years living in the United States, where he recalls having experienced emotional difficulty walking past individuals who appeared to be destroyed. He retired to Victoria while relatively young, and teaches at the University of Victoria, works on a new business venture, and golfs.

"I think I was raised at a wonderful time in Canadian history for someone of my background," he said. "Talent and hard work were rewarded, but the supports were in place so that they could be." That's not to say everyone should be the same, or expect the same success. "Unequal outcomes are an important part of a social democracy," Summerville said. There need to be rewards for entrepreneurship, to encourage people to work hard and take chances that build wealth, he said, adding that at the same time areas like education, health, access to justice and public transit need support. As a political candidate, he said he heard complaints from people who had to pay school taxes even though they didn't themselves have children. There's much to be said for sharing as widely as possible the cost of things that we all benefit from, he said. "If you don't, you probably aren't going to be living in a community that allows for the things you want." Luckily, as a society, we appear to be at the end of the idea that people shouldn't pay taxes for things they don't themselves use, he said.

Summerville says his view that social justice and a strong economy are compatible—and in fact rely on one another—gets a skeptical reaction from his banker friends. Their common view, he has written, is that "since market outcomes were always fair [with] the spoils going to the smartest and hardest working, arguments for social justice and equality of opportunity were simply a cover for the lazy and undisciplined." When Summerville announced he was running for the NDP, "some old colleagues were so offended by my choice of political parties that they didn't return my phone calls then or now. My candidacy was a betrayal."

The merit argument came up when I was talking about inequality with a conservative relative who works in the financial industry in the United States. He asked why the Vancouver Canucks can get along and cohere together when the top-paid player makes many times more than the worst. Despite the possible awkwardness, they seem to gel as a hockey team, he said. He has a point. While the Sedin twins, Daniel and Henrik, were contracted to each make $7 million in 2014–15, their teammate Ryan Stanton would make $550,000, or about $1 for every $13 the Sedins made. Stanton is a defenceman who scored one goal in sixty-four games he played in the 2013–14 season. The implication is that hockey players are paid based on merit, their salaries reflecting their value to the team and their relative contributions to success.

To extend that to the broader economy and argue that pay always reflects merit is a stretch, however. I'm reminded of American baseball player Babe Ruth reportedly explaining why his salary demand of $80,000 was more than the $70,000 that President Herbert Hoover made at the time: "I know, but I had a better year than Hoover." Stanton, who is no Babe Ruth, stood to make about $225,000 more than Prime Minister Stephen Harper in 2014. No doubt there are those who would argue he had a better year than Harper. As Thomas Piketty discusses at length in *Capital in the Twenty-First Century*, in many professions it's not so easy to determine individuals' value to their company or to society. And as Bank of England governor Mark Carney put it in a 2014 speech, "returns in a globalized world are amplifying the rewards of the superstar and, though few of them would be inclined to admit it, the lucky." The best rejoinder may be to point out, as others have, that in the financial crash of 2008 many of the people who helped bring on the crisis received huge bonuses. Whatever that is, it's not a system based on merit.

It's not as if Summerville's ideas about income and social supports make him a radical outlier at a time when inequality is beginning to receive widespread attention. Summerville referenced a series *The Economist* magazine ran in 2012 about "True Progressivism," which came to similar conclusions. "Research by economists at the [International Monetary Fund] suggests that income inequality slows growth, causes financial crises and weakens demand," the series found. The magazine's business editor, Zanny Minton Beddoes, wrote:

> In a recent report the Asian Development Bank argued that if emerging Asia's income distribution had not worsened over the

past 20 years, the region's rapid growth would have lifted an extra 240 [million] people out of extreme poverty. More controversial studies purport to link widening income gaps with all manner of ills, from obesity to suicide.

The cover piece in the same *Economist* series urged governments in relatively "rich" places like British Columbia to do away with "deductions that particularly benefit the wealthy...; narrowing the gap between tax rates on wages and capital income; and relying more on efficient taxes that are paid disproportionately by the rich, such as some property taxes."

Like D'Avignon, despite his criticisms Summerville acknowledged there's much that we get right already. Canada's inequality is high relative to the bulk of OECD nations, but Summerville argued it's unfair to compare this nation with Nordic countries like Denmark or Sweden. Canada is growing relatively rapidly, adding 195,000 new citizens a year, which is higher than anywhere other than Australia, he said. More than one in five Canadians were born outside the country. There is a need to be smart about immigration policies and make sure that new arrivals can integrate into the economy, but the difference should be kept in mind when making comparisons, he said. "There's the comparing us to the rest of the world, and to where we could be," Summerville said. "Canada's doing better than other countries, but the point is Canada should be leading-edge."

One measure where Canada does relatively well is on what's become known as The Great Gatsby Curve, which shows the relationship between inequality and intergenerational mobility (see Figure 2.1). Across countries, as inequality increases, children are generally less likely to earn more money than their parents. Interestingly, however, the curve shows Canada as an outlier from the norm, with better mobility than several countries with lower inequality—including Japan, Germany and Sweden. What we may

FIGURE 2.1: THE GREAT GATSBY CURVE

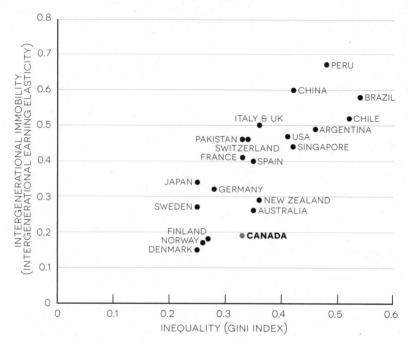

Source: Miles Corak (2013), "Inequality from Generation to Generation: The United States in Comparison," in Robert Rycroft (editor), The Economics of Inequality, Poverty, and Discrimination in the 21st Century, ABC-CLIO

be seeing, however, is a lag between the implementation of policies that cause inequality and when their effects can be observed. In a December 2013 interview on CBC Radio, University of Ottawa economist Miles Corak cautioned that the available social mobility statistics say more about how things are turning out for the baby boomers than they do about what's happening for generations growing up and entering the work force now. With inequality growing in British Columbia and Canada over the past few decades, the question is whether young people will continue to move up and down the income ladder with relative ease. For those alert to reasons for worry, there are plenty.

CHAPTER 3

UNEQUAL OUTCOMES: TRANQUIL ENCLAVES AND HUNGRY PEOPLE

THE PERSONAL FACES OF INEQUALITY rarely stand out in contrast as much as they did for me on the day that the net worth of Jim Pattison—the richest person in British Columbia—was reported to have reached an estimated $7.39 billion, up $1.25 billion from the previous year. On the same day, I bought a man on the street in Victoria a breakfast sandwich from a Subway fast food restaurant and we ended up talking. Perhaps in his sixties, the man—a one-time merchant seaman—had a scraggly beard, greasy-looking hair to his shoulders, and nicotine-stained fingers. As he raised a paper coffee cup to his lips, his hand shook. He said he had a place to live at the nearby hospital. When I told him I was working on a series of articles about inequality, he said that liberals and conservatives are all the same and that it was tough for socialists to get elected, even though that was what was needed.

Later I tried to get in touch with Pattison, whom *Canadian Business* magazine placed fifth in a 2014 list of wealthiest Canadians. The Bloomberg Billionaires Index for that year ranked him as the richest person in the country, by the way, which if nothing else shows the difficulty of estimating the wealth of the very rich. With assets of $9.5 billion, then eighty-four-year-old Pattison had overtaken David Thomson, whose family wealth came from media and publishing businesses. Asked if Pattison would talk with me about income and wealth, his long-time assistant Maureen Chant said, "No, he wouldn't…He just doesn't talk about that kind of thing."

In British Columbia much of Pattison's rags-to-riches life story is already well known. Pattison was born in 1928 in Saskatchewan— just before the effects of the Depression reached Canada—and moved west in 1935. He grew up poor in East Vancouver, where his father went door-to-door "de-mothing" pianos according to various printed accounts. He started out in business as a sales- person at a downtown Vancouver car dealership and still works long hours running a conglomerate with interests that stretch from Europe to Asia.

An article by Gordon Pitts that ran in *The Globe and Mail*'s business section in January 2013 made clear that Pattison's success depends heavily on the tastes and means of consumers, a con- clusion that one can also draw when reading through the list of Pattison's business interests on his company website. I recognized several brands my family and I had used in the past year, including Ocean's tuna, Great Wolf Lodge, Save-On-Foods, Western Family products and SunRype juice. It's hard to get away from Pattison products: even when we bought a car, after shopping around we made the purchase at one of his dealerships. We called around to others, but he had the best price, so got the business. We looked at vehicles made by different companies, but the local dealerships tended to be part of the Pattison empire. He also deals in used cars.

In *Pattison: Portrait of a Capitalist Superstar* (1986), journalist Russell Kelly wrote that it had become a maxim that "You can't live a week in BC without putting money in Jimmy's pocket." And he quoted Claude Richmond, the former cabinet minister who had been responsible for Expo 86, the world's fair in Vancouver that Pattison chaired, saying, "It is difficult to do business in BC without dealing with one of Jim Pattison's companies." The book goes into some detail on Pattison's hardball negotiations with unions, the controversy over sales of pornography that dogged him at the time, and the use of a bank the group owned in Switzerland to avoid paying taxes.

According to the Jim Pattison Group website, in 2014 some 39,000 people worked in Pattison's companies generating $8.4 billion in annual sales, making him a major employer in British Columbia and elsewhere, a significant contribution to communities. Pattison also sometimes gets credit for making donations to worthy causes. When BC Conservative Party leadership candidate Rick Peterson invoked Pattison's name to make the point that it's unfair that nearly everyone pays the same Medical Services Plan premiums in the province, both David Schreck, a former New Democratic MLA and strategist, and Norman Spector, a former federal Progressive Conservative adviser, agreed in an exchange on Twitter that the rhetoric was unwise given Pattison's philanthropy. His donations have included a $20-million gift to the Vancouver General Hospital for a prostate research centre. (That amounts to 0.21 percent of the wealth Bloomberg estimates Pattison has.)

In his 1987 book *Jimmy: An Autobiography*, written with journalist Paul Grescoe, Pattison expressed some distaste for paying taxes. "After watching how many bureaucrats spend the public's money, I've been rethinking my own position as a taxpayer," he wrote, reflecting on his time as chair of Expo 86. "Knowing how some of the government people think, I have a new incentive to minimize my taxes as much as possible."

The book also gave the strong impression that Pattison saw his success in business largely as the result of the strength of his will and his commitment to aim high. "Even though you may reach what some people think is the peak, I believe that you have to extend yourself and continue climbing," he wrote at a time when his annual sales were about 18 percent of what they would reach in 2014. "Whatever else I may be, I'm determined. Once I get involved in a venture that I believe in, I won't quit." And tellingly, in comparing himself to business owners elsewhere, he observed that any success is relative, even for the richest person in the province.

"Measured against many business people, I don't feel that successful," he wrote.

The second-richest person in British Columbia according to the *Canadian Business* list for 2014—yoga clothing retailer Chip Wilson—didn't respond to messages either. Wilson, who owns a large portion of Lululemon's shares and who had been publicly battling with the company's management, had a $3.73-billion fortune, according to the magazine. The rest of the top five richest British Columbians were identified as Mansoor Lalji and family, who have $2.56 billion from their Larco Investments Ltd. real estate development company; Bob Gaglardi, with $2.24 billion from Northland Properties Ltd., which has interests in the Sandman Hotel Group, The Sutton Place Hotels, Moxie's Grill & Bar, Chop Steakhouse & Bar and the Dallas Stars NHL hockey team; and Brandt Louie, with $2.18 billion from wholesale grocery distributor H.Y. Louie Co. Ltd.

Bloomberg, which counts wealth slightly differently than *Canadian Business* does, identified Sherry Brydson as Canada's richest woman. A member of the Toronto media and publishing family that started Thomson-Reuters Corporation, she reportedly owns 23 percent of the company that manages the family's assets and has holdings in the order of $6.5 billion. She lives in a Victoria-area house at the end of a point overlooking the Strait of Juan de Fuca (putting her within easy walking distance of the one-room cabin I rented for $275 a month as a university student). By my calculation, if Brydson were to live another forty years without making another nickel, she could spend nearly $450,000 a day before going broke.

Pattison, Wilson and Brydson are at the very tip of the wealth pyramid in British Columbia. We also have our share of the "super-managers," the CEOs and other top corporate executives that Piketty identifies as driving top incomes ever higher. According to *The Globe and Mail*, the median total compensation for CEOs in Canada rose by 11 percent in 2013 from a year earlier to $5.6 million. At BC-headquartered companies in 2013, Charles Jeannes at Goldcorp

Inc. made $10.2 million, Telus Corp.'s Darren Entwhistle made $10.1 million, Don Lindsay at Teck Resources Ltd. made $9.9 million, Randy Smallwood at Silver Wheaton Corp. made $6 million, Scott Thomson of Finning International Inc. made $5.6 million and Paul Wright at Eldorado Gold Corp. made $5.6 million. The biggest raise went to the CEO at logging company Canfor Corp.— Don Kayne, who saw a 185-percent increase from the year before to make $2.2 million in 2013.

Less visible are the people who form the rest of the top 1 percent of earners, but Statistics Canada did some work to determine who they were nationally, using figures from 2010. Nearly 80 percent of them were men, the StatsCan article "Education and Occupation of High-Income Canadians" reported. Men also made up 74.4 percent of the top 5 percent of earners and 69.1 percent of the top 10 percent. About 62 percent of the top 1 percent were between the ages of forty-five and sixty-four and almost 84 percent were living with a partner in a marriage or common-law relationship. Two-thirds of them lived in either Alberta or Ontario—mainly in Toronto, Calgary and Edmonton—but they also made up 1.2 percent of the population of Vancouver. Out of a Greater Vancouver population of about 2.3 million, that works out to about 27,000 people. As a group, they were well educated. More than 87 percent had a post-secondary qualification. Of those, more than 29 percent had studied business, 14.5 percent had degrees in a health field and 11.4 percent had graduated in engineering. "Of all fields of study, postsecondary graduates who studied in dental, medical and veterinary residency programs were most likely to be in the top [1 percent], with 25.7 [percent] of them doing so," Statistics Canada found. "This was followed by legal professions and studies, where 7.4 [percent] of graduates from this major field of study were in the top [1 percent]."

Massive wealth and stark poverty exist side by side, often within a few blocks of each other. In Vancouver, for example, within a block you can go from payday loan places and shops with bars over their windows to high-end jewelry stores, noted Iglika Ivanova, an economist in the BC office of the Canadian Centre for Policy Alternatives. "It's so obvious." She talked about teachers she knows who work in Surrey and in West Vancouver. The schools in the wealthier area have more engaged parents and more success fundraising, and they have newer buildings and better materials. "It's like in different countries," she said. "We do have stratification within the city and it's not that far away."

In many parts of Victoria, high-end condos have sprouted up around a park that a few years ago was taken over by homeless campers. Prince George has a downtown that's seen better days, yet it's a short drive to a bustling mall, then out half an hour to an area where homes sell for more than a million dollars each. Kelowna has yachts and luxurious hotels on the lakefront, as well as people pushing their belongings in shopping carts. The Cowichan Valley on Vancouver Island has homes listed for a couple of million dollars each, as well as winery tourism and First Nations reserves and other rural areas where derelict vehicles and other junk surround the houses.

BC had three of the richest neighbourhoods in the country on a top-ten list in 2011 on the Montreal lifestyle website *Ask Men*, while the area around Hastings and Main in Vancouver has been identified at times as Canada's poorest postal code.

"Clearly there's enormous wealth around," Raise the Rates coordinator Bill Hopwood observed in an interview. "Part of it is standing back and saying, 'hold on a minute. This landscape I see, this human landscape, do I have to accept it?'" He described walking past Coal Harbour in Vancouver. "I don't know how many million some of those boats are." None of the conspicuous excesses of wealth strike him as necessary, nor does the province's prevalent poverty, and he noted that governments are able to find money for some things but not others. "Poverty is not a God given, if you'll excuse the expression. It's a set of political decisions." But instead of taking a collective responsibility, we tend to blame the individuals, Hopwood said. "It's your fault you're poor, it's your fault you're in the sex trade—whatever it is—rather than say it's social issues." Hopwood champions increased compassion towards people who are living in poverty. "People don't choose this," he said. "People end up here. Often through tragedy."

The same kind of inequalities are outlined in *Charting BC's Economic Future*, a discussion guide that was prepared for a 2013 Simon Fraser University Public Square. The annual gatherings always focus on an international or local issue that is of concern to the public. "British Columbia's prosperity is not being shared equally between population groups (notably, Aboriginal groups, low-income families, and new immigrants in low wage jobs)," the guide found. Job growth is uneven across the province, concentrated more in Metro Vancouver than in rural BC, and many residents/businesses do not pay their fair share of taxes."

At the lower end of the spectrum, according to the *Income Composition in Canada* report from Statistics Canada, people in the bottom half of earners received more money from the government in transfers in 2010 than they paid in income taxes. For families headed by single moms with children under six years old, the portion of income from transfers was the highest, with just 55 percent of their money coming from employment. For people in the top 10 percent of earners, by comparison, 98 percent of income came from employment and they paid 25 percent of their earnings for income taxes.

A twenty-five-year-old I spoke with while working on this book figures that after paying rent he lives on $9 a day through disability payments from the BC government. According to the provincial government, in 2011 some 476,000 British Columbians lived below the so-called low income cut-off (LICO), a government measure below which families would likely have to devote a larger than average share of their income to food, shelter and clothing. The difficulty paying for necessities is often used as a measure of poverty. "At the end of the day poverty is a cash problem," the twenty-five-year-old said. "For what you trade in terms of stigmatization and the Big

Brother of government poking into your life all the time, it's a very small amount of money." We spoke on the phone for about an hour before he asked me not to publish his name, saying he feared retribution from the people who run the system. "The rules are so complex...if they want to do you in they can do you in."

There is no single measure that everyone agrees on to gauge inequality, but it's clear that inequality is growing and is more extreme in British Columbia than just about anywhere else in Canada. One approach for measuring inequality is to compare the top 1 percent to everyone else, the bottom 50 percent of earners or the bottom 10 percent, said economist Iglika Ivanova. (The so-called Gini coefficient is useful to give an idea of what's happening in the middle, and is discussed later in the chapter.) The fact that there is no single number that everyone uses for discussing inequality causes problems because people prefer simplicity, Ivanova noted. Interest in the share of income going to the 1 percent is relatively new, she said. "The reason we talk about it right now is that's where the action is." It's also clear there's stagnation in the middle, she said. "When you look at how much our economy has grown over the last thirty years and how little the incomes in the middle have grown, I think that's problematic."

A 2012 report released by BC Stats—the central statistics agency for the province—discussed income inequality in the province in the wake of the Occupy movement. Written by Dan Schrier, a manager at BC Stats, the report found that inequality had increased in Canada and that among provinces, British Columbia was the second least equal for after-tax figures. "Based on data from 2008, the average income of the top 10 [percent] of Canadians was ten times higher than the bottom 10 [percent], which is a significant increase from the early 1990s, when the ratio was eight to one," Schrier wrote.

The most recent Statistics Canada figures available as of this writing, based on 2011 tax filers, found that in the years since Schrier's report the share of income going to top earners has dropped slightly in Canada as a whole and in BC, but it still remains significantly higher than it was three decades ago. The Schrier report had said that, "among the provinces, only Alberta registered more after-tax income inequality than BC in 2009." The statistic is particularly interesting considering BC ranks better before money is redistributed through the tax and benefit systems, it said. "British Columbia ranked fifth and Alberta seventh in terms of inequality when market income is used (i.e., excluding government transfers and before taxes)." In other words, other provinces have more unequal wages, but do a better job of redistributing money and reducing income inequality. The result is that BC, with about 13.2 percent of Canada's population and despite being a "have" province, is home to 14.6 percent of the nation's people living in poverty.

Canada-wide, according to figures from Statistics Canada's 2011 *National Household Survey*, the median income nationally in 2010 was $27,800. Half of us earned more than that, and half earned less. To be in the top 5 percent required an income of $102,300 and to be a 1 percenter a person would have had to make $191,100. The average income for the bottom 90 percent of earners was $28,000.

Aside from directly comparing incomes, one of the standard measures of inequality is the Gini coefficient. A lower number shows a more equal distribution of income; a score of 0 would indicate everyone made exactly the same amount of money. A jurisdiction would have a Gini coefficient of 1 if all income went to just one person or a tiny group. "Through the 1980s and 1990s the Gini coefficient of income inequality for British Columbia averaged 0.29, but from 2000 to 2009, it averaged 0.33," Schrier wrote in his 2012 report, using data from Statistics Canada.

In the quarter-century before 2001, the Gini coefficient for British Columbia after taxes and transfers was lower than the one for Canada sixteen times (see Figure 3.1). Around 2001, the BC figure spiked from below the Canadian average to well above it, where it has remained ever since. In eight of the ten years ending in 2011, the

FIGURE 3.1: GINI COEFFICIENTS, 1976–2011

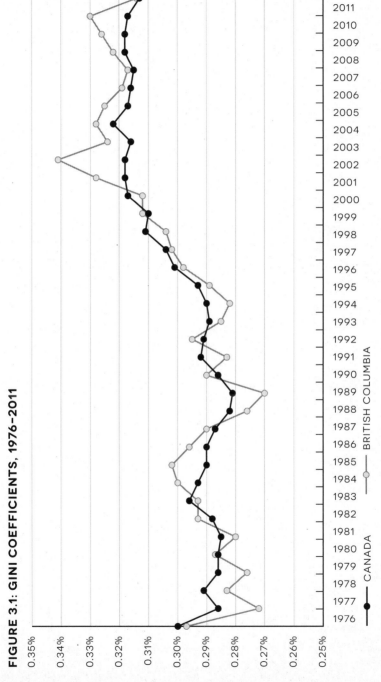

Source: Statistics Canada, CANSIM table 202-709, after-tax income of individuals, all family units

after-tax Gini coefficient for BC has been either highest or second highest among provinces, with the only serious competition coming from Alberta.

The surge in inequality appears to be part of a wider international trend. The OECD found in a 2011 report that inequality had grown in most member countries and attributed the increase to the disparity in wages between high- and low-paid workers, the increase in self-employment, and the drop in redistribution of income through taxes and benefits. British Columbia fits the pattern and then some, having had a government that has aggressively cut taxes on incomes, corporations and financial institutions while cutting transfers to those in need. (See also Chapter 5.)

One could also blame the decline of unions, which has been more dramatic in BC than in the rest of the country. Between 1981 and 2012, BC registered the biggest drop in Canada in the percentage of workers who were members of unions, going from 43 percent of the workforce to 30 percent, according to Statistics Canada. Jim Sinclair, at the time president of the BC Federation of Labour, said that while union density has declined in BC from a high in the 1950s, some 70 percent of large job sites where more than five hundred people work remain organized. "There's no doubt the union movement is alive, kicking and well," he said. The decline matters, he acknowledged, but he said the union movement is still instrumental in raising wages and working standards and pressing for a better deal for all workers.

Many factors are at play in the background, but it's the provincial and federal governments' focus on tax cuts that deserves the most scrutiny. "While tax cuts have benefited people of all income levels to some extent, they have had less of a positive effect on the lowest income earners," Schrier wrote. "This is because these lower-income individuals pay very few income taxes to begin with and are more reliant on the benefits and services that are paid for with tax revenue." The 1 percent—the people targeted by Occupy—had particularly benefited from the tax cuts, Schrier found. "According to the OECD, the richest 1 percent of Canadians earned 13.3 [percent] of total income in the country in 2007, well up from the 8.1 [percent] share they received in 1980."

The challenge, Schrier wrote, is for governments to decide how big a gap between the top and the lowest income earners is acceptable. Social tensions that are visible in such events as Occupy demonstrations suggest the gap is already too big, he concluded.

Along with income levels, which thanks to tax records are relatively easy to study and are regularly reported, it is worth looking at accumulated wealth, though it is more difficult to determine and less frequently updated. Statistics Canada releases findings every five years. In the figures published in early 2014, BC had at $344,000 the highest median net worth in Canada for "family units." Net worth includes the value of all of a family's assets, minus whatever they might owe. The 2012 figure for BC was more than double what it had been in 1999, when the province ranked fourth. It was also more than double the 2012 median net worth for Prince Edward Island, which was $150,300. BC was also far ahead of the $271,400 median in Saskatchewan, $267,500 in Alberta and $265,700 in Ontario.

Statistics Canada also compared the distribution of wealth between those at the top and the bottom. Families in the bottom 20 percent had a median net worth of $1,100 in 2012, which was down a couple of hundred dollars since 1999. Those families in the top 20 percent, in contrast, had a median net worth of about $1.4 million, or about 1,300 times the wealth of the folks at the bottom. Since 1999, families in the top 60 percent had seen their median net worth grow by about 80 percent. A summary of the findings put the differences down to home ownership and the amount of money people hold in private pension assets such as Registered Retirement Savings Plans.

The Broadbent Institute, an independent organization that advocates for reducing inequality, bought more detailed data

**FIGURE 3.2: SHARE OF WEALTH FOR WEALTHIEST 10%
COMPARED TO SHARE FOR BOTTOM 50% OF CANADIANS,
BY REGION, 2012**

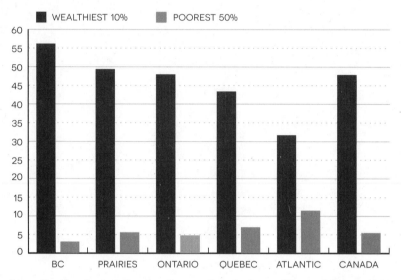

Source: Broadbent Institute, data from Statistics Canada, Survey of Financial Security, 2012

from Statistics Canada than the government agency had publicly released. According to those figures, BC had the greatest wealth disparity between people at the top and at the bottom (see Figure 3.2). The bottom half of the population, about 2.25 million people, held only 3.1 percent of the province's wealth, with the poorest 10 percent owing more than they owned. The top 10 percent in BC, some 450,000 people, held 56.2 percent of the wealth (see Figure 3.3). Those at the top had a median net worth of over $2 million in 2012. At the bottom end, the median net worth for the poorest 10 percent was a debt of $10,700. That median debt had grown from $4,800 in 2005 and $1,400 in 1999. (See Appendix 1: "Inequality by the Numbers.")

Jonathan Sas, the director of research for the Broadbent Institute, said in a phone interview that real estate is the biggest factor, especially in Vancouver. "Those assets are not very evenly

FIGURE 3.3: DISTRIBUTION OF WEALTH IN BC BY DECILE,* 2012

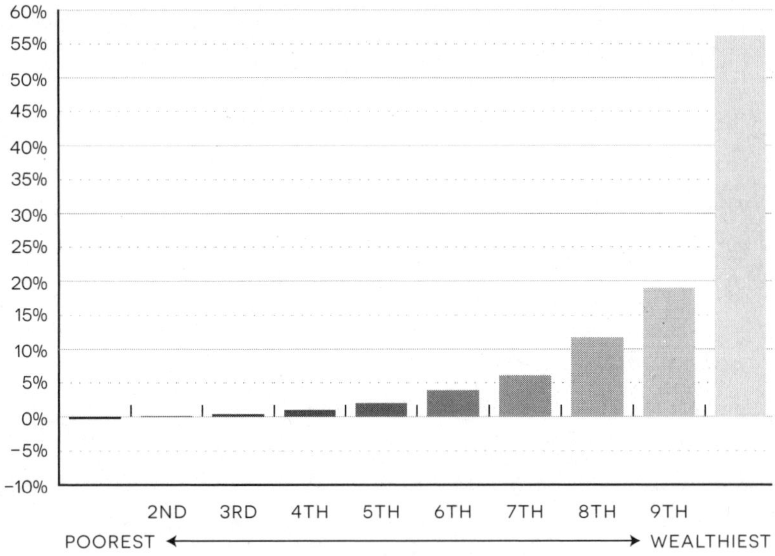

* *Each of the 10 deciles includes 10 percent of the population.*

Source: Broadbent Institute, data from Statistics Canada, Survey of Financial Security, 2012

distributed," he said from Toronto, where he is based. Part of the story is age, with younger families tending to be at the lower end, but the groups at the bottom are seeing their share of the wealth decrease over time, he said. That suggests it's becoming more difficult for them to share in the country's growing wealth.

While the wealthy people making top incomes have more than they could ever need, it's clear those at the bottom are suffering. There are many people the system fails, said a contact who asked to have his name withheld from publication. "We've created systems where if your mind and body isn't close to the average…that will amplify that difference and make things harder than they already are." He has Asperger's syndrome, an autism spectrum disorder where people have trouble with social interaction and nonverbal communication. He sees the system also hurting people who are weaker, more sensitive or even smarter than the average. "People will get caught in the gears of the machine and the response is, 'Let's keep the machine running until we crush them,'" he said. "You spend a lot of time feeling suicidal. You don't feel like there's any way to get through it."

The pattern of inequality extends beyond British Columbia's borders and globally, of course. When I asked Chris Shaw—an author, activist and University of British Columbia professor—where he sees inequality, he said, "Where don't you? Racial, gender, economic…it is still, in North America, white males running the world. And, to a large measure, in spite of the suntan of the current president, blowing it up."

Globally, going back more than a century, the income inequality graph looks like three-quarters of the Golden Gate Bridge. According to work by economists Thomas Piketty and Emmanuel Saez concentrating on the United States and Europe, income inequality peaked in the 1920s, declined through the Depression, then took a sharp fall during the Second World War. It was flat for four decades, before beginning to trend upwards again around 1980. By 2007 the share of income going to the top 10 percent was back where it had been in the 1920s before the crash. Piketty suggests the postwar years were an aberration and the current distribution of wealth continues a long-time trend. Others argue that careful policy decisions could return us to the level of fairness our parents and grandparents took for granted.

According to figures from Credit Suisse AG, a financial services company, half the people on the planet had individual net assets worth less than $3,650 (US) in mid-2014. A net worth of about $77,000 would put you in the global top 10 percent and $798,000 in the top 1 percent. (See Appendix 1.) As bad as things are for many in British Columbia, on a global scale many of us are among the world's richest people and we include a disproportionate number of the people in the top 1 percent of the world's wealthy. The question is: Which way are we going?

CHAPTER 4

CONSEQUENCES: FROM UNFILLED PRESCRIPTIONS TO ECONOMIC WEAKNESS

RESEARCHERS AT THE UNIVERSITY OF British Columbia who looked into the reasons why sick people sometimes fail to take their prescribed medicines discovered something surprising. Where patients live is one of the factors that make a difference as to whether or not they follow through on their doctors' advice, and British Columbians were more likely than other Canadians to say cost was a reason they didn't get their medicine. "Not having insurance coverage for prescription drugs, being in poor health, having a low household income, being under the age of 65 years and living in British Columbia" were all associated with what the researchers termed "cost-related nonadherence" in their 2012 article on the study, "The Effect of Cost on Adherence to Prescription Medications in Canada," published in the *Canadian Medical Association Journal*.

The author researchers—Michael Law et al. from the UBC Centre for Health Services and Policy Research—used data from Statistics Canada's 2007 *Community Health Survey*. They found that on average one in ten of the Canadians surveyed said that due to cost they had failed to fill a prescription or not taken a drug in the year before the survey. The number was one in six for people in British Columbia.

"Drugs have really become a core component of the treatment of disease and it's puzzling why they aren't included in medicare," Law told me in a phone interview after the study's release. "Prescription drugs are the most glaring omission from medicare today." The *Canada Health Act* requires provinces to provide universal public insurance so that all medically necessary hospital services and doctors' fees are covered. Drugs for people outside the hospital, which Law said was a small part of medical expenses when medicare began in the 1960s, are not covered. Today two-thirds of Canadian households spend money out of their own pockets for drugs each year, which adds up, the researchers found. "These payments totaled $4.6 billion in 2010, or about 17.5 per cent of total spending on prescription drugs." The *CMAJ* article does not say which medicines people aren't taking, though it noted the majority of spending on prescriptions in Canada is for drugs like heart medications that are intended for long-term use.

The BC health minister at the time wasn't available for an interview, but a health ministry spokesperson responded to questions about the study. "Through PharmaCare, British Columbians have access to one of the most comprehensive universal pharmaceutical programs in Canada," Ryan Jabs said in an email. "Deductible levels are set up to reflect patients' ability to pay—the lowest income earners pay no deductible or drug costs at all." That includes people on income assistance or living in residential care, he said. About 10 percent of the people registered with PharmaCare, or 274,000 patients, are eligible for 100-percent coverage of drug costs. BC fully covers psychiatric medications and protects all residents from catastrophic drug costs, he said. The province has the best drug coverage in the country for cancer, renal, transplant and HIV/AIDS patients, he said. Still, ministry officials would take time to review the UBC study, he said. "This study shows us that we may need to take a closer look at why some residents report having challenges accessing prescriptions."

PharmaCare deductibles are based on a percentage of a person's income. Someone making under $15,000 a year pays 2 percent of their income, or up to $300, before coverage kicks in to pay 70 percent of the cost. For a person making $30,000 a year or more, the deductible is 4 percent of their income, or at least $1,200. "That's coverage, but for a lot of people who are taking prescriptions every month, even that deductible can form a barrier," Law said. For people who may have several prescriptions to fill, the total adds up quickly, he noted.

There may be good reasons for a person to stop taking the medicines that are prescribed to them—such as adverse reactions or a harmful interaction between two drugs—but cost is not one of them, Law said. When people decide they can't afford the drugs they've been prescribed, they may end up sicker and costing the health care system more in the long run, he said. There were also costs to individuals, employers and society as a whole, and "keeping people healthy through the use of these drugs…is in everyone's best interest." Governments have options to make drugs cheaper for patients, he noted—they could lower the deductible, negotiate better prices or make more medicines free, but they could also start a national plan and take advantage of bulk buying.

The high rate of non-adherence in British Columbia was a surprise to the researchers, but could be the result of PharmaCare's high deductible or the fact that personal debt levels are higher in BC than in other provinces, the article said. "We're not exactly sure what's going on in British Columbia," Law said, though he noted that a 2011 TD Economics special report on *Assessing the Financial Vulnerability of Households Across Canadian Regions* found British Columbians had the highest level of financial vulnerability in the country.

Adrian Dix, who was leader of the NDP when the article on the UBC study on drug affordability came out and is also a former health critic, observed in an interview that governments in recent years had set policies that favoured pharmaceutical companies over patients. The study "shows the need to take some steps to protect consumers, to address these questions of affordability," he said. Over a decade, PharmaCare's share of the money spent on drugs in the province had shrunk from 50 per cent to 33 per cent, he said. "People in BC, dramatically more than people in other jurisdictions, are not taking the drugs they need because of cost....It reflects a good amount of what we've been saying about inequality in the province."

Difficulties in paying for drugs are just one of many signs that people are struggling in British Columbia. The TD Economics report that Law referred to used six indicators for financial vulnerability to compare the provinces. British Columbia led the country on four of the indicators in 2010 and had the highest vulnerability score for all of the twelve years the researchers looked at, going back to 1999. "Reflecting the lofty costs of homeownership, households in British Columbia record the highest vulnerability," said the report, written by Craig Alexander—TD senior vice-president and chief economist—et al. "In particular, BC residents on average register the highest debt-to-income ratio, debt-service cost, and greatest sensitivity to rising interest rates. What's more, BC is the only province where the average savings rate is negative."

TD defined the savings rate as "the share of each dollar of disposable income that is not spent" and noted that saved money could be used to deal with a financial surprise, providing households with some security. In 2010 British Columbians had a savings rate of negative 4.2 percent, the report said. That compared with a national average of 3.9 percent and a country-leading high of 15 percent in Alberta.

British Columbia has long been an outlier, however, the authors found, and the report suggested there could be factors special to this province that were not caught in the data. "For example, the province's relatively large economic reliance on its service sector and self-employment—two areas that tend to have higher-than-average incidences of non-reported income—might be superficially driving down income and driving up the various sub-index readings." Also, the report said, coping mechanisms like renting out basement apartments appeared to have become common in the province, but might not be fully reported in the income figures.

The report still found reason to worry: "Even if these factors are part of the story, they don't address the fact that British Columbia's index level has recorded the second fastest rate of increase among the provinces over the past half decade." With higher interest rates on the horizon, as many as one in ten households in the province was dealing with the real threat of financial stress. One mitigating factor, the report found, was that thanks to rapidly rising home prices, British Columbians had a better than average debt-to-asset ratio, meaning that compared to other Canadians they owed a smaller amount compared to the values of their properties. However, the authors argued, that advantage shouldn't be relied on to continue: "With the home price-to-income ratio pointing to some ongoing over-valuation in the housing market, stable BC home values are far from assured."

There's no question debt looms large in the finances of families in British Columbia. Economist Iglika Ivanova of the BC office of the Canadian Centre for Policy Alternatives, talks about her single-mother friends who work full-time but still need to borrow on credit cards to get by. People get into a financial hole that keeps growing as they end up paying penalties such as bank service fees or charges for bounced cheques that those with more money avoid, she said. "On the bottom you have debt, you have negative wealth."

Ivanova said inequality can lead people to take on debt as they try to keep up with the consumption they see around them. It's a common observation that poverty and inequality are in many ways dependent on how people are doing around you. When my kids see other children being dropped off in big, expensive-looking

German vehicles at the private school down the street they ask why we're poor, despite the fact that we are financially secure. A friend who makes about five times my salary tells me that when he walks around his neighbourhood he feels like his family is average or even relatively poor. Having visited places like Honduras, Venezuela, Kenya and Uganda where there is abject poverty, and with work that brings me into contact with people across the income spectrum, I tend to feel well off. The point though is that aside from what can be measured, rich and poor are feelings. How you're doing often has as much to do with how your neighbour is doing as it does with the state of your own bank account, and that can affect the decisions we make.

People in need, or trying to keep up with their neighbours, borrow money at rates that are unfavourable, whether on credit cards or through payday loans. When the federal Financial Consumer Agency of Canada looked into the payday loan industry in 2005, they discovered that people living in BC were the most likely in the country to use such a service. The companies, which emerged some time in the 1990s, provide small, short-term loans at relatively high rates of interest or fees. In one example the federal agency gives, a sample $400 loan paid off seventeen days later had an effective annual interest rate of 1,242 percent. While about 7 percent of Canadians told the surveyors they had used such a service, the rate was about 50 percent higher in British Columbia, where 11 percent said they had. The other western provinces—Alberta, Saskatchewan and Manitoba—were also above the national average. Also likely to use a payday loan company or cheque-cashing outlet were people who were younger, poorer, less educated, urban and male.

A 2006 federal government research report, *Payday Loan Companies in Canada: Determining the Public Interest*, found that "shared federal-provincial jurisdiction over payday lenders has meant that they are essentially unregulated." In 2009, after years of pressure from critics, the BC government took a step that made the hole people get into borrowing from payday lenders just a little shallower: a new regulation reduced the allowable charge on a two-week loan to 23 percent of the amount borrowed, down from 30 percent. Calculated over a year, that left the annual rate at 600 percent.

John van Dongen, the solicitor general of the day, didn't pretend that payday loans were a good option for people. "It's certainly not a form of credit we would encourage consumers to use," he said. "It is a high interest rate." He did add that the BC rate strikes a balance between protecting borrowers and allowing lenders to do business. "Some payday lenders believe this rate will not allow them to be viable," he said. The changes also required lenders to set out all charges and fees, including the annualized rate, in loan agreements and on posters in their outlets. And borrowers were given the right to cancel a loan at no charge by the end of the following day. The province set penalties at up to $50,000, but the government had no intention of actively enforcing the law. "It will generally be complaint-driven," said van Dongen. "If people can't resolve a problem with their lender they can apply to the consumer protection authority for assistance."

Rob Fleming, the New Democratic MLA for what was then Victoria-Hillside, now Victoria-Swan Lake—who represents some of the Capital Regional District's poorer neighbourhoods—had for several years advocated tighter restrictions on payday lenders. He found the government's regulations fell short. "This is a growing, exploding industry in British Columbia," he said. "This legislation ensures that payday lenders will continue to prey upon people in British Columbia." There are more payday lender storefronts in BC than anywhere else in Canada, Fleming said, and yet the province has been one of the slowest to regulate the industry. "Consumers have been left in the lurch for years," he said. "This government has landed on a figure that's totally in the interests of the big corporations that are in the payday lending business now and it's ignoring the needs of consumers."

The 2006 federal government's research report, by the way, was inconclusive about what if anything should be done. "The payday loan industry presents an interesting situation for policy makers, where both the public interest and the best course of action are somewhat unclear," it said. "Some members of the payday loan industry appear to be charging usurious rates of interest, in violation of section 347 of the *Criminal Code*." And yet the report advised against enforcing anti-usury laws since the industry appeared to be filling a need for some borrowers. "Criminal prosecution...could eliminate the payday loan industry and—in the absence of increased servicing by traditional lenders—leave some consumers without access to the credit or convenience they desire," it concluded.

Another likely sign of general financial insecurity in BC, at least among people with more wealth, turned up in *The Canadian Money State of Mind Risk Survey 2014*, which The Brondesbury Group conducted for the Investor Education Fund, a non-profit funded through Ontario Securities Commission settlements and fines. The survey found Vancouverites were much more likely than other Canadians to say they were willing to take above-average risks with their investments. They were also more optimistic about how those investments would perform. "Vancouverites are the most economically optimistic people in Canada, more likely to see better investment returns on the horizon than people anywhere else in Canada," the study said. "They also express the fewest concerns about the future of their personal investments. This seems a fitting mindset for a city known for its venture capital. Vancouverites are risk takers." Some 43 percent in Vancouver said they would accept the higher risk, compared with 29 percent across the rest of the country. For the study, stocks, hedge funds and limited partnerships were classified as higher risk, while GICs and savings bonds were seen as lower risk.

Vancouver Sun columnist Barbara Yaffe wondered what would make Vancouverite investors differ from other Canadian investors:

"Living on the edge? A frontier mentality? Home to many high-risk mineral exploration plays?" She did find one clue in the study, particularly for people over fifty-five years of age who were trying to supplement their incomes: "Investors aiming to earn investment income for day-to-day living are prone to take disproportionately more risk than many others." If they weren't earning enough income, they would risk more than other people their age do, the study suggested. Yaffe asked, "Could this be what is happening in Vancouver? Are people feeling pressed for cash in an expensive city, pushing their investment strategies to the limit to address an affordability challenge?"

"We have data and we have speculation between the lines," Tom Hamza, president of the Investor Education Fund, which commissioned the study, told me from Toronto in a phone interview. He said he would love to do more research on what's behind the trends, but hadn't yet. There were various factors he could see that he figured contributed to Vancouver's risky investing. The presence of a stock market and a "stronger investing infrastructure" than elsewhere was one. A greater number of young people at a stage in their lives where they could afford to take greater risk was another. He cited a prevalence of immigrants who had already taken risks to get to Canada and might be more willing to take further risks. He also said that some people might be trying to catch up on retirement savings after taking losses or be trying to keep up with neighbours by generating income to spend. "That's an element for sure."

Choosing to forgo their medicine because of cost, taking on high debt levels and making risky investments are a few of the ways inequality seems to play out in British Columbia. The 2013 Simon Fraser University discussion guide on BC's economic future (mentioned in Chapter 3) identified other ways inequality creates challenges for the province. "Despite the many social and economic advantages British Columbians enjoy, the imbalance in the sharing of wealth creation, and the social inequalities this produces, represents a huge challenge for social cohesion," it found, and added:

> Child poverty, cost of living, affordable housing, and unfair taxation all jeopardize BC's social fabric, especially in the Lower Mainland where housing affordability undermines social equality, restricts the ability of BC to attract talent, and is one of the key reasons why people leave the province. In addition, the lack of success to date in fully integrating BC's Aboriginal population and new immigrants into the market economy continues to represent a key missed opportunity for the province.

A contact surviving on disability benefits in Vancouver described feeling as though his freedoms are curtailed in ways that other people don't experience. "If you're on disability you don't have the rights normal people do," he said. For example, despite Canadians having the right to move between provinces, he can't leave BC without risking losing disability payments. "I'm virtually a prisoner of British Columbia," he said. "It's not the worst prison to be in, but I can't even afford my cell."

"There's a growing literature that shows there are impacts of inequality," economist Iglika Ivanova said. Some of those results are long-term, passed from one generation to the next. In the United States, for example, the people who get into Ivy League universities are much more likely to have parents who went to those same schools and are very unlikely to come from the non-elite, she said. Add in the fact many of the people in the US government went to those same Ivy League schools and it's clear the pattern is unlikely to change, she said. Money and inequality also corrupt the political process, she added.

There is, by and large, consensus that wide inequality is bad for everyone in a society. In *The Spirit Level*, British authors Richard Wilkinson and Kate Pickett show that more unequal societies do worse on a whole range of indicators—including life expectancy, mental health, teen pregnancy, violence and crime. The poor results harm people living in poverty, but also the wealthy, they found. "If you fail to avoid high inequality, you will need more prisons and more police," they wrote. "You will have to deal with higher rates of mental illness, drug abuse and every other kind of problem."

Malcolm Gladwell illustrated the point well in "Million-Dollar Murray," a 2006 *New Yorker* magazine article that told the story of Murray Barr, an ex-Marine who was homeless in Reno, Nevada. Gladwell reported that two police officers who dealt with Barr realized:

> *If you totted up all his hospital bills for the ten years that he had been on the streets—as well as substance-abuse-treatment costs, doctors' fees, and other expenses—Murray Barr probably ran up a medical bill as large as anyone in the state of Nevada.*

One of the officers observed, "It cost us one million dollars not to do something about Murray."

And there are many Murrays. The BC Poverty Reduction Coalition says poverty costs the BC health care system $1.2 billion a year, noting that those among the poorest 20 percent of the population are 60 percent more likely to have a chronic health condition than are people in the top 20 percent. Adding in all the costs associated with poverty the annual bill gets up to as high as $9 billion, it says. In comparison, adopting a "comprehensive, preventative poverty reduction plan" would be relatively cheap at between $3 billion and $4 billion annually.

Nor is massive inequality good for the economy itself. As American political economist Robert Reich put it in his book *Aftershock*, "At what point does an economy imperil itself politically, as large numbers conclude that the game is rigged against them? Most fundamentally, what and whom is an economy for?" Chrystia Freeland, a reporter who became a Liberal member of parliament, reached a similar conclusion in her book *Plutocrats*, that the future earnings of the people at the top depend very much on people in the middle having healthy finances. As others have pointed out, no matter how much money a rich person has, he or she needs only a finite amount of pillows, cars, groceries, homes or anything else. On the other hand, putting money in the wallets of people who don't have much virtually guarantees it will be spent, keeping the dollars flowing in the economy.

Mark Carney, the former governor of the Bank of Canada who was named governor of the Bank of England in November 2012, made a case about the economic dangers of inequality in a 2014 speech to the Conference on Inclusive Capitalism. "Inclusive capitalism is fundamentally about delivering a basic social contract comprised of relative equality of outcomes; equality of opportunity; and fairness across generations," he said. Carney identified three reasons to pursue those goals, the first of which was economic, and he noted that there was growing evidence that relative equality was good for economic growth. "At a minimum, few would disagree that a society that provides opportunity to all of its citizens is more likely to thrive than one which favours an elite, however defined," Carney said. Also, he said, research was pointing to the conclusion that greater equality tends to lead to happier populations, and that wherever there is a stronger sense of community people are generally more likely to experience feelings of well-being. Finally, he said, relative equality appeals to "a fundamental sense of justice" and a broadly shared feeling that the system is fair. "Mistrust in market mechanisms reduces both happiness and social capital," he said. The capitalist system has many benefits, but should not be taken for granted, he continued. "Prosperity requires not just investment in economic capital, but investment in social capital...It is necessary to rebuild social capital to make markets work."

The arguments for addressing inequality thus run from the moral to the practical. Societies can reduce the suffering of individuals, but at the same time also save public dollars and keep their economies strong. From a BC perspective, we are somewhere in the middle of the pack with some people thriving and many doing all right, but also many who are struggling. More worrisome though is the trend that has seen inequality rising since the 1970s. If that trend continues, where will we end up? What will our province be like in another forty years? We have a choice.

"THEY WOULDN'T LET ME ... GO TO THE BATHROOM"

Sometimes inequality is not just about how much money we make, but about the conditions of our employment. I was struck a few years ago by the story of Ron Jeffries. A former security guard, he believes working conditions at the health ministry building in downtown Victoria caused him to lose a kidney. "They wouldn't allow me to leave," said Jeffries, who was fifty-nine years old when we spoke in 2010. He was assigned to guard the health building when he worked for a private security company that had the contract to protect the ministry in 2005. "I was working security, front desk at the Ministry of Health and they wouldn't let me leave to go to the bathroom."

As Jeffries looked back at what had happened to him, he discovered that BC law fails to explicitly state that employers have to allow bathroom breaks, an oversight he brought to the attention of then premier Gordon Campbell in a January 2010 letter that was forwarded to minister Murray Coell shortly afterwards. While a labour lawyer says it's illegal to deny a worker a chance to use the bathroom, changes the government made in 2001 left workers to advocate for themselves, something many are uncomfortable doing.

Knowing he wouldn't have access to a bathroom at work, Jeffries said he decreased the amount of fluids he drank. "I'm not going to sit there and drink all day if I can't go to the bathroom and relieve myself," he said. The dehydration led to a kidney stone, then surgery to remove the stone and ultimately the loss of the kidney. "This shouldn't happen to people," said the former forester and navy member who had years ago run marathons, adding he was so sick he was in intensive care for six days, in bed for three weeks and unable to work for nine months. The job paid $9.25 an hour.

The doctor who removed the kidney, Victoria urologist Iain McAuley, wrote in a 2006 letter to Jeffries that he couldn't say for certain that the work situation had started the problems, but that it was a possibility. "In your circumstance I could theorize a possible scenario, which could apply," he wrote. "You decreased your fluid intake because of poor washroom access. This caused dehydration, which was a new situation for you." Dehydration frequently leads to kidney stones and Jeffries had a "malformed" right kidney that may have been prone to forming stones even though he had never had one before, the doctor wrote, adding:

> The combination of poor drainage of the kidney and dehydration caused you to have the stone. The stone in your malformed kidney then resulted in damage to the ureter during the operation and this resulted in you losing your kidney.

He concluded, "I cannot tell you categorically that your stone was caused by lack of bathroom access, but it is a possibility."

When Jeffries worked at the health ministry building, the security company that was his direct employer had a head office several kilometres away. Jeffries said he didn't feel he could insist on having someone come over to cover for him just for a few minutes. Instead, he said he believes it should have been up to the building manager to allow for a break. "I told him and he said, 'I don't have to give you breaks.'" As Jeffries looked deeper into what happened to him, he discovered that BC's *Employment Standards Act*, one of the main laws governing workplaces in the province, covers meal breaks but is silent on bathroom breaks. The building manager appeared to be right, he said. "The law's an ass in this situation."

The building manager and the security contractor have both changed since Jeffries worked at the ministry. The current building manager referred questions to the media branch at the Ministry of Health. A spokesperson there referred questions to the Ministry of Labour. A spokesperson for the labour ministry confirmed the *Employment Standards Act* doesn't cover bathroom breaks, but said it is the kind of thing one would assume would be unnecessary to legislate and can normally be worked out between an employer and an employee. When I asked Murray Coell about the situation, he said, "It's not something I'm aware of." It would be "common sense" that workers would be allowed bathroom breaks, he said.

"I've not run across this specific issue before," said Charles Gordon of Vancouver, a labour lawyer with the firm Fiorillo Glavin Gordon. "Usually these sorts of thing get straightened out pretty quickly." While employment standards don't include washroom breaks, such breaks would be covered as a matter of occupational safety under the *Workers' Compensation Act*, he said. That act says that washroom facilities have to be available to employees, he said, though it doesn't spell out that employees have to be given a break to use them. "The implication would seem to be they get to use them when they need to use them." Told of Jeffries' situation, he said, "Clearly in that situation they're obligated to provide him with washroom facilities."

That they are obligated does not automatically mean it would happen though, he said. The security industry can be difficult for workers, with many people working by themselves, often at night, he said. Security guards are often immigrants or others who may feel reluctant to stand up for themselves, he said. "Many workers feel if they try to advocate for themselves, they'll get fired. Sometimes that's true." Situations like Jeffries' were made worse by changes the government made after 2001, he said. "There was a time when things like employment standards were enforced by employment standards officers who went out in the field." After 2001, they stopped proactively working with employers and moved to a self-help model of enforcing employment standards, he said. "That put a lot of workers in a difficult position."

When Jeffries wrote to then premier Campbell in January 2010, he described what had happened and asked Campbell to change the employment laws. "The employer was following what was written but I believe that no one thought that any employer would follow what was written so closely as to abuse his or her employees," Jeffries wrote. "In my case this resulted in the loss of my kidney, which has affected the quality of my life. On three occasions this resulted in my near death."

Campbell responded to Jeffries by offering his condolences and saying he was passing the issue on to Labour Minister Coell. On February 19, Coell wrote back. The act allows for meal breaks, he noted. "Other matters related to breaks, such as leaving the work station during the break, are left to arrangements between the employer and the employee," he said. "It is my view that employers and workers need to come up with arrangements that work for them using common sense reflecting mutual respect," he said. "There are no plans at this time to change these provisions, but policies are monitored regularly and your concern will be noted should amendments to the Act be considered in the future." He suggested some aspect of the *Human Rights Code* might apply, and provided contact information for the BC Human Rights Tribunal.

Jeffries said he was pleased to hear back from Campbell and Coell, but was disappointed they declined to make any changes to protect other workers who might be in a similar situation. "They're not going to do anything about it," he said. "As I said to my wife, [Coell] basically said, 'Sorry to hear about your troubles, but fuck off.'"

CHAPTER 5

DEEP ROOTS: RESOURCE CLAIMS, FOREIGN WORKERS AND SHIFTING TAXES

ARCHAEOLOGICAL RESEARCH IN BRITISH COLUMBIA has fuelled an ongoing debate about the early roots of inequality and the rise of the 1 percent. One camp suggests inequality rose in times when resources were abundant. Another camp argues that it's actually when resources are scarce that some are inspired to try to prosper at the expense of their neighbours. Perhaps both are correct.

When Simon Fraser University archaeologist Brian Hayden examined semi-subterranean pit houses that were used 2,500 to 1,100 years ago on what is now known as Keatley Creek near present-day Lillooet, he found a large variation in size, journalist Heather Pringle wrote in "The Ancient Roots of the 1%," a May 2014 article for *Science* magazine. The population of about 1,500 people lived in homes that varied from as small as a tiny urban apartment of today to as large as a medium-sized modern house, Pringle wrote. "To understand these disparities, Hayden and his colleagues examined ethnographic records of historic aboriginal societies in the region, which were divided into nobles, commoners, and slaves," she wrote. The team found that the highest-status families would own resources such as fences for driving deer into hunting traps or they had the best fishing rocks on the salmon-rich Fraser River. "Owners built fishing platforms out from these rocks, and so could fish in deep waters where the biggest salmon swam," Pringle wrote. Meanwhile people from lower-status families could only fish using dip nets from public areas on the banks of the river and could only reach smaller fish.

Hayden and his team found that 75 percent of the fishbones in the larger of the pit houses came from big chinook and sockeye salmon that would have been four or five years old. In the smaller houses, all of the bones came from smaller salmon that would have been two to three years old and were likely caught from the riverbanks. "The findings suggest that inequality began at Keatley Creek some 2500 years ago when a few ambitious, aggressive people capitalized on the salmon's bounty," Pringle quoted Hayden as saying. Some people were intent on building up their own wealth and power at the expense of others, Hayden suggested, building fishing platforms from key fishing rocks and claiming private ownership so they would have more food than their neighbours. "These aggrandizers controlled bigger food surpluses than others, but no one stopped them—as can happen to those who refuse to share in other hunting and gathering societies—because there was plenty of food for all." The greatest inequalities emerged at the most productive fishing locations where huge surpluses were produced, and that was no coincidence, Hayden said in Pringle's article. Other archaeologists held different views. Anna Marie Prentiss from the University of Montana, Missoula studied another ancient village in the Lillooet area. "It was a shortage of food, rather than an abundance, that sparked inequality," is how Pringle described what Prentiss and her research colleagues found. Looking at evidence from the Bridge River site, the researchers concluded that the first elites had emerged about 1,200 years earlier, following a decline in the number of salmon returning to the river and a large drop in the village's population. "Some families responded to scarcity by closing off public access to hunting and fishing resources and holding feasts to attract workers to their depleted households, tactics that allowed them to amass more food than their neighbours."

Hayden responded to this idea that inequality is a by-product of people trying to feed their families during lean times by observing that such scarcity is what breeds revolts and demands for greater equality. "When times are good—for example in a booming modern economy like China—people seem more tolerant of inequality," Pringle quoted him as saying.

It is of course possible that both are correct. Prentiss allowed for the possibility in the abstract to "The Cultural Evolution of Material Wealth-Based Inequality at Bridge River, British Columbia," an article that ran in the journal *American Antiquity* in 2012. She and her co-authors wrote, "Recent studies suggest that the form of emergent inequality may have varied significantly between groups, implying that pathways to inequality may have varied as well." The observation that inequality grows in various circumstances appears to apply equally well to the world today. It's easy to think of modern jurisdictions like Honduras or Uganda with relatively stagnant economies, large disparities in wealth and little sign of the kind of revolt Hayden suggested was likely. At the same time, inequalities are large both in the relatively wealthy United States and in relatively poor Nigeria. That is, it may be that inequality is a constant in both good times and bad, differing perhaps in degree and the severity of the outcome for those at the bottom. It would seem those with the power in a society nearly always do what they can to maximize their self-interest and suppress those they consider lesser than themselves.

Throughout the early colonial period, BC certainly pursued policies that were grossly unfair to one group or another, apparently acting on the promise of Richard McBride—premier from 1903 to 1915—that "British Columbia shall be a white man's province." Former NDP leader Adrian Dix, with the help of the librarians at the BC legislature, identified eighty-nine government bills and forty-nine regulations that discriminated against people of Chinese, Japanese and South Asian origin in the province. The most famous of these were the Chinese head tax and the *Chinese Exclusion Act*. Besides these exclusionary laws, there was the embarrassing *Komagata Maru* incident in 1914 when 376 Sikh and Punjabi people hoping to immigrate were forced to stay on their ship in the Vancouver harbour before being turned away.

Jean Barman, in *The West Beyond the West*, her history of British Columbia, attributed the racism of the time to an economic fear among white labourers of being undercut. "Unions long opposed Asian immigration on the grounds of unfair competition, and it is probably a fair generalization that working people were at the forefront of popular opposition," she wrote.

During the Second World War, British Columbians with Japanese ancestry were removed from their homes on the coast, had their property taken and were sent to internment camps in Interior towns like Kaslo, Slocan and New Denver. British Columbians with German or Italian ancestry—in other words, with roots in countries Canada was also at war with—suffered no such forced exclusion that time around. However, around the time of the First World War, between 1914 and 1920 thousands of European Canadians were forced to live in internment camps. An announcement from the BC government in 2014 about the province's role in a cross-Canada commemorative plaque program said the markers would be hung in Ukrainian, Croatian, Serbian, German and Hungarian churches and cultural centres, including fourteen in British Columbia. "More than 8,000 people...were sent to live in crude internment camps with poor living conditions where they were used for forced labour," the government's announcement said. "They were also subjected to other federally state-sanctioned censures including losing the right to vote and having what little wealth they had confiscated."

Add in the dispossession of First Nations from their land after colonists arrived, the creation of the residential school system, and the banning of the potlatch among measures aimed at breaking their cultures, and it's clear this has always been a highly unequal, as well as unjust, place. And it continues to be. In a 2014 Vancouver newspaper opinion piece on apologies for historic wrongs, Dix pointed out there is still much discrimination in our province. "We are reliving some of this history in the present time," he wrote in the *Georgia Straight*. Federal and BC provincial policies had previously denied a path to citizenship to people from China, Japan and South Asia who were brought here to work, he wrote. "In the present day, a majority of immigrants to Canada are Temporary Foreign Workers, who are denied, should they wish it, any path to citizenship." TFWs are vulnerable because of their legal status, Dix wrote. "TFWs regularly work under threat of deportation, a fact that undermines the enforcement of even base employment standards." Despite the province's growing inequality, BC had failed to train enough skilled workers, so importing workers was likely to create resentments, the same as the practice had in the past, Dix wrote. He also said:

> *Our society and economy has been most effective when laws are applied equally, ensuring fair treatment to all workers and fair competition. And it has worked most effectively when people who come to BC and Canada are allowed to become citizens. This is a lesson that history teaches us. Our racist legacy targeted Chinese Canadians and stunted our growth as a province. Learning this lesson will help us in our present circumstance.*

Jim Sinclair, as president of the BC Federation of Labour, saw the Temporary Foreign Workers Program as a tool to depress wages. "Temporary foreign workers are used to create inequality by corporations who are using them to do that," he said in a September 2014 interview, adding that good pay would attract workers. "There's not a labour shortage, there's a wage shortage." The fact that TFWs have fewer rights than Canadian workers, including no right to quit and find another job, also galls. "If you have no right to say 'no,' and if you say 'no' you're deported, you're now vulnerable to whatever they want to do to you," he said. The BC Fed knew of TFWS who had tried to stand up for themselves only to be threatened with deportation, Sinclair said, adding that TFWS should instead be welcomed as immigrants with all the rights that status would include. "If they're good enough to work here, let them come here and live here."

My *Tyee* colleague David Ball quoted a thirty-seven-year-old fast-food worker from the Philippines who was afraid she would have to go home due to a moratorium on restaurants using the TFW program. She asked not to be named for fear of employment repercussions. For five years she had sent $500 a month home to her husband and two teenage children. "If I can't get my residency, I'll have to go back to the Philippines a failure," Ball quoted her as saying. "I feel like a failure in my life, even though I work so hard…I never stop hoping to live in Canada, because I know Canada is a better place for my kids." She was sympathetic to Canadian workers who blame TFWS for taking jobs and suppressing wages, but said their beef should be with the government policy, not workers who are in an even more precarious position. "I wish I could explain to them, 'I understand you guys because you have a family too,'" she said. "But it's not our problem. Ask the government why this is happening, please don't blame foreign workers."

As inequality has been growing in BC in recent decades, some of the factors commonly blamed for widening the gap are the increasing disparity in wages between high- and low-paid workers; the increase in self-employment; cuts to social programs; and the decline of unions. In British Columbia there was a key shift in 2001 when people of the province elected the BC Liberal Party to a majority government, replacing an NDP government that had held power for a decade. On his first full day in office, newly elected premier Gordon Campbell announced a 25-percent cut in income taxes. With later cuts, this contributed to a 37-percent cumulative cut in the income taxes for all payers. During Campbell's rule the government also cut the corporate income-tax rate from 16.5 percent to 10 percent and eliminated the capital tax on financial institutions.

"The tax-cutting policies have created far more inequality and the jobs that were promised never materialized," observed Jim Sinclair, of the BC Fed. The income and corporate tax cuts that started in 2001 left the government short of money and gave disproportionate benefits to upper-income earners, he said. Effectively, the province ran three years of deficits during an economic boom to give more money to the rich, turning traditional Keynesian economic policy on its head.

The effect of Campbell's tax cuts stick out in the inequality statistics. Throughout the 1990s the province had an after-tax Gini coefficient that was near or below the Canadian average, much as it had been through the preceding fifteen years of Social Credit government. (The Gini is a common measure of inequality; as described in Chapter 3, a 0 would reflect a completely equal sharing of income and a 1 would indicate a single person or very small group received everything.) It did rise through the decade while the NDP was in power, but at a rate close to the rest of Canada. In 2001, however, the after-tax Gini coefficient for BC moved well above the Canadian average and in 2002 it spiked to .341, far above the national figure of .318.

The sudden divergence of BC from the Canadian average says something interesting about the effects of the federal government's policies on inequality. Obviously when the government in Ottawa decides to cut taxes, stop tying transfer payments to social programs, pull the funding for social housing or fail to adopt a national childcare program, it makes a difference. What remains unexplained, assuming provinces are treated more or less equitably and that transfer payments are generally used to level regional differences, is why inequality has grown so much faster in BC than it has elsewhere in the country.

In a 2011 report, *BC's Regressive Tax Shift: A Decade of Diminishing Tax Fairness, 2000 to 2010*, the BC office of the Canadian Centre for Policy Alternatives (CCPA) examined what had happened in the province. Tax cuts saved the richest 10 percent of households $9,200 a year, it said. For the richest 1 percent, the savings were $41,000 a year. Meanwhile, households in the middle got a much smaller gain, about $1,200 a year. For those at the bottom, the tax cuts worked out to just $200.

"I think most people would expect we have a tax system where as you have a higher income you pay a higher rate," said Seth Klein, BC director for the CCPA. Instead the province had unfairly shifted the tax burden onto people with lower incomes over the past decade, he said. The CCPA researchers used Statistics Canada data to look at the total tax people pay, including on sales, income, property, medical services premiums and carbon. In 2000, wealthy people paid a slightly higher percentage of their income as tax than other people did, Klein said. By 2011, they were paying less. "I didn't think we'd see a downward sloping line like that," he said. "I think people would be surprised."

The primary cause of the change was cuts to income taxes, which are applied at different rates depending how much money a person makes, Klein said. "The problem is income tax is only one tax that we pay, and its role within the overall tax system has been shrinking." British Columbia had reduced income taxes over the decade and increased what it takes in from other taxes, he said. "Tax cuts have been the primary policy agenda of the last ten years…It hasn't delivered. That's why we need to rethink this." In 2011, after a decade of tax cuts the government said were intended to stoke the economy, the unemployment rate in British Columbia was the highest in Canada west of the Maritimes. The CCPA advocated a fair tax commission to address these questions. "We shouldn't be doing this in piecemeal fashion," Klein said.

Christy Clark, who replaced Campbell as premier in 2011, has, to the time of this writing, maintained the low-tax mantra, a message that has helped her party win four majority governments in a row, including the 2013 victory that surprised just about everybody. "I will not reach into your pocket for more money, because that just makes it harder for families in British Columbia," she said in a typical 2012 speech to an audience at a luncheon that the Tri-Cities Chamber of Commerce hosted. "Higher taxes and higher deficits chase jobs away." She did waffle somewhat when an audience member asked directly during a brief question-and-answer period whether the Liberal government would raise any taxes. "Would we raise taxes in some areas but not others? It's a difficult question to give answers directly to just because what I'm interested in is the overall tax burden for the province," she said. Then she reminded the audience that the Liberals since 2001 had been focused on reducing taxes. "We are not planning a budget that's going to be a big tax-and-spend budget. It's going to be a balanced budget. It's going to involve a lot of tough decisions." Clark offered reassurance that her government wouldn't be seeking a bigger slice of people's paycheques. "We are going to make sure that we keep taxes down for individuals," she said. "We are going to maintain the lowest taxes in Canada in this province. I just don't think we can continue to add to the burden for the people of British Columbia. We need to leave more money in your pocket."

BC Liberal budgets have tended to make up the money elsewhere to balance tax cuts to individuals and corporations. When Finance Minister Mike de Jong presented the government's 2014–15 budget, he called it a "boring balanced budget" and boasted of BC having the lowest income taxes in Canada. A slide titled "Keeping taxes low for BC families" bragged that BC had the "Lowest Provincial Personal Income Taxes for Individuals Earning up to $121,000" in the 2014 tax year. The budget documents, however, showed the total provincial tax burden going up significantly when Medical Services Plan premiums and other fees were included.

Tables deep in the appendices of the budget and fiscal plan compared the total tax burden to various kinds of families in each province. They add in other provincial taxes, including those on sales, fuel, property and carbon, as well as net child benefits, health care premiums and payroll taxes. A two-income family of four earning $90,000, for example, pays total provincial taxes of $9,922 in BC, slightly higher than a comparable family in Saskatchewan and nearly $2,300 more than the $7,625 that family would pay in Alberta. And a lower-income BC family of four earning $30,000 would pay $3,081 in total provincial tax, significantly more than in Ontario ($2,424), Alberta ($1,324) or Quebec ($590). Of the six scenarios included in the appendix, the only one where BC came out with the lowest total provincial tax was for unattached individuals earning $80,000 per year.

Nor did the taxes outlined in the table include other significant costs that depend on the government's policies, including fees for BC Hydro, the Insurance Corporation of British Columbia (ICBC) and BC Ferries. These have a big impact as well and have been steadily rising. As Art Kube, president of the BC Council of Senior Citizens' Organizations, put it in a press release criticizing ferry and BC Hydro increases, "The rate of poverty among seniors, and particularly among women, is increasing at an alarming rate. The government's actions are making it even worse." The province's revenue from MSP premiums was budgeted to increase by about 5.4 percent in each of the following three years. Revenue from BC Hydro, which had already announced rate hikes of 9 percent for 2014 and 6 percent for 2015 as part of a ten-year plan, was also set to make a significant jump.

Jordan Bateman, the BC director of the Canadian Taxpayers Federation, was at the government's budget presentation in February 2014, at the Victoria Conference Centre. He noted MSP premiums have been an increasing burden on British Columbians. "It's the invisible tax nobody ever talks about," he said. "It's a tax we need to start talking about." It would make sense to eliminate all the "boutique" tax cuts that affect a very small number of people, and instead freeze MSP premium hikes, he said.

David Black, president of the Canadian Office & Professional Employees Union (COPE) Local 378, which represents workers at BC Hydro and ICBC, said the government's claim to balance the budget depended on taking more money from Crown corporations like BC Hydro. The government is increasing electricity bills and using the money to balance the budget, he said. "They're transferring that debt onto the backs of ordinary British Columbians." Or as Jim Sinclair, then president of the BC Federation of Labour, put it: "For average British Columbians, they're struggling to have a balanced budget and that's still the case."

"Any idiot can cut taxes," said Sinclair in a later interview, noting he thinks there's renewed appreciation of the value we get for our taxes. "The tough part of government is delivering the services." The amount of money we spend collectively through the government has been shrinking, which particularly affects the people who depend on the government. The policy leaves people more money to spend on themselves, but it does so unequally, he said. "Working people and ordinary people are squeezed twice." The combined effect of worse services and stagnant wages for many creates more poverty and despair, he said.

Tables included in the provincial government's 2014 *Financial and Economic Review* show that when expressed as a percentage of the province's nominal gross domestic product (GDP), total revenue shrank an average of 0.2 percent a year from 2002 to 2014. Over the same period, spending on social services declined by 2.5 percent a year. The only branch of government to get an increased share of the GDP was health, which grew by 0.2 percent a year.

Economist Iglika Ivanova, of the Canadian Centre for Policy Alternatives' BC office, said British Columbia's legacy of tax cuts had created fiscal problems for the province and led to cuts to services. "We've shrunk our fiscal capacity," she said. "It's made it harder to balance the budget." The minister made a big deal of being in an "exclusive club" of provinces with balanced budgets, she said. "I think most people would be glad if we weren't in the exclusive club of having the worst child poverty."

While public polls generally suggest people like low taxes, and politicians generally shape their pitches to voters based on that assumption, much depends on how the question is raised. In survey results released in late 2012, the CCPA found that some 71 percent of British Columbians said they felt they already paid too much tax. Another 27 percent said they paid about the right amount and just 3 percent said they paid too little. However, when asked if they would pay between 0.5 and 3 percent more of their income to support specific measures, many said they would. Support for the various measures, with overlaps allowed, included 53 percent who would pay more to raise welfare rates, 58 percent who would pay to protect forests and endangered species, 61 percent who would pay to eliminate Medical Service Plan premiums and 69 percent who agreed with paying more to provide more access to home and community based health care services for seniors. The online survey was given to a random sample of 1,023 British Columbians.

"The point of the exercise was to show when you make it more concrete...the answer changes," said Seth Klein, director of the BC office for the CCPA. While a majority of people automatically reject paying more tax, he said, "under the right circumstances, where people understand what they're paying for, you get a different kind of answer." There is already evidence of this in our tax system, said Klein. Compared to the outrage over the introduction of the harmonized sales tax, there has been muted opposition to the steady increase in Medical Service Plan premiums, a regressive tax, he said. Similarly, people seem to have accepted the carbon tax, even though two-thirds of the money it raises goes to cutting corporate taxes. The explanation may be that people don't mind paying taxes when they are tied in their minds to things they support, such as paying for health care and fighting climate change, he said.

The CCPA report says 57 percent supported raising taxes on people making over $100,000 to "reduce income inequality, protect the environment and improve access to public services." And 90 percent agreed with raising taxes for people who make over $250,000. Respondents' voting intention seemed to make little difference to the responses, with supporters of the Green Party and NDP only slightly more supportive than Liberal or Conservative voters of raising taxes to pay for particular services. However, younger people were significantly more likely to approve of such a raise than older people were.

At the very least, people in the province are ready to have the discussion, Klein said. "British Columbians are saying they'd appreciate a more thoughtful debate about taxes."

CHAPTER 6

LIFE AT THE BOTTOM: STINGY SUPPORT AND RISING HOMELESSNESS

R ESTRICTING THE HELP AVAILABLE TO people at the bottom was one way in which the BC government made up for its drop in revenue after 2001, when tax cuts began disproportionately benefiting those at the top of the income pyramid. Jessica Sothcott, who was struggling on disability payments thanks to a government policy clawing back child support (see Chapter 1), is just one of hundreds of thousands of people who have depended on government help to meet their basic needs.

When the Liberals came to office in BC, a total of 252,162 British Columbian men, women and children were surviving with the assistance of welfare. That was already down significantly from 367,387 in 1995, when some 9.7 percent of the population depended on the program, but not far enough for the new government. The BC Liberals dropped the amount of money that welfare would give to people, on top of rate cuts the New Democrats had made, and tightened eligibility requirements. By 2006 the number of welfare clients had dropped to a low of 132,606, about half as many as when the Liberals took office. The largest decline was in the number of people receiving temporary assistance—people whom the government considered to be employable.

By May 2014—in the wake of the 2008 financial crisis, job losses and a tepid recovery—the number of people receiving help had crept back up to 177,040, or about 3.8 percent of the population, still far from its peak. Aside from people who have completely fallen through the holes in British Columbia's social safety net, welfare recipients have among the lowest incomes of anyone in our province. And it's clear that people with low incomes do worse in this province than their counterparts do elsewhere in Canada. In 2011, according to adjusted after-tax figures from Statistics Canada, people in the lowest 20 percent of earners in BC had an average income of $15,500. That was significantly below the Canadian average of $16,900 and far below the Alberta average of $20,200.

The changes made after 2001 included cutting rates for many recipients, especially for "employable" people over fifty-five years of age. A single "employable" person between the ages of fifty-five and fifty-nine saw their cheque reduced to $510 from $557. An "employable" person between sixty and sixty-four years of age faced a cut of nearly 20 percent, to $510 from $608. The National Council of Welfare, which the federal government disbanded in 2012, in 2003 called the BC rates "cruel and punitive," pointing out at the time the rates for a single employable person were 67 percent below the poverty line. They have since gone back up to $610, a level that still mostly ignores thirteen years of inflation. The amount includes $375 a month for rent in cities that have some of the most expensive real estate in Canada.

For everyone except the disabled, the government also eliminated earnings exemptions, which allowed people to keep the first $200 as an incentive to seek employment. Single parents were now expected to work when their youngest child turned three, instead of the previous age of seven. People over the age of nineteen had to prove they had been independent from their parents for two years before they could qualify for assistance. Emergency hardship assistance was no longer available, said the human resources ministry's service plan, "in certain circumstances, such as when a person quits a job voluntarily, or for refugee claimants." The ministry announced plans to lay off some 460 people of a total staff of 3,000, close 36 of its 198 offices across the province and cut its budget by 30 percent over three years. The bonus payment for the deputy minister of the day depended on cutting the number of people receiving welfare.

Consider how the cuts affected Tara Mundy and her five-year-old daughter. They were eligible for about $860 monthly in welfare from the human resources ministry. The rest of their income came from a monthly child tax credit of about $200 from the federal government. They paid $640 a month to rent a two-bedroom apartment in Esquimalt—well under the average for the region—leaving just $420 for the month's utilities, food and any other expenses. Mundy worked part-time at a daycare, but since the Liberals took away the earnings exemption, she found working put her no further ahead. The government cut everything so that when people work it's harder to get off welfare, she said. "To me it seems unfair."

Even one of the ministers who was for a time responsible for welfare, Rich Coleman, would later acknowledge that some of the policies were obviously unfair. Requiring single parents whose children were younger than three years of age to go through a three-week job search before they could get welfare, even though once they gained assistance they would not be required to work, made no sense, he said in 2009. "When I got the ministry…a lot of those questions were my first questions coming out of the box, so we'd already started to change those things," said Coleman, who at the time of the interview was also responsible for housing. "I thought, if you have children under three, and you're going to get social assistance, why [are] we going to send you on a job search when you've got to take care of your kids?"

The cuts to the welfare system most directly affected the poor, but they were made amidst other moves that compounded the difficulties for people living in poverty. Cuts to daycare subsidies made it even harder for single parents to work or go to school. Chopping all but a few job-training programs narrowed the options for people who wanted to develop skills that would make them more employable. Reduced legal aid funding made it hard for anyone who couldn't afford a lawyer to use the justice system; as a result, for example, many people needing spousal support after a separation were unable to pursue their claims. Women's centres across the province closed after their funding was removed. Tuition fees for post-secondary education rose dramatically.

The attack on the welfare system had a huge effect on communities across the province, said Sarah Khan, a lawyer for the BC Public Interest Advocacy Centre. Had the Liberals fixed the problems years ago, or not created them in the first place, she said in a 2009 interview, "there's no way we could have seen the levels of homelessness we see now."

Susan Henry, a community worker and advocate at First United Church in Vancouver's Downtown Eastside, said welfare cuts were driving a social crisis. "It's contributed to where we're at right now with so many destitute people," she said. "When you don't have any income, or this tiny income, how can you afford to have a place?" People who are homeless have been allowed to sleep in the church for some years, and that number exploded after 2002, Henry said. "It was just awful," she said, adding those policy changes were still doing damage.

The social development and social innovation ministry has gone through several name changes and has had by my count at least eleven different ministers in the Liberals' fourteen years in office in the province. The first was Murray Coell, a social worker who in return for his efforts at welfare reform was booted from the BC Association of Social Workers (BCASW) professional organization. In a 2009 interview, Coell defended the changes he oversaw in 2001 and 2002. "In a system that revolves around people, you have to be willing to change as the times change," he said. "In our early part of our mandate of course the job was to get people back to work, which we did." He asserted the drop in the welfare caseload was due to the government's success getting people into jobs, though the Ombudsperson and others have pointed out the government had no evidence to support the claim. "We're now in a different economy, which will have different challenges," Coell said. "At the time we had the best advice we could to make sure people got employment. The economy helped with that. I think the retraining programs really helped."

Asked about the criticism he took personally, including the BCASW censuring, he said, he thought that would happen "anytime you make change, and we made major change to the welfare system, and it needed to be done. You had at one point six out of ten single parents on welfare in British Columbia and one out of ten people on welfare in British Columbia. It wasn't needed. What was needed was retraining and the ability to create jobs, and we did that." Coell also said the reasoning behind some of the tougher changes to welfare, including dropping the rates and ending earnings exemptions, was that being on assistance should be less comfortable than working. The idea was not to support people in need indefinitely, but to help them enough to get them back into the workforce as quickly as possible, he said.

KEEPING THE SEAT WARM: MINISTERS RESPONSIBLE FOR WELFARE IN BC, 2001-15

- Murray Coell, June 2001–January 2004
- Stan Hagen, January 2004–September 2004
- Susan Brice, September 2004–June 2005
- Claude Richmond, June 2005–June 2008
- Rich Coleman, June 2008–October 2010
- Kevin Krueger, October 2010–March 2011
- Harry Bloy, March 2011–September 2011
- Stephanie Cadieux, September 2011–September 2012

- Moira Stilwell, September 2012–June 2013
- Don McRae, June 2013–January 2015
- Michelle Stilwell, January 2015–

In 2008, the Canadian Centre for Policy Alternatives released the results of a two-year study on the effects of BC's welfare policies. The report included many personal stories, published with people's names changed, including one about "Lorraine." After being cut off from welfare for a reason she said was unfair, she had no income. She lost her home, started skipping more meals to save money and returned to working in prostitution. In hopes of leaving the sex trade, she went back to an abusive ex-partner who assaulted her badly enough to break some of her bones. Getting better required surgery and several months in a hospital. "She was clearly worse off since being cut off," observed Seth Klein and Jane Pulkingham, the lead authors of the sixty-nine-page report, *Living on Welfare in BC: Experiences of Longer-Term 'Expected to Work' Recipients.*

Lorraine was one of sixty-two people the researchers followed for two years, between 2004 and 2006. Thirty of the people interviewed for the study were in Vancouver, seventeen in Kelowna and fifteen in Victoria. The government classified each of them as expected to work, and they had all been on welfare for at least fifteen months. A researcher contacted them once a month and interviewed them every six months. While some people's lives improved over that time, others worsened and few escaped poverty. Eventually, after twelve weeks of waiting, Lorraine returned to welfare. At the time of her fourth interview with the researchers she was not using drugs, had stayed away from her ex-partner and was living in a transition house. Six months later she had a room of her own in an SRO (single room occupancy) hotel, was still working in the sex trade and was missing many meals.

"We were interested in isolating those who were being targeted by the work expectations," said Klein, director of the BC office of the CCPA. The idea was to see how the 2002 changes that Coell had argued would move people into jobs were actually working out, the number of "employable" people collecting welfare having dropped by more than 70 percent. "We have tried to construct a study that sticks with those who are most vulnerable to these kinds of changes," Klein said.

At the end of the two years, researchers were able to interview forty-five of the original sixty-two people (of the others, one died, four were working or in school and nothing is known of the rest). Of the forty-five people they interviewed, 48 percent stayed on welfare throughout the study, 27 percent left voluntarily and stayed off, 16 percent left at some point and returned, and 9 percent were cut off. For the twenty-nine who were on welfare at the study's end, twenty were no longer "expected to work" and had been reclassified as Persons with Persistent Multiple Barriers to Employment, having a medical condition that exempted them from searching for a job. The new labels gave them slightly higher assistance rates. "A majority seem to be slightly better off, primarily because most were re-categorized," the report said. "But the degree of housing and food insecurity remains troublingly high. And those who were not re-categorized saw no improvement in their income or other basic needs." The twelve who left voluntarily were better off, with "a sizable increase in their incomes," though most of them still made too little to cross the poverty line.

The four who were forced to leave welfare were "clearly worse off," with a "staggering" drop in income. All four were homeless. "It's through-the-looking-glass stuff," Klein said. "It serves nobody that these people are cut off." Many of the participants had unstable housing. Four out of ten said at the start of the study that they had been homeless at some point in the previous six months. Those who had housing "were much more likely to leave welfare for employment." Few had enough money for healthy food. Three out of four got food from a food bank, soup kitchen or drop-in centre in the month before the interview. By the final interview, many still relied on charity to eat. "Disturbingly, even those who were re-categorized continued to rely on food banks or soup kitchens an average of four times per month," the report said. "And those who were not re-categorized reported a significant increase in their use of food banks or soup kitchens."

The authors made various recommendations, including putting people into appropriate categories in a timely manner so they wouldn't have to meet inappropriate employment requirements; reconsidering policies that allowed welfare recipients to be cut off; and providing people with housing, medical help, addiction treatment, childcare, education and other support they needed if they were to have a chance of finding and keeping jobs. They also recommended raising welfare rates, indexing them to inflation and allowing all recipients to keep at least some of the money they might earn. "We urge that the ministry (and government overall) change its overarching goals, from a narrow focus on welfare case-load reduction and 'moving people from welfare to work,' and move instead to the broader goals of poverty reduction and elimination, and health promotion," they wrote. The report concluded:

> BC's welfare policies do not help people find a path out of poverty. Only a small fraction of the participants in this study left poverty. Those who remain on assistance remain very poor, even if re-categorized. Those forced off even more so. And while those who shifted from income assistance to the labour market were better off, most are now counted among the working poor.

The minister at the time, Claude Richmond, labelled the CCPA's call for a 50-percent hike in welfare rates "unreasonable," even though it would still have left the recipients well below the poverty line. "Now you know if we did that they'd be above the rate some people who work earn and it would cost over $700 million a year," he said. "It's just not reasonable." The ministry meets frequently with advocates, he said, and seriously considers any reports and recommendations. "But that was a request they've been making for the last ten or fifteen years. They always get up and say 'raise the rates by 50 percent.' Do you realize, I have no stats on this—this is an opinion—but how many more people we would have on welfare if we raised the rates 50 percent?...We would become, and you can quote me on this, we would become a welfare magnet."

Already, he claimed, BC had the second- or third-highest rate of all Canadian provinces for most categories of welfare. "If we were to raise rates by 50 percent, and it's totally unrealistic, you know where that would put us? It would put us into the stratosphere as far as anyone else is concerned and we would be a very attractive place to come and be on income assistance."

The minister's claim of generosity, however, was inconsistent with figures from the federal government's National Council of Welfare. A table based on 2006 data compared the household incomes of people on welfare after accounting for tax credits. According to the table, the $6,460 annual income for single employables ranked fifth in the country. A 50-percent increase to people in the category would have put the province just $700 ahead of the top payer, Newfoundland and Labrador. For single parents with a child, BC ranked sixth. For couples with two children, BC was ninth, ahead of only New Brunswick. It was only British Columbians with a disability who fared as well as the minister suggested. The payment of $10,665 was the second highest rate in Canada in 2006, behind Ontario.

Report co-author Seth Klein said he did not believe a 50-percent increase in welfare would attract people to the province. "There is nothing attractive about living on welfare, and people would not move here to get it," he said. Most people who receive welfare do so for only a few months, but anyone who doesn't get a job quickly is likely to be on the caseload for a long time. Therefore, the report said, the rates should be high enough for people to meet their basic needs. "People have the right to live with dignity," it said. "People need to be able to live without resorting to charities, or to desperate measures such as survival sex or petty crime, or remaining in abusive relationships." Nor would minister Richmond have to act alone, Klein said. "If he is really concerned about this, yet prepared to acknowledge that current rates are too low, then why is he not leading a national effort to increase rates in a coordinated manner?"

Richmond, like ministers before and after him, insisted the government's focus on moving people into jobs was working. "We have gone from a culture of dependence and entitlement to a culture of independence and employment," he said.

Despite claims that everyone is working, it has never been clear that's why the numbers dropped so quickly after 2001. A government attempt to distribute "exit surveys" showing what people were doing six months after they left welfare was abandoned after it was pointed out that the surveyors couldn't find the majority of the people involved, many of whom no longer have phone lines.

Sue Hendricks, an income assistance advocate with Victoria's Together Against Poverty Society in the mid-2000s, said in an interview that many of the people she's seen have lost welfare payments because of not doing a job search or complying with an employment plan. There was one client, for instance, who was supposed to go to the John Howard Society for job training. "He missed only one appointment and he was cut off." A single mom with three kids, including a twenty-one-year-old daughter with developmental challenges and two who were younger, faced a similar situation. She was in a job program for women with barriers to employment, but "she missed appointments because her daughter was sick…She just felt she needed to be there for this person, and she got cut off." Eventually the ministry put her back on, but not before causing a great deal of stress.

Hendricks also remembered a woman who was expected to find work even though she was parenting two kids under six years of age. "She didn't have daycare but she had to go on a job search," Hendricks said. The woman wanted to search for a job, Hendricks added, but dragging the children around to do so didn't make sense, so it was impossible for her to meet the ministry's requirement and keep her welfare payments. Finally, "does not meet two-year independence test"—which requires a person to show they've earned at least $7,000 a year in the previous two years—started coming up in October 2002 as a reason why a case was being closed. That reason had been used 2,812 times by January 2005. "The people who are having trouble with it are of course young people. And immigrants," Hendricks said.

The codes ministry staff enter when welfare files are closed show that people leave for all kinds of reasons. The following codes, obtained through a freedom of information request, show that for every six people who left because they got a job, there was one who moved out of the province, one who dropped out of contact with the ministry, one who became a student and one who died. Others were cut off for not meeting the ministry's requirements to look for work.

These are some of those reasons, and the number of times each code was used between June 2002 and January 2005:

- No response to cheque hold or letter: 50,850
- Obtained employment: 37,404
- Moved out of province: 6,325
- Person deceased: 6,065
- Non-compliance—refused request for information: 6,059
- Cheque returned, no client contact: 5,865
- Student in school—secondary and postsecondary: 5,854
- Does not meet two-year independence test: 2,812
- Non-compliant with employment plan: 2,723
- Non-compliance—job search: 2,097
- In prison/halfway house: 1,955
- Quit/Fired/Refused employment: 651
- Immigration—sponsorship breakdown: 351
- Immigration status is non-Canadian, non-permanent resident or not protected (refugee): 261

Most people who collect welfare do so only for a short time, so there is a constant flow off the caseload. When the ministry tightens the eligibility requirements, as it did in 2002, the effect is that of closing a tap so that those who leave are not replaced.

For many of the situations, it seemed obvious where those who left welfare were going—and it wasn't to work. After 2001 the province saw a spike in the number of people with nowhere to live. I first noticed the increase in homelessness, the result of crises in housing and poverty, as a reporter for *Monday Magazine* in downtown Victoria. An alternative weekly, the paper at the time took an interest in such issues. At first it was little more than an impression, then anecdotes began circulating about overflowing shelters, unaffordable rents and increases in the number of people camping in city parks. Similar trends were emerging in other BC cities. Local governments began doing homelessness counts, a method that they stressed provided a minimum estimate for the number of people who were homeless, a snapshot that likely under-counted the true extent of the problem. For Metro Vancouver, from 2005 to 2008 the number of people who were homeless grew from 2,174 to 2,660. Within that figure, the number counted as "unsheltered" grew from 1,127 to 1,574.

There were debates through early 2008 about the true number of homeless people in the province. Citing figures he said came from BC Housing, minister Rich Coleman told me there were between 4,500 and 5,500 homeless people in BC at any given time. The agency said it based its estimate only on the communities that had done official homelessness counts. David Chudnovsky, the NDP housing critic at the time, called Coleman's number "bogus." He had his own "conservative" estimate of 10,500 homeless in the province based on homeless counts and numbers provided by shelters and other aid agencies.

A report by health professors at the University of British Columbia, Simon Fraser University and the University of Calgary, written in 2007 but not released until 2008, came up with a number that was up to triple Coleman's estimate. As many as 15,500 adults with severe addictions or mental illness might be homeless in BC, said the 149-page report, *Housing and Support for Adults with Severe Addictions and/or Mental Illness in British Columbia.* The authors were Michelle Patterson and Julian Somers of sfu, Karen McIntosh and Alan Shiell of u of c, and Jim Frankish of ubc. The report was prepared at the request of the health ministry's mental health and addictions branch; other partners and contributors included the provincial health authorities, the Employment and Income Assistance Ministry, and Coleman's own Forests and Range Ministry. To get their estimate, the authors used data and reports from the Canadian Mental Health Association, the Canadian Senate, the provincial government and academic journals. "No single authoritative source of information is available to derive these estimates," the report said. "However, a number of recent reports offered valuable insights into various levels of housing need."

The report said some 130,000 adults in British Columbia had severe addictions and/or mental illnesses. About 39,000 were "inadequately housed," meaning they met the Canada Mortgage and Housing Corporation (cmhc) definition of being in "core housing need." Of those, about 26,500 didn't have enough support to help them stay in their homes. Somewhere between 8,000 and 15,500 were what the report called "absolutely homeless," meaning they were living on the streets, couch-surfing or otherwise without shelter. The report said the authors confirmed their figures with "local stakeholders and key informants." It also said that despite impressions that homelessness, mental illness and addiction are urban problems, interviews with front-line workers found the same problems were "highly prevalent in rural settings."

While creating supported housing for everyone at risk of homelessness would be expensive, the authors found that the cost of doing nothing would be even higher: "If we focus on the absolutely homeless, non-housing service costs amount to about $644.3 million per year across the province." That figure included the costs to the health care and prison systems as well as emergency shelters. "In other words, the average street homeless adult with SAMI [severe addictions and/or mental illness] in BC costs the public system in excess of $55,000 per year." Providing adequate housing and supports would cut those costs by $18,000 per person each year, it said, saving about $211 million in annual spending. The authors noted they did not include the amount of money that homelessness may cause to be lost by businesses, tourism and cancelled conference or convention bookings. "The inclusion of these and other cost drivers would further enhance the case for change," the report said.

By 2009, the office of then auditor general John Doyle had looked into the problem. He concluded in the March 2009 report *Homelessness: Clear Focus Needed* that homelessness was growing and that the government had failed to develop a plan that would reduce the number of people without homes. Doyle wrote:

> *We found significant activity and resources being applied to homelessness issues but there is no provincial homelessness plan with clear goals and objectives. The foundation of many best practices appear to be in place. However, the absence of clear goals and objectives raises questions about whether the right breadth and intensity of strategies are being deployed.*

The government didn't even have a grasp of the size of the problem, he said. "The lack of good comprehensive information about the nature and extent of homelessness in the province" made it difficult to plan, he noted. The only figures available were from homelessness counts conducted by municipalities and regional districts that likely underestimated the problem, and even they were rising, he said. "The continuing increase in the number of homeless counted suggests a lack of success in managing homelessness, let alone reducing it."

A good financial case could be made for better addressing homelessness, Doyle said. "The cost of public services to a homeless person is significantly higher than to that same person being provided with appropriate housing and support services." He also pointed out that the rise in homelessness had largely come in good economic times. "The recent, dramatic downturn in the economy increases the likelihood of more people becoming homeless."

The government's response, included with the report, committed to eliminating homelessness, though Doyle pointed out the government needed to set clear strategies and a time frame to make it happen.

Rich Coleman, a powerful minister in both the Campbell and Clark cabinets, has had responsibility for the housing file since 2008. In general he has overseen renewed spending in the area and in late 2014, as this book was being readied for production, numbers had begun to drop—though not as fast as many hoped. Coleman has at times been unapologetic on the subject. In a speech in the legislature just days before the opening ceremonies of the 2010 Winter Olympic Games, which BC hosted, Coleman acknowledged that he was getting questions from foreign reporters about the housing and homelessness crisis in Vancouver. His strategy, as he explained it, was to respond by telling reporters covering the Olympics that the situation was worse wherever they came from. "One of the reporters said to me: 'What do you do about social housing?'" the Hansard transcript quoted him as saying in the House. "And I said: 'Well, I believe that in your city you're presently bulldozing some projects that you built, that you called social housing that became slums because you perpetrated something on the society.'"

He described another case where he went on aggressive defence with a reporter from an unnamed city of two million people:

I won't name [the city] because it's not fair to the poor reporter. He came to me and said, "You know, you've got 2,500 to 3,000 homeless people here."

I said: "Yes, that's true. It's about that [many]. We have shelters for them, and we have housing that we're building for them. But when you go to write your story, think about this. You've got, actually, according to your records, 13,500 homeless people in your jurisdiction where you come from.

"How many integrated supports have you got out there for people with mental health addictions and homelessness? How many shelters do you have?

"Ask these questions. How many units have you gone out and renovated and taken on to turn around for people? What do you have for a plan to build new? Do you have any outreach workers that go out and connect people to medical services and housing and supports, to deal with their mental illness and issues?"

I said, "Let me try and explain to you the story of British Columbia. In the last few years we've had homeless outreach people in 49 communities across the province of British Columbia—49 communities. They've connected 8,700 people to supports and housing as of January 2010."

As we did that… these were folks that were homeless or at risk for homelessness that we've actually connected to housing and supports, and 80 percent of those people are still housed today.

(Hansard, *February 10, 2010*)

Coleman said the "neatest part" of the two weeks before the Olympics was having the "opportunity to educate some jurisdictions around the world about how they should handle their own housing, mental health, addictions and homeless issues."

Despite Coleman's bluster, there has been little progress since.

In 2014, the regional count for Metro Vancouver found 2,770 people who didn't have homes. About a third of them identified as members of First Nations, a far larger representation than the 5 percent in the city's total population. The overall number of people who were homeless was up by just 150 from the number found in 2011 in the last count. "We've stemmed that rapid increase we saw in the mid-2000s," Deb Bryant of the Greater Vancouver Regional Steering Committee on Homelessness was quoted in the *Metro* commuter newspaper as saying at the news conference to announce the results. "The picture isn't fabulous, but at least we're sort of holding."

The February 5, 2014 count by the Greater Victoria Coalition to End Homelessness found 1,167 people who were homeless, not including people who were couch-surfing, sleeping in cars or tenting in parks. The number included 70 families, 116 children and 89 youths. The report said shelters turned away 78 people that night, most of whom were women and 11 of whom were children.

In 2012 the government made modest changes to the welfare system that were welcomed by anti-poverty advocates. These included re-instating the earnings exemptions of $200 a month for people on regular welfare and raising the exemptions for people on disability assistance. At the same time the government extended the mandatory work search from three weeks to five, therefore extending the time people would need to wait for help. "It just feels punitive and penny-pinching," said Seth Klein of the CCPA, who described some of the other changes as positive. "It just creates a lot of hardship for people." Welfare is understood as a last resort and people don't tend to apply until they're in desperate need, he said. "All indications were the three-week wait was a dysfunctional rule, and they've chosen to expand it."

By 2013 the ministry responsible for administering welfare remained a common source of complaints. Ombudsperson

Kim Carter is the independent officer of the legislature who can investigate whether people are treated fairly by the government. Nearly 20 percent of the files her office opened in 2012–13 involved the social development ministry, up slightly from a year earlier. Those 983 files put the ministry well ahead of the runners-up: the children and families ministry (641 files), justice (591 files), Workers' Compensation Board (304 files), Insurance Corporation of British Columbia (296 files) and health (135 files).

Carter's *Annual Report 2012/2013* included many stories that pointed to the petty bureaucratic decisions that made people's lives more difficult. One was about "Evan," a long-term recipient of disability assistance who was living in northern BC—the Ministry of Social Development had underpaid benefits to him for nearly three years. The ministry admitted staff made a mistake, but would only reimburse Evan for one year, telling him tough luck for the other two. The report said:

> The ministry confirmed that, due to an error on its part, an underpayment had occurred on Evan's file for 34 months. The ministry did not have a specific policy or legislative direction about reimbursing for an underpayment, but indicated that its usual practice is to reimburse the person for a maximum of 12 months, as it had done in this case.

The social development ministry reviewed the matter and agreed to pay Evan what it owed him for the full time it had underpaid him, but only after the Ombudsperson's office questioned the policy.

"Ludmila" also required help from the Ombudsperson's office to get the Ministry of Social Development to apply common sense. Living in the north, she had received income assistance in the summer, but was returning to school in the fall hoping to improve her chance of finding a job. As a full-time student she would be eligible for loans and other financial aid, but not for income assistance.

Ministry staff counted August as the month she started school, disqualifying her for benefits a month earlier than she would have been otherwise. However, this is how the Ombudsperson's report described her August school event:

> *The instructors of the post-secondary program she enrolled in had invited students to attend an orientation day on August 31. Ludmila attended this event, which she described as non-compulsory, informal, introductory, and non-instructional. At the event, she met her instructors and fellow students, and participated in organized social events with students from other programs. No classes were held. Classes began the following day, on September 1.*

Carter's report documented that the Ombudsperson's office "reviewed the program syllabus and related correspondence and discussed these documents with the ministry, as they appeared to confirm that no classes were held before September 1." The ministry reversed its decision.

In another case, "Max" had no food and couldn't pay his rent, but the social development ministry required him to go through a three-week job search before they would help him. The Ombudsperson's report stated:

> *Max told us that the ministry did not consider his need to be immediate as he had not been able to produce an eviction notice from his landlord. Max said that it was not possible for him to produce an eviction letter as it was his roommate who was evicting him.*

With the Ombudsperson's involvement, the ministry agreed to accept an eviction notice from Max's roommate and acknowledged it should have given him food vouchers. It also waived the job-search requirement.

"Peter" moved and told the ministry that was providing his disability benefits in plenty of time, but the ministry sent the $300 payment to his former landowner. "He said that the ministry told him to contact the former landlord and ask for the funds to be reimbursed. Peter contacted his landlord but the landlord refused to cooperate." Meanwhile he had to pay his new landlord out of his disability cheque, leaving him little money for food. With the Ombudsperson's involvement, the ministry agreed it had made a mistake in paying Peter's former landowner and paid Peter back the amount that had been deducted from his benefits.

On the broader question of why so many of her office's files involve the social development ministry, Carter offered various thoughts. "The people who are most dependent on the government are the most likely to come to us," she told me in an interview, noting that in many cases the main public bodies she addresses all deal with people who are at a point in their lives when they are in need. Justice, the third biggest source of Ombudsperson file openings, includes both the BC Family Maintenance Enforcement Program and the provincial corrections system. In many cases the people complaining to the Ombudsperson's office would be unable to afford to hire a lawyer, so coming to her office is a way to get help without that barrier, she said, and added: "It's a reflection of imbalance in not only power between the government authorities and the people who are dependent on them...sometimes there are people who just can't plug into the new processes." In some cases a ministry believes it has a policy, but it's not communicated clearly to staff on the front lines who deal with clients, Carter said. In others, the staff on the front lines have discretion in how to deal with situations, but there's a lack of direction on how to apply it, she said. "You may have places that have shortages of staff."

It has become harder to get help that would have been easily given a few years ago, said Renée Ahmadi, an advocate with Victoria's Action Committee of People with Disabilities, in a 2010 interview: "There are now things people have to appeal for that before were not an issue." Getting classified as "disabled" is often a point of contention, she said. The label entitles a person to more money from the ministry, almost $300 a month for a single person as of late 2014, according to rates that have been in place since 2007. But the ministry was refusing many people who should have been entitled to disability assistance, Ahmadi said. "It's laughable [who is turned away]. People with cerebral palsy, people who are obviously disabled."

Kirsty MacKenzie, an advocate with Vancouver's Downtown Eastside Residents' Association, described the situation this way in an email:

> It has become far too easy to highlight the gross disparities between what this government will spend on elite recreation and luxury development and the resources it extends in support of the most vulnerable members of our society … skyrocketing income inequality in the midst of plenty is Gordon Campbell's biggest legacy to this province.

THE TRUFFLE WITH RESTRAINT: SOME BELTS ARE TIGHTER THAN OTHERS

Despite tight budgets in recent years, there have been priorities. In 2010, as unionized public-sector workers and welfare recipients were asked to tighten their belts, the Crown corporation BC Hydro hosted a reception at the Union of British Columbia Municipalities (UBCM) convention in Whistler. The main attendees at the annual conferences are mayors and councillors from throughout the province, but guests also include MLAs, municipal and provincial staff members, reporters and others. The total bill for the reception from Tourism Whistler, the conference centre operator, came out at $62,000 and included:

- 1,135 glasses of wine ($6.25 each)
- 351 servings of domestic beer ($5.75 each)
- 171 micro-brewed beer ($6.25 each)
- 210 servings of fruit juice
- 59 San Pellegrino sparkling water
- 10 de-alcoholized beers
- A tip of $8,061.27

I got the details through a freedom of information request. John Horgan, then the NDP energy critic and at the time of this writing its leader, said the reception was part of a pattern of wasted money at the Crown corporation. "BC Hydro should focus on its core business, which is providing low-cost electricity to ratepayers and not holding receptions for politicians," he said, and suggested it should be "returning benefits to all British Columbians, not just politicians congregating at places like Whistler." He added that he doubted BC Hydro's customers would be impressed to hear the company spent tens of thousands of dollars buying drinks and food for politicians. "It further enrages people who see their bills going up and up and up," he said.

A BC Hydro spokesperson defended the spending. "BC Hydro's generation, transmission and distribution activities cover the entire province, affecting virtually every person, community and local government in BC," said Susan Danard in an emailed statement. "Most locally elected officials attend the Union of BC Municipalities Conference, offering BC Hydro an efficient and cost-effective way to meet as many of them as possible in one location." Roughly 1,300 conference attendees came to the reception, she said. "Alternative options would involve additional BC Hydro staff travel time and resources that would cost more than hosting everyone at one event," she added.

Discussions at the conference covered a broad range of topics of interest to BC Hydro, she said. They included the reliability of electrical service, the development of alternative energy, local infrastructure projects, opportunities for conservation and reducing costs for local governments, and "ways to improve collaboration to attract industry to more remote communities," she said. BC Hydro representatives also had formal meetings with mayors, councillors and regional districts at the conference, participated in a clean-energy workshop, and set up an educational booth at a trade show that was part of the conference. As well, there were informal meetings, she said. "Over the course of four days, we conservatively estimate that more than 2,000 points of contact were made with local government officials."

Whatever kind of opportunity hosting the event was for BC Hydro, it wasn't good enough for them to do it the next year at the 2011 UBCM conference in Vancouver. That year the $50,000 tab for the reception was picked up directly by the provincial government instead. The bill listed:

- 1,475 glasses of wine at $6.75 each
- 496 bottles of domestic beer at $6.75 each
- 7 bottles of de-alcoholized beer at $6.50 each
- 88 soft drinks at $4 each
- 54 bottles of fruit juice at $4.25 each
- 49 bottles of water at $4 each
- 25 dozen prosciutto and asparagus with white truffle: $950
- 25 dozen smoked sablefish skewers with herb butter: $1,000
- 25 dozen pan-seared spicy prawn crostini: $1,000
- 25 dozen smoked chicken with papaya salsa on bagel chip: $950
- 20 dozen chevre and roasted vegetable tarts: $760
- 25 dozen two-colour tandoori chicken skewers: $925
- 48 dozen pizza points: $1,440
- 48 dozen pakoras: $1,440
- 48 dozen chicken drumettes: $1,920
- 20 dozen vegetable spring rolls: $740
- 4 fresh maki sushi platters: $900

- 11 Italian antipasto displays: $4,400
- Canadian and international cheeseboards: $3,600
- Fresh vegetable crudité with herb dip: $1,800
- Service charge: $6,237.68
- HST: $5,165.03

The following year, for the 2012 UBCM conference in Victoria, the bill for the reception was again paid by provincial taxpayers. The total came to over $32,000, but this time did not include charges to the government for beer and wine, though it noted that eight cash bars had been set up at the event. The menu was notable for the fact that two dishes this time featured truffles—fungi that in Europe are traditionally sniffed out by pigs. The tally for the 2012 event at the Crystal Garden included:

- Truffled mushroom bruschetta, 65 dozen: $2,470
- Grilled vegetable and truffle goat cheese tart, 65 dozen: $2,470
- Crab cakes, 80 dozen: $3,360
- Beef skewers, 80 dozen: $3,360
- Chicken satay, 80 dozen: $3,200
- Tempura prawns, 80 dozen: $3,360
- Antipasto platters: $4,320
- Warm flatbreads: $2,560
- Gratuity on food and beverages: $3,765
- Taxes on food and beverages: $3,463

In the three years that I reported on the menus and invoices at publicly funded UBCM receptions, the bills dropped by about half. Most mayors and councillors, and the other convention attendees, aren't exactly the 1 percent, but by and large they're doing okay and it remains unclear to me why the public should be buying them gourmet treats.

CHAPTER 7

SOCIAL ASSISTANCE: DOING WELL AND NOT DOING SO WELL

EACH YEAR BILLIONS OF DOLLARS flow through the ministry that runs British Columbia's welfare system. With the focus on welfare-to-work in recent decades, large payments have gone to the companies that run employment programs for the government. The owners have done exceedingly well, in some cases amassing fortunes in the millions. And yet for those who desperately need the ministry's help, aid is parcelled out in small amounts. People like Rochelle Bergman, a former truck driver, struggle to survive on disability payments. Meanwhile ministers who make salaries twenty times greater than what an individual receives on welfare have tended to have little sympathy for the conditions of those dependent on the system. One of them, Moira Stilwell, declined to advocate for a raise in rates that would have helped many. She did, however, find another cause she could get behind, demanding a change in a government policy that would have benefited a very small number of people who just happened to include her own son.

In my years reporting on the badly damaged welfare system in British Columbia since 2001, I have found one person who appeared to be doing extremely well. Ian Ferguson was the president and CEO of WCG International Consultants Ltd., the company he founded to run JobWave, the largest of the job placement companies charged with helping people move from welfare to work. While people struggled on welfare, or failed to meet the ministry's new eligibility requirements, Ferguson and his colleagues made millions in British Columbia delivering a program that Ontario later tried and abandoned because the results weren't good enough to justify the expense.

In 1999, *BC Business* magazine estimated WCG's annual revenue at $2.5 million. By the 2001–02 fiscal year, the province's public accounts indicate, BC taxpayers were paying the company more than ten times that amount with annual payments ballooning to $26.4 million, a level they stayed at through much of the decade. Ferguson said in an April 2003 interview with me that the company does 60 percent of its business consulting with the private sector, but didn't provide details when pressed. Assuming Ferguson was correct, the company would have had revenue of some $66 million, or more than a twenty-five-fold increase from just a few years earlier.

By Ferguson's own estimation, he has "done well by doing good." When we spoke in April 2003 he had a home on a leafy cul-de-sac near the University of Victoria and was building a new house, with waterfront views, nearby. He also kept a place in Los Angeles and was racking up frequent-flyer miles commuting to meetings in Victoria every couple of weeks. He and his wife, Elizabeth, also a partner in WCG, bought themselves matching Mercedes-Benzes, although Ferguson said he mainly drove a leased 2001 Infiniti. Ferguson had previously been an IBM account manager. "It's not like selling 1,000 computers," he said of the job-placement business. "That's nice too, but if you can help 26,000 people change their lives, that's the right thing to do."

To some, Ferguson was a hero, a social entrepreneur whose company played a big role in helping the government move hundreds of thousands of people off welfare and into the workforce. The Fraser Institute's 2002 report card on BC welfare reform praised JobWave. "The use of private sector providers and their particular competencies in delivering welfare and welfare-related services," wrote Jason Clemens, the institute's fiscal studies director, "represents an enormous step forward in social policy in Canada and should be expanded, both in British Columbia and throughout Canada." The now-defunct *Report* magazine, the long-time voice of Western Canadian neo-conservatism, was also enthusiastic about JobWave's role in a February 3, 2003 article about the BC Liberals' "no-nonsense approach" to welfare. *BC Business* magazine identified WCG as one of the top twenty-five companies in BC to work for and as one of the top fifty "up and comers."

Even Carole James, the former New Democratic Party leader, liked JobWave. The NDP government successfully used the company to reduce welfare caseloads, she told me not long after becoming party leader. Asked if funding JobWave was good public policy, she said, "I think it is." However, she added, the government needed to ensure such programs were accountable and effective.

While the program got its start under the NDP, it expanded greatly under the BC Liberals after 2001, at a time when the government was taking opportunities to turn over public services to the private sector. Aside from the high-profile sale of the publicly owned BC Rail to CN Rail, the government signed large contracts with companies such as Telus, IBM, Maximus and EDS Advanced Solutions to provide public services. In 2013, BC's auditor general identified eleven such deals the government had signed with a total value of about $2.4 billion.

The success of JobWave and its ballooning revenues attracted the attention of more than a few critics. They saw Ferguson as an aggressive businessman, with a knack for getting government contracts, who became rich by providing a fast-food-style service of questionable value. The phenomenal growth of private placement services and the high taxpayer-funded revenues such services enjoy are reason enough to cast a wary eye on WCG and the JobWave program, said Marge Reitsma-Street, a social work instructor at the University of Victoria. "I think it's really problematic," she said. Reitsma-Street acknowledged that she may be "a bit old-fashioned" in thinking our "common interests" should be looked after in the public sector. However, she argued that when health care is done for profit, for example, evidence shows that quality goes down while the expense goes up. With a small budget for administration, Reitsma-Street said, the same results that JobWave gets could be achieved by a public institution, like the old Manpower offices that listed jobs and helped people with job searches. With a small amount of help, she said, many JobWave clients could get jobs on their own.

The natural churn in jobs in British Columbia was referred to at the September 2002 open cabinet meeting by then-human resources minister Murray Coell. "There are ongoing opportunities through the 500,000 jobs that are typically changing hands in BC in an average year," he said. "These vacancies are created by people changing employers, retiring, going back to school or leaving work to raise a family. Because the labour market is so dynamic, it creates opportunities for British Columbians to get their first jobs or to re-enter the workforce after a time away." Garnett Picot, author of a Statistics Canada report on welfare leavers, put it this way: "At any given time the people who exit welfare are, of course, the most employable ones." While the total number of people on welfare may not normally change much from month to month, there's a normal cycle where individuals leave welfare for jobs and new claimants arrive.

The human resources ministry's own research said it was normal for two out of three welfare recipients to leave within six months. It's also true that of those who leave, two out of three are back on welfare within two years. This raises the question of whether wcg is often just a broker in the middle of a regular cycle, turning a tidy profit from the normal process of people moving between welfare and work.

wcg managers, however, said they were proud of the service they provide. "We so appreciate [the human resources] ministry because they've been a solid partner in our pilot and we've all worked together for the betterment of the people under Murray

[Coell]'s care," said Darlene Bailey, wcg vice-president and partner, in a 2003 interview in JobWave's Victoria headquarters. "I think that's what sustains us in this work. We feel like we're making a difference." Asked how much money the company makes, Bailey said: "The bottom line is we really are proud of what we do." When pushed to answer, she said: "It's profitable, and thank heavens it is."

In 2001, the company had a goal of placing 3,500 people, but Bailey said they actually placed 7,000. Her numbers raised several questions. How could a company help twice as many people as it was paid for and still turn a profit? How many people was Job-Wave actually paid for? "We did a lot of it for free," said Bailey. "We just exceeded it." More answers were not forthcoming. It's a competitive business, said the company's PR guy, who sat in on the interview. The company doesn't want to show its hand to the competition.

Neither the government nor the company wanted to provide a copy of the JobWave contracts. The first arrived on my desk in a brown envelope delivered anonymously to my office. Later I received all the contracts for JobWave and Destinations, the other major placement firm in BC, through a freedom of information request. The December 1999 JobWave contract, which was signed by the NDP government and continued until July 31, 2003, gives some indication of how the company reaped its rewards. The contract defined *placement* as follows:

> *An action that causes a Participant to become independent of Income Assistance, including commencement of employment with a suitable employer who can provide a Participant with sufficient hours of work and income such that the Participant is no longer eligible to receive Income Assistance.*

By this definition, a person who moves to Alberta would be deemed to be "placed," because he or she would no longer be receiving income assistance in BC. So would a person who went back to the welfare office and didn't meet eligibility requirements, ended up homeless, or even died. Ferguson said they were able to track clients "twenty-four hours a day, seven days a week," but in practice the only thing they really knew was whether the person was back on welfare. As long as the person wasn't drawing the dole, WCG would get paid.

Might the company be paid for clients who slipped through the social safety net? "There's a full range of circumstances in people not being back on income assistance in BC," Ferguson replied. He insisted, however, that "the vast majority are back at work."

Yet the government's own exit surveys of people who have left welfare consistently show that after six months the phone numbers for nearly half the people they seek to interview are out of service. Only 1,013 of the 4,762 people in the February 2003 survey actually told the surveyors they had work. Of those, it's unclear from the report how many hours they were working. In addition, in 2003 Statistics Canada released a national study based on income tax information. It showed that for people who left welfare in the 1990s, one out of three had earnings two years later that were lower than the amount they had received on welfare.

Besides the loose definition of *placement* in the contract, WCG benefited from a generous payment schedule. For each person "placed," the original contract specified that the government would pay WCG a maximum of $4,865. While the company didn't get paid in full until the participant has been off income assistance for nineteen months, WCG received $3,500—or 72 percent of the total—in three instalments after just seven months. The seventh and final payment, made at nineteen months, was a mere $185. The contract also allowed for advance payments of $900,000, and at least one ministry employee was seconded to the company at the government's expense.

A later contract was a little bit tighter, according to information provided by the human resources ministry, offering the company "approximately $3,400" per placement. The company still got 25 percent of the total amount after the person was off welfare for just one month, and collected 70 percent of the sum after nine months. (One key difference between the 1999 and 2002 contracts is that under the later contract welfare referrals could no longer be released from the program at their request.)

Would the company get paid for everyone it placed if it exceeded the targets? "Traditionally the answer was if there was money in the government's budget you did," said Ferguson. "If there wasn't you didn't." Ferguson added that "overplacing" was part of JobWave's strategy. "To take the cycles out of the business.... We will always to the best of our ability place as many as we can."

Seth Klein, director of the BC branch of the Canadian Centre for Policy Alternatives, said the government's big bill with JobWave made little sense. "People are always leaving and finding jobs. There's nothing new in this." At the same time, the government had radically altered the job coaching industry, he said, by rewarding volume and requiring all job training agencies to move to performance-based funding where payment depended on people finding jobs. This created an incentive for the agencies to help only the easiest people to employ, Klein said, and to abandon anyone who might have a hard time finding a job.

Tina Griffith, an instructor-counsellor with Workstreams, a non-profit job training agency, confirmed that the industry had shifted, and that many of the people who had worked in it a long time found the change difficult. "We're in the business of social services, not capitalizing on people finding work," she said. The new payment model might suit JobWave fine, she added, but she didn't like it. "Basically there's a price tag on everyone who comes through here."

Over the years, evidence that JobWave might not be providing value for money piled up. WCG launched a chain of JobStores that offered services to the public that were similar to those provided to welfare clients, including resumé writing and interview preparation, but failed to find a market and soon closed the JobStores. The Ontario government tried a pilot project with wcg starting in 2005, but, unlike BC, studied the results and in 2008 decided that the company saved the public no money and did no better a job than the government could by providing the service through public employees.

In 2010 I obtained investigation reports that showed BC investigated wcg after it was discovered the company was billing the government for helping clients even though the clients were "no-shows." The ministry's office in Prince George raised questions about why wcg International HR Solutions' office in the city had already billed the ministry for intake for clients it later described as "intake no-shows." The discrepancy arose because the office was using a two-step intake process, the report found. The office was requiring clients to come for an orientation then return "some time later" for an intake interview, it said. "The intake fee is billed at the orientation step," it said. "This practice…has resulted in over-billings and delays in identifying clients that should not be accepted into [the BC Employment Program]."

The investigators identified $2,800 in overbillings. Also, of the eight intakes they looked at from January and February of 2009, just one was done within the twenty-one days allowed under wcg's contract with the government. The investigators compared the two-step process with what was happening at seven other wcg offices and found the others were completing their intakes in a single step.

Darlene Bailey, wcg's president and CEO—who had replaced Ferguson—responded to Tracy Orr, director of the BC Employment Program (BCEP) in a May 7, 2009 letter. "Delivery staff have received additional training on the requirement that the entire intake process needs to be completed prior to either accepting or declining a BCEP client," Bailey wrote. "Regional management and our quality assurance team will closely monitor to assure that no further examples occur." wcg would deduct the amount overbilled from its next invoice for the area, she said.

A PricewaterhouseCoopers review of the BCEP, I reported in 2009, found some 12 percent of the money was paid in situations where the contractors did not meet the documentation requirements.

Ferguson by then had moved on, having sold WCG in 2007 to a publicly traded company, Arizona-based Providence Service Corporation. The sale came just four days after the BC government started a new five-year, $40-million contract with the company, Jagrup Brar—the NDP's employment and income assistance critic— pointed out in the legislature during debate of the ministry's $1.5-billion budget for that year. He suggested the government had helped prepare WCG for sale, something the minister at the time— Claude Richmond—said he found "offensive."

During the debate Brar detailed some of the connections between WCG and the Liberals. "One of the vice-presidents of WCG is Mr. Robin Adair," he said. "Mr. Adair...directed communications for Liberal candidate Sheila Orr in the 2001 election." The lobbyist registry said Adair had visited various Liberal MLAs, including premier Gordon Campbell, Brar said, and he noted that another vice-president was James Rae, who worked as a deputy minister to Richmond in the 1980s. "Above all," Brar said, "WCG has donated over $95,000 to the BC Liberal party since 2001. Can the minister confirm these facts?"

Adair, by the way, later ran and narrowly lost in the 2009 election for the BC Liberals in the Saanich South constituency. He was quoted at the time as saying he had nothing to do with the operations of WCG and his role was merely to be the public face for the company.

Responding to Brar, Richmond said: "I can confirm that I have known Dr. Rae for a long time on and off since he was a deputy minister for me. That was back in 1982 for a short while, and then I was out of government for ten years and didn't really see him. It's a very friendly relationship but certainly not a very close one." He said he did not know about Adair's involvement or WCG's donations. "The first I've ever heard of donations is what you just told me today," he said. "I have no knowledge of that. Beyond that I can't comment."

The contract tendering process was open and transparent and WCG received no special treatment from the government to make the $30-million sale possible, Richmond said. "I find those words 'with the help of the ministry' offensive." He added all that had been sold were the shares in WCG, not the government programs. The contract continued to be run by the same people, despite the change in ownership, he said, adding that if Providence failed to meet the contracted requirements, the government could always terminate the agreement.

Richmond said he didn't know when he first found out about the sale. WCG and Providence requested a meeting with him, he said, but he had refused, saying it was a private deal between two companies and he was not going to get involved. "I said that if the deal goes through, then they can explain to me what has happened."

It was Providence's first foray into Canada from the United States, where its core business is delivering social services on contract to governments. Payment to Ferguson and his partners included $10.1 million cash and $7.8 million in Providence shares, according to Providence's financial filings. There was also provision for a further $10.1 million depending on WCG's earnings. At the time Providence had revenues of nearly $700 million a year and paid its CEO, Fletcher McCusker, $1.82 million in 2008. That made McCusker's salary about 250 times what a single "expected to work" person on welfare in BC would have received in the year.

As of 2014, WCG was still providing services to the BC government, but the number of contracts going to non-profit job training agencies had increased. In the most recent fiscal year, WCG billed the government $6.24 million, or about a quarter of what it did at its height.

* * *

IF BRITISH COLUMBIANS knew how little money the province provides for people living with disabilities, they would surely support increasing the rate, former long-haul truck driver Rochelle Bergman told me. When she needed it, Bergman was surprised to discover the monthly rate in BC for people with disabilities was just $906, she said. She kept thinking there would be other sources of money available. "It just didn't seem right," she said in a 2012 interview, when she was forty-nine years old. "I thought there was more, but there wasn't."

Disability payments left Bergman with not enough money, month after month. "I can't make ends meet," she said. "Nobody could live on that." The rate needed to come up by at least $700 a month, she said. "I would bring it right up if I could, at least to the poverty line," she said, adding that advocacy groups tended to ask for relatively small increases. "I'm not going to fight this for something underneath the poverty line."

Bergman said she had worked and paid taxes for more than three decades—since she was sixteen years old. A couple of years before we spoke she got tendinitis, a painful inflammation in her arms that made it impossible to continue driving a truck. Since then she had received medical benefits, then federal government employment insurance, then nothing. She had spent her registered retirement savings, she said. She owned a condo in East Vancouver, but said that selling it would increase her expenses as she would need to find rent each month. She took part in a job-training program and ended up with a certificate in marketing and communications from the British Columbia Institute of Technology, but had not found work in her new field. "It's not like I've been sitting around sucking my thumb. I've been trying to do things."

At her doctor's suggestion, she applied for disability benefits through the provincial social development ministry, which also provides temporary welfare for people who are out of work, and began receiving benefits in February 2012.

The following summer Bergman wrote a three-page brief for journalists on her situation and what people with disabilities face.

"The stress of not having enough money is building up inside me," she wrote, adding:

> *I wake up now with migraines every day. My depression is now deeper than before and my anxiety attacks come more often. My sleep patterns are all over the place, I hardly sleep or I sleep too long… My eating patterns are now weirder than before. I sit in front of the toilet and wait till I get sick because of my nerves. My stomach goes into grips of pain where it tightens up so much, I feel like I cannot breathe. I am biting my fingernails till most of them bleed.*

On the phone, Bergman said she was getting stomach aches, backache and nausea, and that was making a challenging situation worse. "My whole body is falling apart. The stress is killing me."

The briefing told her own story, but also included information from Statistics Canada, news articles and advocacy groups. She quoted the *Canadian Charter of Rights and Freedoms* sections that declare everyone's right to life, liberty and security. Bergman circulated her document to media throughout the province. Asked if others had responded to her, she said, "So far no, you're the only person. You're the only one so far who's sent anything back to me." And yet she remained optimistic that people would listen, and that when they did they would see the injustice of the situation. Somebody had to change the situation, she said, and "it might as well be me."

When I spoke with Bergman, the minister responsible for the welfare and disability system was Moira Stilwell—a medical doctor by profession whom Premier Christy Clark had appointed a few months earlier. Stilwell was sympathetic to a point and said she could understand why Bergman was finding living on disability benefits difficult. "I'm not surprised a person who had a steady job and steady paycheque is going to face a change in lifestyle when they become disabled," she said. "I think being unemployed after you've been self-sufficient is very stressful."

It's worth noting that as a cabinet minister, Stilwell made around $150,000 a year, which was likely a step down from what she would have made as a radiologist at St. Paul's Hospital in Vancouver before she was elected. At the time this book was being written, she had been demoted to the backbenches, where she was making about $100,000 a year. Stilwell and her husband appeared to be doing okay, though. Her recent public disclosure statements, which she by law has to make as an MLA, said her investments were in a blind trust. When she entered politics, her 2009 statement included a long list of investments, held either directly or through her medical practice's corporation. They included lots of Canadian, American and international index funds, but also stocks in household names like Sears Canada Inc., CISCO Systems Inc., General Electric Co., Home Depot Inc., Intel Corp., Oracle Corp., Power Corp., TD Bank and Krispy Kreme Doughnuts Inc. Through a partnership Stilwell also owned some stock in Netflix, Inc. in 2009, which has gained nearly 1,000 percent since then. Stilwell's 2013 disclosure said she and her husband owned a recreational property in Whistler.

In the ministry Stilwell oversaw, disability assistance rates had been stagnant since 2001, with the exception of a one-time $120-per-month increase in 2007. In 2012 the province made "modest" changes that allowed people with disabilities to earn more money by working, raising the earnings exemption from $500 a month to $800 and introducing a policy that let recipients spread any income over a year to allow for fluctuations. A person who earned up to $9,600 at a seasonal job, for example, could now keep more of the money he or she earned. The government did not at that time raise the rates, however, and Stilwell said the tight provincial budget and deteriorating fiscal situation restricted what could be done. "An increase in rate is not likely in the short term," she said.

In the 2014–15 fiscal year, the most recent available at the time of this writing, the social development ministry budget was just over $2.5 billion, making it less than 6 percent of the provincial budget. For every dollar spent on welfare, two are spent on elementary education and seven go to the health ministry.

The system has to balance between helping people who are vulnerable and what is affordable for the BC public, Stilwell said. "It's not perfect and I'm not going to make it out to be," she said, but added that overall the system was good and provided the fourth-highest level of support in the country. "I certainly think people in BC want all individuals to live with dignity and be as independent as possible." The policy changes would be helpful, and there are already subsidies available for housing, child care and bus passes, as well as employment programs, she said. "Across the board we take seriously our responsibility to provide support to vulnerable people and their families."

When then BC auditor general Russ Jones looked at disability assistance in a May 2014 report, he concluded the program was difficult to navigate and that the government was fuzzy about its goals. "The ministry has not defined clear objectives and measurable targets that define what it means to meet the basic needs of clients," he found, adding:

> Ministry information indicates that given the level of assistance provided, some clients' basic needs may not be met. Clients may need to turn to charitable donations, family support and other sources of assistance to obtain appropriate shelter and other basic necessities.

Carole James, who was then the NDP's social development critic, said the government had treated people with disabilities appallingly. "I don't think there's anybody who would look at income assistance rates and say it makes it a good living for anybody," James told me. At the time it looked likely the NDP would soon win a majority government. "No commitments, but we need to be sure we review it," she said. She also expressed skepticism about increasing earnings exemptions, saying that while they helped some people, "it can look like you're providing huge support when in fact most people can't utilize it."

Or as former truck driver Bergman put it, "Not everybody could work part-time. It's a dumb program. What are they talking about? We can't work, hence we're on it."

In July 2012, the Disability Without Poverty Network—a coalition of five advocacy groups—released *Overdue*, a position paper calling for increased rates. "There is a significant gap between the income needed to cover the cost of basic essentials and the assistance available under BC's PWD [persons with disabilities] benefit," it said. "Without action that gap will continue to grow. Our proposal to increase the PWD benefit would play a significant role in helping close the gap and improving the quality of life for people with disabilities in BC."

The groups in the disability network are the BC Coalition of People with Disabilities, the BC Association for Community Living, the BC division of the Canadian Mental Health Association, the Social Planning and Research Council of BC and the Community Legal Assistance Society. They proposed raising the rate of disability assistance to $1,200 a month, indexing it to inflation so it keeps pace with increases to the cost of living, and introducing a shelter assistance program to help people with disabilities pay their rents. The Disability Without Poverty Network polled British Columbians, the report said, and found 88 percent said $906 a month would not be enough for people to live on. "In addition, 90 per cent of those surveyed indicated that they would support an increase in the assistance provided to people with disabilities," it said.

Raising the disability rate to $1,200 would at the time have cost about $300 million a year. Bringing it up further, say by the $700 a month that Bergman advocated, would add about $700 million a year to the ministry's costs. The provincial government's total annual revenues were over $42 billion in 2012 (and have since risen), or about sixty times the amount Bergman was talking about.

"What needs to change is people's attitudes," Bergman said. "I want people to understand we are people, we still have problems like everyone else. The government should give us dignity and respect."

Bergman said she has had to rely on the food bank to eat and that she knows many people with disabilities who are either broke or who have had to choose to live with their parents. For adults, it's a life with little dignity, she said. "I want all BC to know this is what we get and we can't live this way.... Maybe with the public's help something could be done."

When I asked Stilwell about the coalition's proposal to index the rates, her answer was in effect "not now," similar to her answer to the question about raising rates. "We're always re-examining our policies and putting them up against the resources," she said. "I don't think at the moment that indexing is affordable."

THE CABINET MINISTER WHO ADVOCATED FOR A FAMILY CAUSE

In the same year in which Moira Stilwell refused requests for raises to assistance rates, there was another group to which she was willing to lend her support. Before becoming the minister for social development, Stilwell was the minister of state for health, a junior position helping out then minister Mike de Jong. In that role she championed the cause of Canadian medical students studying in foreign countries who wanted greater access to training positions at home. It would eventually be revealed that her son was one of that small group.

Advocates for the students, known as Canadians studying medicine abroad or csAs, wanted them to be allowed to compete against graduates of all North American medical schools in the first round of matching students to internship positions. The issue goes back decades and the CSAs had always had to wait until the second round to apply for internships, and many were impatient to find a position since they are often carrying as much as $400,000 in debt from their studies. A group based in Vancouver said in 2012 it knew of 350 CSAs and believed there could be as many as 500.

Stilwell picked up the cause and wrote a lengthy report titled *Action Plan for Repatriating BC Medical Students Studying Abroad.*

"These students and their parents have expressed significant difficulty in returning to their home province after completing their undergraduate medical school training," Stilwell wrote. She added:

> *When they apply for residency positions specifically in British Columbia, they face unique barriers which virtually exclude them from placement in those positions, barriers not faced by UBC graduates, Canadian medical school graduates or applicants from the United States. To make this a fair, merit based process now through changes in policy costs nothing!*

She suggested increasing the number of residency positions by fifty-seven, a move that no doubt would have come with a cost to the public, and then opening all of those positions to British Columbians who graduated from medical schools outside North America. Access to those positions had been based on education, with preference given to graduates of schools in North America that all go through the same accreditation process. Stilwell instead suggested, as did the lobby group Society for Canadians Studying Medicine Abroad, making entry to the competition based on place of birth or citizenship. "Our population needs these gifted young physicians," she said.

The recommendations in Stilwell's report would have taken BC in a direction the province had in 2011 considered and abandoned, since treating people differently based on where they were born would open the government up to challenges under human rights legislation. As health minister, de Jong—a lawyer by training—expressed similar concerns about the fairness of treating CSAs differently from other international medical graduates.*

In recent years the Canadian Resident Matching Service (CARMS) began surveying CSAS to find out more about them. While some CSAS are long-time Canadians, others came to Canada with their families before going abroad for school, said Sandra Banner, the agency's executive director and CEO. "It's a very, very diverse group," she said. "We see them graduating from fifty different countries and ninety different schools." Half go to schools in Caribbean countries and the other half are spread around the globe, she said. While North American medical schools are all tested and meet the same standards, she said it would be unwieldy for Canadian authorities to review and accredit the many schools CSAS were attending. Often the schools the CSAS attend are exactly the same ones other international medical graduates (IMGS) have been to, giving the students equivalent education, she said. "We can't say they're different educationally."

According to a summary, the CARMS survey found that "21 per cent of the students are children of Canadian physicians who did not get accepted into a medical school in Canada" and the largest number were from BC and Ontario. They had a median debt of $160,000, more than double the $71,000 for medical students in Canada. "Ninety percent of respondents expressed frustration over the perceived barriers to getting medical residencies in Canada once their studies were over. Caribbean students were the most frustrated," it said.

From an inequality point of view, not only was Stilwell advocating for a group that includes a significant number of children of physicians who failed to get into Canadian schools, but it turned out Stilwell's own son, Kevin Lichtenstein, was part of the group.

---

* In her report, Stilwell argued that CSAs were being treated unfairly and that the government should also be worried about human rights complaints from them.

He was studying medicine in Ireland at the time, something she had failed to mention in interviews with me on the subject, or to minister de Jong while she was working on the report for him.

De Jong told me he was unaware that Stilwell's son was one of a few hundred British Columbians affected by the policy. De Jong said it had been a couple of months since he had asked Stilwell to review the complex issue for him. But when asked if any MLAs had children affected by the policy, he said, "I don't know. I couldn't say for sure. I could check. I know it is an issue, it is certainly an issue that has engaged widespread attention." He talked about communities that need doctors and the "reservoir of talent" that exists in pools of foreign-trained doctors before saying, "I think Moira, who did a report for me—I've never talked to her about children, I'm not even sure how old her kids are—that would be the only person, but I'm not certain what her circumstances are."

Asked why she previously failed to disclose that her son was affected by the policy she had been advocating and advising on, Stilwell said, "It's not about one person, it's about thousands of Canadian kids abroad." A radiologist and nuclear medicine physician, she also said her experience gave her insight into the medical education system. "I've been steeped in the medical training system for thirty-two years. I have lots of perspectives and unique knowledge about it," she said. "I've taught residents for thirty-two years. I've been in the teaching system. I'm aware of it because of my son's situation, but as I say, I don't think it's about one student or another." Her role had been to "shine a light on it" and talk to the minister about the situation and suggest solutions, she said.

It is also worth noting that things turned out relatively well for Stilwell's son. In 2013 he received a residency position in cardiac surgery at St. Paul's Hospital through the University of British Columbia, where his father, Samuel Lichtenstein, was then the head of the division of cardiovascular surgery. Samuel Lichtenstein was also then director of cardiovascular and thoracic surgery at St.

Paul's, a position he held for twenty years, and the medical director for the regional cardiac science program at Providence Health Care and Vancouver Coastal Health.

Attempts to reach Kevin Lichtenstein through St. Paul's Hospital were unsuccessful and messages left for Samuel Lichtenstein were not returned. My message to Stilwell generated a response from Kimanda Jarzebiak, a public relations specialist with Ascent Public Affairs who worked on Stilwell's successful 2013 re-election campaign in Vancouver-Langara and on her unsuccessful 2011 bid to lead the BC Liberals. Kevin applied for one of the "leftover" positions that are open to international students, Jarzebiak said. "I do know there was an independent process put around that," she said, adding neither Stilwell nor her husband were involved. "It's nothing to do with Dr. Lichtenstein or Moira. It's a UBC process."

But David Snadden, who as the executive associate dean of education oversees the selection process for UBC's faculty of medicine, confirmed there were concerns about how the residents in cardiac surgery were chosen that year. "If we feel there's been any irregularities, we do go in and look," Snadden said. "We are always looking to see if the processes are fair." He said privacy concerns restrained him from talking about specifics. "We have a young resident we're responsible for," he said, without naming names. "It would be unfortunate for them to be involved in a way that would damage their training. That's what would concern me."

In general, however, the school would make sure the selection committee for each discipline was fairly balanced and using selection criteria that were equitable, he said. "The departments do set the criteria."

If the school found a problem, they would appoint an outsider to work with the selection committee and make sure the people on that committee were free from conflicts of interest, he said. If necessary, the school would convene a new selection committee, he said. He said he couldn't say what steps the school had taken regarding the cardiac surgery positions, though he confirmed steps had been taken. "So far we haven't found anything untoward," he said. "We are confident the processes were fair and equitable, as far as we could see." Snadden made it clear, however, that the investigation was limited: "I can only work with the information we have…With the information available to me we would feel any concerns were alleviated."

Asked if Samuel Lichtenstein was involved in the selection process that awarded his son a position, Snadden said, "I don't know the answer to that question." He said, "I know he was not on the selection committee and the selection committee makes the decisions." Whether Lichtenstein exercised influence in some other way, Snadden said, "I don't work in the department, so I wouldn't know."

To understand the context for Kevin Lichtenstein's good fortune, it's worth considering the experience of someone who couldn't get a training position in three years of trying: Monica Herrera, president of a group representing IMGs, the Association of International Medical Doctors of British Columbia. Herrera grew up in Chile and went to medical school in Colombia before immigrating to Canada. She said she passed the exams needed to practise in Canada, but was unable to get a residency position in three years of applying. "It's a costly process," she told me, noting she knows of three hundred others in the same situation. "This group is not a group who is swimming in money."

Herrera never got a residency position and instead ended up with a job in workplace health and safety for the Fraser Health Authority. "I'm happy with my life, but I have that nostalgic feeling," she said, adding that as a child she played at giving her dolls medical treatment. "For me it's taking a little bit out of your identity to not be able to do this." Aside from the stereotypes of doctors driving taxicabs, there are physicians from Eastern Europe who are in Canada working in construction, she said. "I think if the system is fair to everybody it's okay…What we want is one process everybody can go into."

When the well-connected son of one family of 1-percenters gets a "next to impossible" training position and another person with comparable training can't get one during several years of trying, it sure looks unfair. The same goes for when a provincial cabinet minister advocates on behalf of a group that includes her son, but declines to act for people struggling on disability payments, a system for which she was for a time responsible.

CHAPTER 8

DEMOGRAPHIC DIVISIONS: MIDDLE-AGED WHITE MEN AND ABORIGINAL GIRLS

N OT LONG AGO, I RAN into a neighbourhood mom whose daughter used to be in the same class at school as mine, though her daughter had since moved to a private school. When I mentioned I was working on a project about inequality, she asked, "What, like between men and women?" Not exactly, I said, explaining that I was looking more at inequalities in income, wealth and opportunity, and that while that often lines up with gender, race and other identifiers, that wasn't really my focus. She was, however, not the only one to raise the identity question with me, and as an able-bodied straight white middle-aged male, I'm aware it would be easy for me to miss the ways in which who people are affects how they do in our economy and society. As noted in Chapter 3, top earners tend to be well-educated, urban, married, middle-aged men, pretty much making them my peer group (aside from the top-earner part). On average, they are clearly much better off than, for example, indigenous female children. Literally, we are of course all unequal, each of us with a position somewhere on the spectrum, but that inequality tends to work out worse for people in some groups than it does for others.

The West Coast Legal Education and Action Fund (LEAF)— a non-profit that advocates to make Canada more equal for women—in 2009 released a report examining to what extent British Columbia had met the United Nations Convention on the Elimination of all forms of Discrimination against Women (CEDAW). It gave the BC government a *D* for women's equality. "Gender's no longer a priority for this government provincially or federally and it's showing," said Alison Brewin, executive director of West Coast LEAF. "What we're trying to illustrate is there are international standards around gender and equality that aren't being met here."

British Columbia's top mark, a C, was for efforts to stop violence against women and girls and for how women and girls are treated in prison. The reviewers gave the province *D*'s for its housing system, the weakness of its social assistance program and for access to child care. The province received failing grades for its failure to fully investigate the cases of missing and murdered indigenous girls and for access to justice.

The report led to questions in the BC legislature. Michelle Mungall, MLA for Nelson-Creston, said she would prefer to put questions about the report to a minister of women's equality, but could not since the BC Liberals disbanded the ministry in 2001. Instead she addressed a question about missing and murdered indigenous women to then solicitor general Kash Heed, who later left politics. "Our primary goal has always been to ensure that we have front-line services available for people who become victims of violence in society," Heed said. "We are investing $43 million into programs to ensure that we have victim assistance available, whether it's members from a disenfranchised group in life or who fall victims of violence."

Burnaby-Deer Lake MLA Kathy Corrigan picked up on the other *F* awarded to the province, in the area of access for women to the justice system. She asked, "Why has this government gutted legal aid services and allowed critical services like the Family Law Clinic to close their doors?"

"Actually, the member is incorrect," responded Mike de Jong, the then attorney general. "Funding for legal aid services from the government have actually gone up again this year."

Drawing on the LEAF report, Corrigan said: "Just this year the Family Law Clinic was axed, dispute resolution referrals eliminated, extended services for family law cases suspended and the Legal Services Society gutted." She asked how "dismantling the legal aid system" would help women, particularly single parents, who need the services.

The question brought a tougher attack from de Jong. "I think it's a vitally important subject," he said. "But I also think that the member as a legislator and an occupant of a seat in this chamber has a duty to check her facts…She chooses either deliberately or inadvertently to bring information to this House and present facts that are not facts." Funding for the Legal Services Society has actually increased, he said. "Now that may not fit within the parameters of the political story that the member chooses to advocate, but it is a fact."

Speaking a few hours after the exchange, Brewin said de Jong and Corrigan were both correct. "Funding to the Legal Services Society has not been cut," she said. "Services to families that need legal aid have been cut…The funding wasn't cut but the services were." The shortfall goes back to the huge cuts the provincial government made to legal aid in 2002, which she said has been "consistently underfunded" since then. "Family law legal aid virtually doesn't exist in BC right now."

The question needs to be considered in the context of how the government's policies have affected women in a variety of areas, she said. Lack of child care makes it hard for many women to find and keep jobs, she said, and women are more likely than men to be poor. "We have the highest poverty rate in Canada here in BC and women are hit hard by that…It's the combination of all those issues that makes equality a problem in BC."

Marjorie Griffin Cohen is a professor of political science and gender, sexuality and women's studies at Simon Fraser University.

In a 2012 paper, BC *Disadvantage for Women*, written for the BC office of the Canadian Centre for Policy Alternatives, she looked at the wage gap, comparing women to men, but also women in British Columbia to women across the country. In 2010 in BC, women made 65 percent of what men did, according to Cohen's paper, which was even worse than the Canadian level of 68 percent. Women's incomes had caught up somewhat with men's since 2000, but not as quickly as in the rest of the country, she said. "While earnings for women in BC are slowly improving, they are not keeping pace with the average for women workers in Canada," she wrote. In an Organization for Economic Co-operation and Development study of twenty-six member countries, Canada ranked the sixth worst for income inequality between genders, she noted. "Within a country that has a poor showing for women's equality in earnings, women in BC have fallen behind the Canadian average."

Looking for causes of the gap, Cohen found plenty. "Both levels of government in Canada have a responsibility for the policy directions that relate to earnings inequality," she wrote. "At both the federal and provincial levels, public policy for women has been undermined by neo-liberal approaches to government." Citing Canada's signing of the United Nations' CEDAW, which aimed to eliminate discrimination against women, she started with an assessment of the federal Liberal government's budget from 1995:

This budget marked a massive shift in direction for social programs in Canada, a shift that accelerated a federal government direction that had begun during the years of the Brian Mulroney Conservative government. It created a situation where more of the burden and less of the funding for social programs went to the provinces.

BC had made the problem worse. "When the Liberal government in BC was elected in 2001 it began concerted efforts to make labour more 'flexible' and responsive to employers' needs," she wrote, and continued:

> It also instituted measures to reduce what it considered to be a high wage economy. The effect on labour was direct and brutal and it often appeared to target women. The changes that occurred in BC public policy toward labour and low-income groups coincided with the increase in income disparity between groups and the disadvantage women in BC experience in earnings.

Cohen singled out the 2002 legislation that set aside a contract for hospital support workers so the government could privatize their work. "About 8,000 health care workers who did cleaning, food preparation, laundry, and other hospital work lost their jobs," she wrote. "The vast majority of these workers were women, and while the private multinational companies that took over the work rehired some, the wages initially dropped from about $17.50/hour to as little as $10.00." The provincial government also took away many bargaining rights for some groups of workers, notably teachers, most of whom are female, she said.

That kind of gender income inequality can have serious consequences. Tracy Porteous, the executive director of the Ending Violence Association of BC, was quoted in a 2014 *Globe and Mail* article linking income disparity between the sexes with an increase to violence against women. Along with the largely transient male workforce and the prevalence of drug and substance abuse, it was particularly a problem in places dominated by resource-extraction industries like forestry and mining, she said, while stressing that the vast majority of men working in such industries don't commit violence. In the northeastern BC city of Fort St. John, during the heart of the province's oil and gas boom, men made an average wage in 2006 of $56,000, more than double the $27,000 women made. The article quoted Porteous as saying that the income disparity

FIGURE 8.1: CHILD POVERTY RATES BY PROVINCE, 2011 DATA

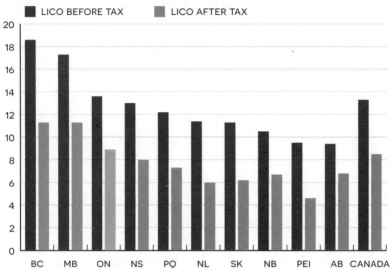

Source: *First Call, using Statistics Canada, Income of Canadians, 2011, Table 202-0802, Persons in low income families, annual*

results in women becoming financially dependent on their partners and thus vulnerable.

Meanwhile, the expression of outrage at British Columbia's dismal record on child poverty has become an annual affair in the province, with the perennially worst off being children living in households headed by single mothers. Each year Statistics Canada releases figures showing British Columbia is either the worst in the country or close to it on poverty in general, and on child poverty in particular. The opposition MLAs rightly point out the performance is shameful and the government responds by saying things are getting better and the statistics are out of date. The advocacy group First Call's report from November 2013, showed BC with a child poverty rate of 18.6 percent, using the before-tax low income cut-offs from Statistics Canada as the measure of who is poor, making it the worst in Canada (see Figure 8.1). "British Columbia also had the most unequal distribution of income among rich and poor families with children, the report said. "The ratio of the average incomes of the richest ten percent compared to the poorest ten percent was 12.6—the worst of any province." A year later, four provinces had passed BC to have worse child poverty rates, but First Call's 2014 report stressed that didn't mean BC was doing well. "Our first provincial report card containing data for 1994 showed that one in five (over 170,000) BC children were poor. It is profoundly disappointing that 18 years later the data still shows that one in five (169,420) BC children are poor," it said (see Figure 8.2). The figures point to real suffering, whether it is children who go to school without breakfast, families that strain to afford basic necessities, or adults who can't afford a place to live.

There are other layers to inequality in British Columbia, including regional disparities that are worth noting. When the government cancelled the ferry route from Port Hardy to Bella Coola while leaving comparable routes in southern British Columbia untouched, the owner of a lodge that depends on tourist traffic to the Chilcotin region described the decision as being regionally unfair. "It looks like remote communities are supporting great service for islands with holiday homes for Victoria decision makers," Beat Steiner, the owner of Tweedsmuir Park Lodge, said in an interview as the 2014 tourist season began. And when planners and local politicians in the Capital Regional District looked for somewhere to put sewage-treatment facilities, they considered various options, including a plan that would have distributed several small plants around the region. Eventually, though, they recommended just one large plant in Esquimalt, which happens to be below the regional average in terms of both average incomes and property values.

When the recession started in 2008, its effects were felt unevenly across the province. Regular Employment Insurance benefits are accessible to people who have lost their jobs through no fault of

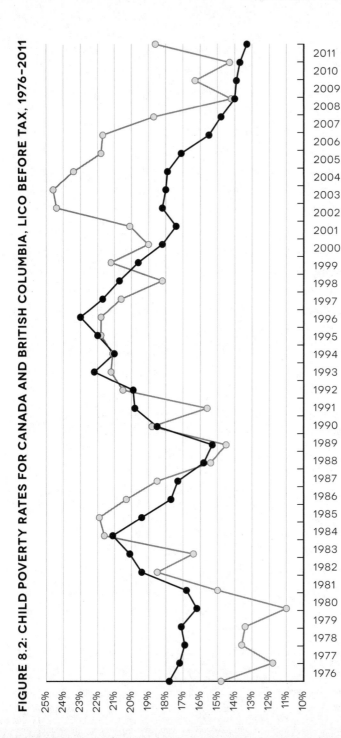

FIGURE 8.2: CHILD POVERTY RATES FOR CANADA AND BRITISH COLUMBIA, LICO BEFORE TAX, 1976–2011

Source: First Call using Statistics Canada, Income of Canadians, 2011, Table 202-0802, Persons in low income families, annual

their own and are available and able to work, but can't find a job. Many communities were close to the provincial average increase of 25 percent in the number of EI recipients from a year earlier, but there was much regional variation. Fort St. John, an oil and gas centre, was at one end of the spectrum. Despite the recession, the number of EI recipients had actually decreased, with 18-percent fewer people receiving benefits compared with a year earlier. At the other end of the spectrum was the beleaguered forestry town of Mackenzie, where in a year the number of recipients almost tripled from 130 to 380. Other resource centres saw similar expansions of people needing help. The number of recipients in the Cowichan Valley went up by 114 percent, in Houston by 83 percent, in Lillooet by 80 percent and in Bulkley-Nechako by 77 percent. In the Lower Mainland, the growth was below the provincial average in Surrey (18 percent) and Vancouver (21 percent), and highest in Port Moody (50 percent) and Maple Ridge (67.9 percent). Urban centres including Kamloops, Kelowna, Prince George and Victoria registered above-average increases of around 35 percent. Communities where the gains were 50 percent and higher included Duncan, Parksville, Courtenay, Vernon, Armstrong, Enderby, Salmon Arm, 100 Mile House, Port Hardy, Esquimalt and Langford.

While the EI figures are a snapshot that indicate some of the variations in the province's labour market, many of the trends are long-term. People living in Kaslo or on Lasqueti Island have been much more likely to have incomes below the low income cut-off than have people in Elkford, New Denver or Belcarra.

According to BC Conservative Party leader Dan Brooks, between 1996 and 2011 the number of people living in rural British Columbia fell by 58,000. Over the same period the province's cities gained 733,000 people, he said. Brooks blamed the provincial government, which had done nothing when sawmills were shuttered in Houston and Quesnel, or when coal mines closed in Chetwynd and Tumbler Ridge.

Another layer of inequality is seen in the role immigration plays. In 2005, according to census data from Statistics Canada, Canadian-born men with university degrees in British Columbia earned a median of $57,788. Men who had immigrated from elsewhere to Canada, who also had university degrees, earned a substantially smaller median in BC of $39,059. If they had arrived recently, which Statistics Canada defined as the past five years, they earned just $27,807. A recent immigrant with a university degree could therefore expect to earn less than half the income of his Canadian-born counterpart.

Women were worse off, whether born here or elsewhere. Canadian-born women with university degrees had a median income of $40,054 in the province, substantially less than their male counterparts who were also born in the country—about the same as male immigrants, but quite a bit more than the $28,664 immigrant women with university degrees earned or the $17,990 earned by similarly educated recent female immigrants. At the bottom end were recent female immigrants without a university degree who in BC earned a median of $13,822. Canadian women who hadn't been to university earned about double that. Canadian men without degrees earned triple, at $43,000. A 2011 Royal Bank of Canada report argued that fixing the gap would be good for the country's economy. The increased wages would add 2.1 percent to the nation's gross domestic product, it said.

In recent years we've seen a new wave of people into the country: temporary foreign workers who are welcomed to fill labour shortages, often in low-wage service sector jobs, but who are not given the same rights as other workers. Their jobs, for example, are tied to the employers who bring them in, making it impossible to seek better positions if something goes wrong and giving them significantly fewer rights than workers who are Canadian citizens. There is even inequality in who gets to fill those marginal jobs. In the summer of 2014, the United Food and Commercial Workers, the union I'm a member of, filed human rights complaints in BC, Ontario and Quebec because of the low number of women who were being brought from Mexico to work on farms. Employers have been allowed to request workers based on gender, something the union said amounted to discrimination. Thousands of people come to Canada as migrant farm workers, but just 4 percent of them are women, the union said.

People with disabilities also fare worse than others in the economy. While 8.8 percent of all Canadians were below the low income cut-off after tax in 2011, the rate for people with disabilities was 23.5 percent. That compared with 19.7 percent of lone parents, 17.3 percent of Aboriginal people living off-reserve and 16.4 percent of recent immigrants.

It is also clear that the people descended from those who were here first tend to do poorly under the current system. In a 2010 paper, *The Income Gap Between Aboriginal Peoples and the Rest of Canada*, prepared for the national office of the Canadian Centre for Policy Alternatives, researchers Dan Wilson and David Macdonald looked at the income gap between people from Aboriginal populations—a definition that includes First Nations, Inuit and Métis—and other Canadians. "Not only has the legacy of colonialism left Aboriginal peoples disproportionately ranked among the poorest of Canadians, this study reveals disturbing levels of income inequality persist as well," they wrote. "In 2006, the median income for Aboriginal peoples was $18,962—30 [percent] lower than the $27,097 median income for the rest of Canadians." One piece of cautious good news was that the gap had been narrowing, they found:

> The difference of $8,135 that existed in 2006, however, was marginally smaller than the difference of $9,045 in 2001 or $9,428 in 1996. While income disparity between Aboriginal peoples and the rest of Canadians narrowed slightly between 1996 and 2006, at this rate it would take 63 years for the gap to be erased.

The income gap was consistent across the country, Wilson and Macdonald found. "Income inequality persists no matter where Aboriginal peoples live in Canada." The income gap between Aboriginal peoples and the rest of Canadians, they found, was "$7,083 higher in urban settings and $4,492 higher in rural settings. Non-Aboriginal people working on urban reserves earn 34 [percent] more than First Nation workers. On rural reserves, non-Aboriginal Canadians make 88 [percent] more than their First Nation colleagues."

Wilson and Macdonald found the promise of education complicated. "The study also reveals income inequality persists despite rapid increases in educational attainment for Aboriginal people over the past 10 years, with one exception," they wrote, and added:

> *Aboriginal peoples with university degrees have overcome much of the income gap between them and the rest of Canadians. The income gap between Aboriginal peoples and the rest of Canadians who have earned a Bachelor's degree diminished from $3,382 in 1996 to just $648 by 2006.*

The thing is, a relatively small number of Aboriginal people earned bachelor's degrees or higher—about 8 percent, compared with 22 percent of the rest of Canadians—the authors wrote. And for those without degrees, the consequence to income was significant: "Below the Bachelor's degree level, Aboriginal peoples consistently make far less than the rest of Canadians with the same level of education."

Within the indigenous population, Macdonald and Wilson noted some "new and significant trends are emerging between men and women." Aboriginal women were more likely than Aboriginal men to finish secondary school and get university degrees, they wrote. "Aboriginal women are also earning median incomes closer to those of Aboriginal men—a trend that isn't being replicated in the general Canadian population." They also found that Aboriginal women with bachelor's degrees actually had higher median incomes than non-Aboriginal Canadian women with the same qualifications. "This is the only segment of Aboriginal society that exceeds the median incomes of their non-Aboriginal counterparts," they wrote, adding:

> That said, educational attainment among Aboriginal peoples still lags well behind averages for the Canadian population as a whole. Non-Aboriginal Canadians are far more likely to complete high school and to get a university degree and the gap between the groups is growing.

Aboriginal people were more than twice as likely as other Canadians to lack a secondary school diploma or fail to go on to post-secondary education:

> The 28 [percent] of non-Aboriginal women who have a university degree or higher is double the rate for Aboriginal women and the situation is even worse for Aboriginal men, where only 8 [percent] have a university degree or higher, which is less than a third the 25 [percent] rate for non-Aboriginal men.

The authors cited the 1996 *Report of the Royal Commission on Aboriginal Peoples*, which estimated "the cost of doing nothing"— that is, keeping the status quo in federal government policy towards Aboriginal people, at $7.5 billion a year. "This figure included $5.8 billion in lost productivity and the remainder in increased remedial costs due to poor health, greater reliance on social services and similar program expenditures."

Wilson and Macdonald called for a "comprehensive approach to the problem" that would go beyond leaving a solution solely up to the market or relying on education to narrow the gap. "It starts by acknowledging the legacy of colonialism lies at the heart of income disparities for Aboriginal peoples," they wrote, and continued:

> *Without doubt, First Nations, Inuit and Métis women are among the poorest people in Canada. Tragedies that have befallen Aboriginal women—for example, the high rates of victimization and violent crime, including more than 520 missing or murdered across Canada— rightly raise concern over the vulnerability that is created by their unique position at the bottom of income earners in the country.*

The outcomes for indigenous people are particularly important in British Columbia, where according to the 2006 census from Statistics Canada, First Nations make up about 5 percent of the population, a bigger portion than the 3.7 percent nationwide. The provincial statistics agency has looked into how indigenous people fare in the province's economy. "Non-Aboriginals were more likely to work full-year/full-time (33.4 [percent]), compared to Aboriginals (22.0 [percent])," said the most recent BC Stats report available on the subject as of this writing; it used data from 2001. The report said:

> *Among those who worked full-year/full-time, average employment income for Aboriginals was considerably lower at $34,696 compared to non-Aboriginals at $44,552. Comparisons within total income groups show the Aboriginal population concentrated at the low end, with 63.8 per cent making less than $20,000, compared to non-Aboriginals at 45.3 per cent. The total median income of Aboriginals is $13,242, compared to $22,535 for non-Aboriginals.*

In August 2014, the Canadian Council of Child and Youth Advocates wrote a letter to the Council of the Federation, which is made up of Canada's provincial premiers and territorial leaders. The CCCYA is an alliance that includes government-appointed children's advocates from nine provinces and one territory. "In our work, we see the devastation of deep-seated intergenerational trauma in Canada's Aboriginal peoples," they wrote. "Aboriginal children have poorer health status, they lag significantly in educational outcomes, and they are too often the victims of sexual exploitation and violence. Many of them live in deep poverty." The advocates expressed frustration that though they had raised the same issues in reports in the preceding years, there had been no discernible action.

The government body Public Safety Canada found that Aboriginal women and girls are "easy prey" for people who traffic in humans since they are more likely than others to live in poverty, suffer from drug addictions and have mental health problems, according to a report that The Canadian Press obtained.

Poverty, inequality and marginalization of indigenous women can have severe consequences, as Wally Oppal, formerly the BC attorney general and a BC Supreme Court judge, made clear in *Forsaken: The Report of the Missing Women Commission of Inquiry* in 2012. Oppal was the commissioner of the inquiry. "Aboriginal women experience higher levels of violence in terms of both incidence and severity and are disproportionately represented in the number of missing and murdered women across Canada," the report said. "Aboriginal women as a group have a heightened vulnerability to violence simply because they live in 'a society that poses a risk to their safety.'" Vulnerable and marginalized women in BC and around the world suffer a higher risk of violence including sexual assault, murder and serial predation, Oppal wrote. "The phenomenon of missing and murdered women is one stark example of this exposure and is seen as part of a broader pattern of marginalization and inequality," he wrote. "The increased vulnerability of certain groups of women, such as women involved in the sex trade, play an important role in providing victims for serial killers."

The report began as an inquiry into the disappearance of sixty-five women from the Downtown Eastside of Vancouver and the failure of the police to properly investigate, then extended to murders on the so-called Highway of Tears in Northern BC. "Each missing and murdered woman had a unique life and story," the report said. "At the same time, this group of women shares the experience of one or more disadvantaging social and economic factors: violence, poverty, addiction, racism, mental health issues, intergenerational impact of residential schools and so on." Not every woman who had gone missing or been murdered had experienced each of those conditions, the report said, but added: "Most had experienced several of them." Marginalization contributed to making the murdered women vulnerable to predation, Oppal wrote. "Three overarching social and economic trends contribute to the women's marginalization: retrenchment of social assistance programs, the ongoing effects of colonialism, and the criminal regulation of prostitution and related law enforcement strategies."

Indigenous women make up 3 percent of the BC population, but constitute about 33 percent of the missing and murdered women, Oppal noted. Of thirty-three DNA samples investigators identified on the farm of serial killer Robert Pickton, twelve came from indigenous women. "The over-representation of Aboriginal women within the women who disappeared from the DTES [Downtown Eastside] must be understood within the larger context of the legacy of colonialism in Canada," Oppal wrote. By "colonialism" he said he meant the "historically unjust relationship" between Aboriginal peoples and governments through the years in Canada. That included the government's policy of assimilation, which purposely targeted Aboriginal women, the report said. "The long-term impact of these colonialist policies continues to be keenly seen and felt by the over-representation of Aboriginal peoples in nearly every measured indicator of social and physical suffering in Canada."

Following the 2014 murder of Tina Fontaine in Winnipeg, amid calls for a national inquiry into missing and murdered indigenous women, retired judge Ted Hughes told *The Globe and Mail* that the

Children are often "denned up" in substandard housing, unable to get to appointments or to where services are available, said British Columbia's Representative for Children and Youth, Mary Ellen Turpel-Lafond. There's a lack of engagement when there's no money to participate in sports or recreation, or in paid child-care settings. They may end up feeling rejected in their own community, particularly in places like Vancouver where they are surrounded by significant wealth. "The face of poverty, the face of children in poverty in British Columbia, is a pretty common face." A lot of children are starting off far behind. Will they catch up? Do they have a fair chance to succeed in the education system? Are they able to get health care when they need it? "It's not all a policy debate. It's about people."

That so many children are doing poorly in British Columbia says much about how we are doing as a society. One of the key differences between children and adults is that children are in many ways restricted from making choices that would improve their situation. "The largest group without autonomy in Canadian society is children," as David Green and Jonathan Kesselman put it in the 2006 academic book *Dimensions of Inequality in Canada*. There are good reasons children don't have full autonomy, they wrote, but that means adults have to be even more careful to make sure children are treated justly. "If justice is a sovereign virtue, then fairness toward those who do not have the means to defend, or even define, their own interests must surely be a marker of a just society."

CHAPTER 9

CRUSHING COSTS: REDUCED SALARIES AND THE HOUSING SQUEEZE

O N A NOVEMBER 2013 AFTERNOON that was bitingly cold by Victoria standards, a couple of dozen activists gathered on the sidewalk in front of the Ministry of Social Development office on the outskirts of downtown hoping to give away a food basket and other prizes. They were there for "Welfare Wednesday"—the day the ministry hands out cheques—to find the person who had spent the longest on the wait list for social housing so they could give her or him the award. It was good-natured street theatre with a serious point.

People struggling on meagre benefits from the government, waiting for a better place to live, are in trouble in a market that's also tough for people earning low wages and even for those making above average incomes. It's a similar story across the province, especially in Vancouver, where tales of families earning $100,000 a year who feel priced out of the real estate market are common. Many face the choice of continuing to rent, commuting from the suburbs or living somewhere else altogether. Between 2011 and 2013, some 14,449 people left British Columbia for other provinces. The bulk of the shift, Statistics Canada reported, was made up of young people leaving to find work in Alberta and Saskatchewan.

A discussion guide prepared for the 2013 Simon Fraser University Public Square on BC's economic future concluded that high housing prices are a drag on the provincial economy. "Affordability is a key issue, notably in the Metro Vancouver area, and risks driving away talented individuals who could contribute economically," it said. "This growing economic divergence undermines productivity, increases household debt, reduces the tax base to pay for government services, and puts the brakes on consumer consumption as a driver of growth."

The BC housing crisis is also a major driver of inequality in the province. In Vancouver, nearly half of all households spend more than the 30 percent of their income on housing, the percentage that's considered affordable. Ownership is even more expensive. A 2013 housing affordability report from the Royal Bank of Canada found that someone earning a typical Vancouver wage wanting to own a detached bungalow (or average home) would have to pay 84.2 percent of their pre-tax income to cover their housing costs, including mortgage, utilities and property tax. That compared to 55.6 percent in Toronto, 38.3 percent in Montreal, 37.3 percent in Ottawa, 33.7 percent in Calgary and 32.9 percent in Edmonton. As Victoria renter Sharon Keen put it to me one afternoon, as we talked about housing prices in BC, "You need one and a half or two incomes just to have a roof over your head. It's way out of whack. It's not right."

Meanwhile those who have been able to afford a home have also had an opportunity to build their wealth. My wife, Suzanne, and I bought a bungalow in a nice part of Victoria in 2000 for $220,000, a price that seemed steep but affordable at the time. Within a few years the assessed value doubled, in some years going up by more than what I made by working. The value has continued to increase, we've made some improvements, and the home is now somewhere around $700,000. We know the bubble could burst at any time and the value of our home could drop. Towards the end of 2014,

Bank of Canada Governor Stephen Poloz warned that Canadian homes were overvalued by 10 to 30 percent. Where a house cost three times an average annual income in 2000, the figure had risen to five times. For us a collapse in prices would be a bit of "easy come, easy go," but we'd be all right. People who bought before us did even better, and some who bought after have also done quite well, though in many cases they had to take on large mortgages to make it work. Not all have been so lucky, of course, either with their timing or with amassing the money to get into the market.

Hosting the November 2013 Victoria housing protest outside the welfare ministry, Kym "Hothead" Hines introduced Ted Hawryluk by saying he had been on the social housing wait list for fourteen years. It had been longer than that, Hawryluk said after he took the microphone: "I've been waiting about eighteen years on the BC Housing list." Hawryluk has been a familiar presence downtown, where he sold copies of *The Street Newz*. The paper has since folded and been replaced by a local version of Vancouver's *Megaphone*. Hawryluk has wispy facial hair, shoulder-length dark hair and I've never seen him without a baseball cap. He gets around in an electric scooter, his small black dog riding in the basket.

He said he figures a few things have kept him from getting into subsidized housing, where he would spend less of his disability benefits on rent. He already has a roof over his head, he has a dog and he smokes cigarettes, he said. "That puts me at the bottom of the housing list." The ministry is trying to house the most vulnerable first, but it leaves a lot of people paying more than $500 a month to "poverty pimps" who rent out substandard places, he said.

Hawryluk outlined his budget. His disability benefits were $906 a month. Out of that he paid rent, hydro and his phone bill. "I've got about $56 a month left to live on," he said. Thanks to selling *The Street Newz* and the policy that allowed him to earn some money without reducing his benefits, he was able to survive, he said. His biggest expense was rent. The ministry allowed $375 a month, an amount for which there was virtually nothing available in much of the Capital Regional District. "Our rental [support] rates are frozen at 1998 rental rates," said Hawryluk. Rents are allowed by law to go up 4 percent a year, but the benefits don't keep pace, he said.

Politicians know Victoria is an expensive city for renters, Hawryluk noted. "We've got MPS and MLAS staying here in Victoria and they get a big bonus, living allowances and that," he said. "The government can come up with a whole lot of money for people who are already rich, but when it comes to the actual poor they're not even pegging us at inflation."

He's correct about the MLAS. In 2014, the provincial representatives who lived outside the Capital Regional District were entitled to bill as much as $17,000 a year to stay in hotels in Victoria.* Those who rented or owned a home in Victoria and had receipts to show what they'd spent were eligible for up to $19,000 a year. Even without providing receipts they were entitled to $1,000 a month, or $12,000 a year. The policy, set in provincial law, allows MLAS to buy Victoria properties that they may continue to own personally when they leave office. Annual public disclosure statements show that many MLAS have grabbed the opportunity to own property in Victoria over the years—a nice bonus for doing the people's business.

A few months into 2014, I sat with Hawryluk while he called BC Housing for an update on his file. His application was on hold, the woman on the phone line said. They hadn't heard from him in over six months, so it was paused, she said, before she reviewed with him his contact information and the kind of benefits he was receiving. She told him that with the call he would be good for another six months on the wait list. According to BC Housing's records his current application started in November 2005, which the agent agreed was "very long, yes." Now that he was over fifty-five years

---

* It's worth noting that in 2014 the BC legislature sat just seventy-one days, which was up from thirty-six days in 2013 and forty-seven days in 2012.

of age his chances would be "not bad" but, she advised, "you have to follow up." While she was sympathetic and her phone manner was kind, ultimately all she could do for Hawryluk was confirm he remained on the wait list.

The high cost of housing and the difficulty getting help is a common story from those trying to survive on disability or welfare payments. There is insufficient social housing to fill the need, partly the result of a lack of investment in the sector by both the provincial and federal governments in recent years. A woman passing on the street during the November 2013 protest said, "It took so long for me I just gave up on it." At the time she had a newborn. She had spent two years waiting. "We were in a place that had mould and mice and everything." And a young Vancouver man with a disability told me he had been on the list for subsidized housing for two years. "As time goes by you realize it's a holding pattern," he said. "Nothing's going to happen."

David Tat, a member of the Victoria advocacy group Committee to End Homelessness, said he had been on the social housing list for many years. "I know people that are paying $725 in rent and they're getting $900 [in benefits]," he said. He himself was spending just under $600 on rent, he said, but added, "It's still an awful lot out of $900."

As the protest ended, the organizers handed out the prizes and the winners shared them around with the non-winners, leading Hothead to observe that sharing is what people who are living in poverty do when they can.

The high price of housing came up repeatedly in interviews about inequality in British Columbia. One Vancouver contact, who asked to have his name withheld from publication because he fears retribution from the people who run the disability system, said that after paying his rent and a few other fixed costs, he's left with $9 a day for food. By being careful he can survive on that, he said, but observed, "Poverty is an issue of cash, strictly."

Sharon Keen had reached retirement age when we talked about housing prices, but was still working so she could keep a place to live in Victoria. "To me it's all got to do with housing," she said. "Maybe we need a big crash." Payments she was receiving from the Canada Pension Plan and Old Age Security came to about $960 a month, she said. Rent on her one-bedroom Victoria apartment, which she also worked out of, was $900. The apartment was smaller than one she had previously, from which she says she was "renovicted"—forced to move so the landowner could renovate. To make up the space she needed she found it necessary to rent a $200-a-month storage locker. That drove her housing cost to $1,100, which was an average rent in 2013 in Victoria, according to the Canada Mortgage and Housing Corporation. "I should be paying half [my income]," said Keen, naming the level that to her would feel affordable. Asked what she would be likely to find for $450 a month in Victoria, she said, "You can't. That's what I'm saying."

Canada needs a national housing strategy and incentives for developers to build rental housing, she said. More than half of Victorians rent, as do a similar number in Vancouver. "The renters keep getting the short end of the stick, right across the country, whether it's Halifax or here," Keen said. Many other people struggle with housing payments, she said. "We're locked into perpetual slavery making monthly rent and mortgage payments as far as I'm concerned. The shit's going to hit the fan one way or another pretty soon here. Something's got to give." Keen said the pressure had to be taken off somehow: "To me we have a choice. We either double pensions, or you cut the rents and mortgages in half."

Such a collapse would, of course, be devastating for people who own homes and might be counting on using the property's value to fund their retirement. It would be even worse for those who have signed on for large mortgages in recent years and might well find themselves owing more than their property is worth. So-called underwater mortgages are a predictable result of housing crashes, such as the one Toronto experienced around 1990 or the more recent one in the United States. In 2014, six years after the housing bubble burst in the United States, some 9.7 million Americans owned homes that were worth less than the amount they owed on them, according to an article on the *Forbes* website. As things are in BC, though, there's a large divide between renters and owners. The split is between rich and poor, to some degree lucky and unlucky, but also to a large extent falls along generational lines. One of my Vancouver colleagues at *The Tyee*—a hard-working young reporter named Katie Hyslop who writes about education and social justice issues—says on her biography page that she has "the goal of making a living substantial enough to rent a place above ground again some day."

There has been much debate about the causes of skyrocketing real estate prices in Vancouver. Some have argued that foreign buyers are driving up prices, particularly by purchasing Vancouver condos as investments that are likely to hold their value. The evidence, however, seems to be largely anecdotal and the topic has become charged with some in the real estate industry accusing critics of racism. Also, a 2014 Frontier Centre for Public Policy study by Wendell Cox argued for rolling back the Agricultural Land Reserve (ALR), which has protected farmland in the province since the 1970s. Cox argued that anti-sprawl policies increase urban poverty and make cities less affordable, as well as limiting ethnic diversity. The *Province* newspaper quoted Tsur Somerville, director of the University of British Columbia's Centre for Urban Economics and Real Estate, as saying that eliminating the ALR could improve affordability by a maximum of about 15 percent. "The major containment factor in Vancouver is God," he said. "The mountains, the sea and the border is what causes about 70 percent of the land [around Vancouver] to not be developed."

For our purposes, *why* real estate prices are high is less important than that they *are* high. Combined with lower wages, worse job prospects and more expensive education, high property values are one of the main factors that prevent young people today from enjoying the same kind of expectations for financial well-being that their parents and grandparents—or even people just a decade or two older—used to have.

"We all know housing prices are higher now than they were a generation ago," said Paul Kershaw, a UBC professor focused on social care, citizenship and the determinants of health. He is also the founder of the Generation Squeeze advocacy group and enthusiastically shares statistics to support his argument. When we spoke in 2013, he was thirty-nine years old. His manner was engaging, though he gave the impression of having been through the material so many times that as he talked he built the kind of momentum that makes it difficult to interrupt with questions. Between 1976 and 2013 the price of residential real estate had gone up by 240 percent in Metro Vancouver, said Kershaw, citing Canadian Real Estate Association data. Average housing prices were up by $165,000 in Canada and by $350,000 in BC after accounting for inflation, he said.

For people like his mother who own their homes, that's great, he said, but it's "crushing the dreams" of their kids and grandkids.

Young people today are more likely to go to college or university than previous generations, but tuition fees have doubled over the same period, he said. Although young people are twice as likely to have degrees, that distinction has been achieved with high levels of student debt. At the same time job prospects have diminished, with many young people working as unpaid interns or in low-pay positions to get established, Kershaw said. Compared to 1976, using inflation-adjusted Statistics Canada figures, the typical wage for twenty-five- to thirty-four-year-olds has dropped by $3 an hour across the country. The drop in British Columbia has been even larger, with a decline of $4 an hour, Kershaw said.

The advantage of having a university degree has, by the way, narrowed. For a 2014 study, *Wages and Full-Time Employment Rates of Young High School Graduates and Bachelor's Degree Holders, 1997 to 2012,* Statistics Canada compared young people who finished high school between 2010 and 2012 with people who had come through a decade earlier. The researchers found that in the later group male high school graduates earned 75 cents for every dollar earned by males with bachelor's degrees. That's a significant gap, but not as big as ten years earlier when the high school grads made 68 cents for each dollar made by the degree holders. Over the same period, female high school graduates went from earning 64 cents to each dollar earned by females with bachelor's degrees to earning 68 cents.

Marc Frenette and René Morissette, the study authors, attributed much of the change to the stagnation of wages for male degree holders, the rise in the number of people with degrees, the oil boom in the early 2000s and increased minimum wages. Demand in the oil industry had raised the need for less-educated workers more than it had for more-educated ones, they wrote. "Gains in real minimum wages accounted for about one-third of the narrowing of the wage differential among young women, but had no discernible impact on the wage differential among young men," the report said. "This was because young female high school graduates were more likely than their male counterparts to have hourly wages at or near the minimum wage rate." For both men and women, having a degree did, however, make them more likely to be employed.

In a piece published on the Broadbent Institute's website, Economics Professor Lars Osberg, of Dalhousie University, picked up the question of whether education can solve inequality. "For the age group 25–64, Canada's post-secondary education attainment level (51% in 2010) substantially exceeds that of the United States (42%) and is in fact the highest in the OECD," he wrote. "Canada's investment in education has been a 'good thing' for many other reasons, but it has not prevented the stagnation of middle class household incomes in Canada and has not solved the problem of ever-growing income gaps." Providing "better education" is a good thing, Osberg wrote. "Just don't expect it to solve the problem of rising income inequality anytime soon."

Kershaw's Generation Squeeze website summarized the burden on young adults who are raising young children, noting they are squeezed both for time at home and for essential services like child care, which can cost more than university. "They are squeezed for income because housing prices are nearly double, even though young people often live in condos, or trade yards for time-consuming commutes," the website said.

Other observers are similarly alarmed about the reduced prospects for young people. A personal finance column by Rob Carrick in *The Globe and Mail* reported on research by Markus Moos, an assistant professor at the University of Waterloo. In 1981, the average income for people between the ages of 25 and 34 was $38,335 in Metro Vancouver, he wrote. By 2006, after adjusting for inflation, that had fallen to $31,844, a drop of 16 percent. That's unsurprising to young people trying to get established. As a 25-year-old contact of mine with Asperger's syndrome who is receiving disability payments put it, "There's a lack of work for young people...A lot of jobs now are based on the ability of people to put a big smile on their face and be a good service worker."

Jonathan Sas, director of research for the Broadbent Institute, did a master's degree in political science in Vancouver before settling into a job in Toronto, not far from where he grew up in London, Ontario. He had various reasons to return east, but said, "I had the perception, and this was prevalent in my university cohort, that there are more jobs in Toronto and Ottawa."

There is also a trend towards more temporary work, particularly for young people, as Andrew Longhurst told Emily Fister at *The Tyee*. Longhurst was in the second year of his master's in human geography at Simon Fraser University, and while on an internship with the Canadian Centre for Policy Alternatives wrote the report

Precarious: Temporary Agency Work in British Columbia. Using Statistics Canada data, he found the number of people working for temp agencies in BC had doubled from 8,848 in 2004 to 19,580 in 2013. In 2004, only 24 percent of new jobs in the province were temporary, but by 2013 the portion had grown to 40 percent. The trend was particularly worrying considering survey numbers show temporary workers receive only about a quarter of the pay that permanent employees earn.

Longhurst illustrated with an anecdote:

> *One of the young women I interviewed is a woman of colour. She talked about the fact that her parents worked all their lives in the public sector, in unionized government jobs. They had pensions to fall back on in their retirement. She said that, "When we were growing up, we were pretty stable, pretty middle class." And now she's in her early 30s and nowhere near that place, doesn't even come close to it. She talked about not having enough employment through temp agencies to pay her bills. As a response, she was taking on debt, using [her] credit card as the safety net. For her, the temp work wasn't sufficient or adequate to make ends meet. The labour market is really changing, and turning towards this growth in precarious and temporary employment.*

According to *The Globe and Mail* in October 2014, across Canada some 80 percent of new jobs created in the previous year were part-time, and those jobs typically didn't come with the security, benefits or predictability that allowed people to save money, start families and buy homes. About 19.3 percent of jobs were part-time in 2014, up from 12.5 percent in 1976. While some part-time workers are of course happy with the arrangement, for 27.3 percent of them the situation was involuntary, according to 2013 Statistics Canada figures.

Greg D'Avignon, president and CEO of the Business Council of British Columbia, noted that Canada has reduced poverty among the elderly to a level that's among the lowest in the world. A 2013 United Nations report that ranked the social and economic well-being of senior citizens in ninety-one countries around the world found Canada was in fifth place. Sweden was at the top and Afghanistan at the bottom of those included. Various policies have helped seniors, including publicly funding health care and the way we deal with property taxes, D'Avignon said. "We're clearly putting disproportionate resources into that age group," he said, observing that as a group seniors are relatively good at making their voices heard on issues that affect them. Meanwhile many young people are in need, he said. The unemployment rate for youth was around 14.5 percent, more than double the rate for people between the ages of twenty-five and fifty-four, he said. "Again, that's where some of that frustration comes in."

Mark Carney, governor of the Bank of England, mentioned the generational nature of inequality in a 2014 speech. "Intergenerational equity is similarly strained across the advanced world," he said. "Social welfare systems designed and enjoyed by previous generations may prove, absent reform, unaffordable for future ones. And environmental degradation remains unaddressed, a tragic embarrassment now seldom mentioned in either polite society or at the G20."

Jim Sinclair, then president of the BC Federation of Labour, said in a 2014 interview that the baby-boom generation who benefited from cheap education and other public supports had been pulling them away for the generations following behind. To Mathew Kagis, an activist in his forties, the generational divide is largely about whose voices get heard. "The boomers currently dominate the political discussion," he said in an interview.

Others, however, see dwelling on the generational divide as a distraction. "I think it's about class, not generations," said Bill Hopwood, an organizer of the Raise the Rates Coalition, when I asked him about Paul Kershaw's message on generational inequality. "It's not that we're stealing from the future, it's that the rich are stealing from all of us."

And Sharon Keen, who at retirement age is financially stretched just to pay her rent, said she objects to Kershaw's thesis. Two out of three baby boomers don't have any pension from working besides the mandatory Canada Pension Plan, she said. "Especially the women, like me."

Isobel Mackenzie, BC's Seniors Advocate, said in her October 2014 report *The Journey Begins: Together, We Can Do Better* that it's important to have an understanding of the true economic picture for seniors. "While some want to portray the senior of today as affluent and well-resourced, genuine poverty is common among BC seniors and that poverty harms their health and well-being."

Kershaw agrees inequality exists along various lines. "I think we often have inequality when we have different power dynamics," he said, adding that those points of inequality could include gender, class, income or race, for example. In Canada, and in BC in particular, they include a colonial legacy where people of First Nations descent are worse off than the general population on most any indicator of health, education or well-being. "They're all characteristics of our identities that intersect," he said.

Seniors, for the most part, however, are doing much better than a generation ago when one out of three of them had a low income, Kershaw said. Governments of the day responded to the crisis, he said, and the public now spends $45,000 a year for each person over the age of sixty-five through programs including health care, Old Age Security and the Canada Pension Plan. That compares to $12,000 per year per person under forty-five years of age, he said. And while many young people suffer to make ends meet, Canada has one of the lowest rates of poverty for seniors in the world at 5 percent, Kershaw said. The country, he noted, has a history of responding to seniors' poverty and other social challenges. "Right now we're not doing that for younger generations...We seem unwilling to modify that adaptation for Gen-x and Gen-y."

These questions are in many ways non-partisan, said Kershaw, if only because all the parties are ignoring the needs of youth. During the 2013 provincial election both main parties would have increased spending on health care, which mostly goes to older people. At the same time neither was prepared to spend $1.5 billion to make child care affordable. "It reflects the reality of power politics," he said. "Platforms are going to get organized around who shows up." There are well-organized and vocal groups like the Canadian Association of Retired Persons that represent the interests of seniors, a demographic that votes in large numbers, but not young adults, said Kershaw. "It's not on the radar of any political party."

Even the Occupy movement did little ultimately to highlight the challenge young people face, he said. "I think the Occupy movement totally distracts from generational issues," he said, noting the slogan "We are the 99 percent" masks large variation. People who are over fifty-five years of age today are the richest that age group has ever been, he said. He gave the example of his sixty-seven-year-old mother, who despite time out of the workforce and not receiving a full pension was comfortable thanks to doing well on real estate. In the year before our interview she had been to Vietnam, Laos, Panama and Costa Rica, he said. "That's not the middle class being eroded…Canada's middle class isn't being squeezed per se. Canada's younger generations are being squeezed." There needs to be a public push for a better deal for younger generations, said Kershaw. "We could mitigate it by trying to keep tens of thousands in their pockets in their early adult years."

Housing prices and wages are determined by markets, making them relatively difficult to change, he said, "unless you're talking about breaking up capitalism, and I don't think many of us are." Government policies that help people when they're starting to have children would make a big difference, he said, and it would be possible to lengthen parental leave to eighteen months and to raise the dollar amount of benefits. The public could also subsidize child care to bring fees down to $10 a day, he said. That would still be above the rates in Quebec but much better than they are now in British Columbia, where daycare can cost more than university tuition.

Such policies could save young people as much as $50,000 at a key point in their lives, allowing them to pay off student debt, accumulate a down payment on a home or save for retirement, Kershaw said. It's insufficient for the government to say it's creating jobs for people, he said. Jobs are important, but middle-income jobs pay less than they did a generation ago, while housing prices have gone up and pensions have become less common.

He blamed the failure to act at least in part on neo-liberalism and the hollowing out of government. Programs like health care that now exist are allowed to grow, but anything new is seen as too expensive. That in turn has young people feeling disconnected from their governments and realigning their expectations.

CHAPTER 10

"GET A JOB" FALLS SHORT: NEW EXPECTATIONS FOR A NEW ECONOMY

WHETHER THE QUESTION IS ABOUT alleviating poverty or reducing inequality, the answer from BC political and business leaders has for many years been "jobs, jobs, jobs." Not everyone thinks that is enough, though. Much depends on the quality of the available jobs and on what happens to people who are outside the workforce.

Relying on jobs as the big answer goes back to previous governments. Here, for example, is how then premier Gordon Campbell in 2009 described the government's position on fighting poverty: "A job is, by far, the best social program you can have." At the time, he was responding to a caller's question about mandating poverty reduction targets as he took part in the leaders' debate on CKNW radio during an election campaign that his Liberals won handily. Since Christy Clark replaced Campbell as leader of the BC Liberals and premier of the province in 2011, she has repeatedly said good jobs are the best security for BC families. She won the leadership on a vague "Families First" platform: it was unclear which families she meant or what putting them first would mean.* After winning

---

* Asked about Clark's "Families First" platform, UBC Professor Paul Kershaw said, "I liked the language, but we have not seen anything near the policy adaptation that it would take to make that phrase a reality."

the job, she did raise the minimum wage, create a new statutory holiday in February and get rid of parking fees in provincial parks. But soon Clark began connecting the idea of families first with a version of "get a job" that found expression in the BC Jobs Plan and the push to build a liquefied natural gas industry in the province. Education was going to be about "turning learners into earners" and post-secondary institutions were instructed to dedicate more money to vocational training.

Even for people with disabilities, the government's answer has been: "Get a job." In a September 2014 opinion piece that the government sent to media outlets throughout the province, Don McRae—then Clark's minister for social development—said the province aimed to have the highest participation rate in Canada of people with disabilities in the workforce by 2024. "Earning a living is an important part of our life and identity," he said. "It is how we take care of ourselves, provide for our families, and contribute to our community. Our jobs provide us with an opportunity to learn new skills, build relationships and follow our passions." More than 330,000 people of working age living in BC had a disability, and the government estimated that about half of them were employed, the piece said. Where some would see a problem, McRae saw an opening. "There is an opportunity to tap into this workforce and help people with disabilities gain meaningful employment," he wrote, adding:

> We know that many people with disabilities have the education, the skills and experience to help BC businesses thrive. We also know that when barriers are removed, and people with disabilities are able to participate fully in their communities and support their families, everyone benefits.

Few would argue against the benefits that an individual sees from working. But it's also clear that "Get a job" is an extremely limited social policy. It might be enough if we had full employment and there was a decent job for everyone who wanted one, and if everyone arrived at adulthood able to work, but that's not the economy or world in which we live. Pediatrician Barbara Fitzgerald expressed the critique well for an opinion piece she wrote on child poverty that ran in the *Vancouver Sun* in 2014. "Please don't tell me their parents should get jobs," Fitzgerald wrote. "Many parents have one or more jobs that pay a wage that doesn't support the family." In other cases, children are passed from one foster home to another and are denied the chance to get a good education, she said. "They will never have a good job. The children are innocent. They deserve hope and the opportunity to do something different."

Mary Ellen Turpel-Lafond, BC Representative for Children and Youth, observed in an interview in September 2014 that the province has both transitional and deeply entrenched poverty. Transitional poverty is what you see when someone is temporarily out of work, the kind of thing BC has seen more of with the 2008 recession and the slow recovery. That kind of poverty is generally temporary in people's lives and can be relieved as the economy strengthens and jobs are created, but Turpel-Lafond pointed out that the six years that had passed since the start of the recession was still a long time in the life of a child.

The province also has pockets of deep, entrenched intergenerational poverty, particularly in Aboriginal communities, said Turpel-Lafond. "*Poverty* is hardly the word to do justice to it," she said, noting the desperation many face around food, housing and social exclusion. The problems were too deep for job creation to make a difference, she said, adding the focus on job creation failed to consider people's health, the needs of their households or their abilities. "The problem is you never get the job," she said, or the job's wage is so low that it's not realistic to think the money will be enough to help a person climb out of poverty. For many, it's a false promise that a strong economy will improve their lives, she said. "The rising tide lifts all boats, unless you're living in the trailer park, in which case you're flooded out."

After taking office in 2001, BC Liberals consistently insisted they were setting the conditions so the economy could create jobs and make people better off. As proof of their success in those early years, they pointed to the rapidly declining welfare caseload. But a report I succeeded in getting the government to release in 2009 showed that Campbell and his revolving welfare ministers had been wrong on why the welfare caseload was shrinking and that major changes the Liberals made to the system did nothing to improve people's incomes. Seth Klein, BC director for the Canadian Centre for Policy Alternatives, looked over *Income Levels of* BCEA *Clients after They Leave Income Assistance* (BCEA is the acronym for BC Employment and Assistance). "What's interesting about it is it shows no improvement," he said. "[It] stands in stark contrast to the good news narrative we've been fed for the past few years."

The report used federal tax data to track people after they left welfare. It included only people who filed a tax return in every year of the study period. About 30 percent of people who left welfare were therefore not part of the study at all, and as the time frame of the study went on, it included fewer and fewer people. Not even half of those who left welfare in 2000 were included in the study five years later, for example, mainly due to failing to file returns. "If you didn't file at all, you're not captured in this," Klein said. People who are homeless, addicted or otherwise having a hard time are most likely not going to file their tax returns, he said. "What about the people we should be most concerned about?"

Nor did the report have anything to say about the people barred from collecting welfare because they did not meet new eligibility requirements. "We still have a greater interest in what happened to those who were denied and discouraged than we do in what happened to the leavers," said Klein, a co-author of a 2006 CCPA report that found the shrinking of the BC welfare caseload was largely caused by people being shut out at the entrance.

That said, the government's report did offer data that can be compared over time. In general, and not surprisingly, people who leave BC welfare have higher incomes than they would have from government assistance. After Liberal changes to the welfare system, however, they were more likely to remain in poverty. "The income of those who left after the introduction of the BCEA welfare reforms were lower than those who left pre-2002," the government study found, referring to the provincial Liberal government's changes to the system. Also, it said, compared to the federal government's low income cut-offs (or LICOs, the threshold below which a family will spend a larger share of its income on the necessities of food, shelter and clothing than will an average family), "a higher percentage of clients who left after the BCEA welfare reforms have income below the LICOs." The report said both declines could be at least partly explained "by the change in composition of the caseload from more-employable to less-employable clients." As people who were easier to employ left welfare—or couldn't get onto welfare—the people who left later were the least employable and therefore had comparatively lower incomes when they did leave.

The report also showed that getting off welfare is not the same as escaping poverty. A chart on page 8 of the report demonstrated that the number of former clients with a family income below the LICO stayed steady as time passed. Of those who left income assistance in 2000, 34 percent were under the LICO that year. Five years later that figure was down to 33 percent. Put another way, over five years, just one more in a hundred families managed to climb out of poverty. As Klein observed, "There's not much further path out of poverty going on here." The figure speaks to the government's policy of pushing people as quickly as possible into the first job they find, he said. "Because we haven't really given people the kind of training or assistance that would offer them a path into a well-paying job, you're not seeing a lot of progress."

Income levels told a similar story. In 2001, the median employment income for single-parent families who had left welfare the year before was $10,800 (all figures are in 2005 dollars). A similar family in 2005, the most recent year included in the study, made just

$9,000. Men fared better than women, based on median incomes. A single man who left welfare in 2000 was making $18,800 by 2005. A single woman over the same period saw her income drop from $7,800 to $5,600.

"There's nothing particularly positive here," Klein said. "It certainly doesn't show the reforms improved results." It would be wrong to say that the Liberals have succeeded at moving people from welfare to work and that people are better off, he said. "All these findings are at odds with what the dominant narrative has been from successive ministers." A low unemployment rate and getting people working is a good thing, said Klein. It is not, however, enough. "Having a record low unemployment rate does not in and of itself reduce your poverty rate." He also pointed out that the declines reflected in the report came during a time of strong economic growth in the province, suggesting that as the economy declined things would get worse. To move people out of poverty you have to find ways to boost the wages of low-income earners, he said, explaining that's why raising the minimum wage is key. With roughly 3 percent of British Columbians receiving income assistance, a large number of the people stuck at the bottom of the income scale are there despite working.

In real terms, the minimum wage hasn't improved in decades. A July 2014 Statistics Canada report called "Study: The Ups and Downs of Minimum Wage, 1975 to 2013" found the purchasing power of the minimum wage across the nation was just one cent higher in 2013 than it had been in 1975, though it had dipped in the intervening years. The study took a weighted average of provincial minimum wages and expressed them in 2013 constant dollars to negate the effects of inflation. "In 2013, the average minimum wage in Canada amounted to $10.14 per hour," the study found. "The 1975 minimum wage translated into 2013 dollars (that is, the real minimum wage) was almost identical at $10.13." In between it had dipped as low as $7.53 in 1986, rising back up to $8.81 in 1996, then

the rain" to campaign for an increase. "If you stick with it you can win sometimes," he said. "The message has gotten through that good wages are good for the economy." The BC Fed campaigned for at least four years to have the minimum wage raised to at least $10 an hour, a position supported by the New Democratic Party. "I take it an election's coming and our campaign has been successful," Sinclair said, noting that $10 an hour wouldn't go as far as it would have when the BC Fed started its campaign. Even after all the increases were in place, the raise wouldn't be enough, he said. "$10.25 isn't at the poverty level yet," he said. "This will help a small amount, but only a small amount." Clark should have indexed the minimum wage so it would go up with the cost of living, just like the premier's salary does, he said. "If it's good enough for Christy Clark it should be good enough for the lowest-paid workers in the province." By the end of 2014, the BC Fed had launched a new campaign—this time to raise the minimum wage to $15 an hour.

It's also worth noting that minimum wages are of little help if they aren't enforced, and in the murky world of low-paid labour performed by vulnerable people, minimum wages sometimes aren't enforced. As a volunteer with the Victoria Immigrant and Refugee Centre in the late 1990s, I tutored with a family who had recently arrived from Eastern Europe. The couple involved had professional degrees and had held good jobs where they came from. In Victoria they were having a hard time finding work and feeding their children. At one point one of them got a job cleaning a bar in the hours after the drinkers had left. The employer would pay $8 an hour for four hours to get it done. Often, as bars can be, it was very messy. Only one of the couple was paid to clean, but both would go do the job together and it usually took more than four hours to get it acceptably clean. The bottom line is they were each working hard for about half the minimum wage. When I said they could complain to the Employment Standards Branch, they said there was no way they could do that, so desperate were they even for the small amount of money they were receiving.

Other employment standards also make a difference. Sylvia Fuller, a UBC associate professor of sociology, outlined some of the issues in an interview with Emily Fister, one of my colleagues at *The Tyee*. "In a 24-7 economy...you might have workers who are working uncontrollable hours and that's hard to co-ordinate with childcare," she said. Employers in BC can call a worker in for a shift with just two hours' notice, she pointed out, and added:

> *That's really short. So if you're working a retail job or a hospitality job and your employer says, 'Oh, things are getting busy and I'm going to call somebody in,' well, if you have kids, especially young kids at home, it's hard to arrange childcare in that time period.*

That has an impact on the people doing the bulk of the care-giving, she said. Mothers who are looking after children, and who have a harder time than other workers accepting shifts on short notice, are particularly vulnerable to losing their jobs, she said. They may also find it difficult to win promotions, she added. "That's not specifically tied to mothers, but it's the kind of employment standard that really potentially works to the disadvantage of women in lower wage, retail or hospitality positions."

There have been attempts to make low-wage work a better deal, with some BC municipalities deciding to pay their employees "living wages" significantly higher than the minimum, well ahead of Seattle voters' 2014 support of a phased-in $15 (US) minimum. During an early morning session at a Union of BC Municipalities convention in a basement room in the Whistler Convention Centre in 2010, it was clear the Canadian municipalities in question had done so at some political risk. New Westminster Councillor Jaimie McEvoy said he and his council colleagues had been accused of driving up wages, bankrupting their suburban Vancouver city and not actually helping anyone. Their crime was being the first municipality in Canada to mandate that people working for the city be paid a living wage. The idea is to pay enough that people working full-time can rise above the poverty line, based on a local calculation. In Metro Vancouver in 2014 the rate was $20.14 an hour, based on what it would cost two working parents to pay for basics like shelter, food, transportation and child care, after taxes, credits, deductions and subsidies have been taken into account. The rate was about $1.17 lower in the Capital Regional District and $3.08 lower in the Fraser Valley.

"Governments have never been neutral on salaries," said McEvoy, who was talking to an audience of local politicians as part of a panel at the UBCM conference. The wages governments pay have always affected the labour market, he said. They pay their executives well, he noted, and always look carefully at the salaries for councillors and mayors. "It's only for the group of people at the bottom that we don't worry about what they're making or how they're doing," he said. And when living wages are explained as being a way to address child poverty, which is associated with problems such as poor performance in school and various health risks, the idea finds wider acceptance, he said. While people might argue about minimum wage and increasing welfare payments, when it comes to children, "it's never the kid's fault."

Living wages get at a key question: When the province's social policy rests on the directive to "get a job," how are people who work doing? To what extent do minimum wages, or even average wages, line up with what it actually costs to live in a community?

In New Westminster the living wage applies to people working directly for the city, as well as to contractors who spend a significant amount of time on city property. Most city employees were already being paid decently, so bringing everyone up to a living wage cost just $20,000 more a year, McEvoy said. Helping contractors meet the wage requirement—and it turned out there were sixty or seventy of them doing everything from maintaining street lights to shredding paper—required another $150,000 in increased payments. Cities often give business to the lowest bidder, he said. "Then you're part of the problem and we were part of the problem, to be honest." The move found broad community support, but it took a long time to get people used to the idea, he said. "It was really a nine-month process of introducing the idea and getting to the point where we were ready to move forward." While it's a touchy issue, McEvoy said, it's been one the municipality has been able to lead on. "It's a winning issue," he said. "It's very popular with people on the street."

While many of the attendees at the session voiced support for the idea, they said they would find it difficult to convince their colleagues and communities. As one put it, "This is a tough sell for a lot of people here." And it's worth noting that attendance for the discussion was somewhat thin: of the 1,500 delegates at the UBCM conference, only around thirty attended the breakfast-time session.

Some of the attendees were from the Township of Esquimalt, a Capital Regional District municipality, which at the time was poised to become the second local government in Canada to adopt a living-wage policy. Then Esquimalt councillor Bruce McIldoon said he was confident it would pass. "It's a very positive thing," he said. While some councillors have been nervous about endorsing it, he said, young people and blue-collar workers understand and like the idea of paying enough to cover the basic necessities. "We will be the second community to come onside in Canada."

A few months later Esquimalt did pass a living-wage policy, but watered down from the original proposal. The *Victoria News* reported that the new policy wouldn't apply to wages negotiated in any of the township's collective agreements with unions and would only apply to future contracts that were more than six months long or worth more than $100,000. Esquimalt also decided that the policy's hourly rates, costs and benefits would be up for review every three years. The resolution passed in a 4–3 vote, but neither side seemed pleased. Mayor Barb Desjardins told the community paper, "I have to say I'm disappointed because we don't know fully what we're getting into." And Randall Garrison, who was later elected as the MP for the area, said he preferred the original motion. "This is not a question of charity. It's a question of fair pay," he was quoted saying.

The motion in Esquimalt built on the work of the Canadian Centre for Policy Alternatives, which was encouraging local governments to become living-wage employers. It has published a resource book to help other municipalities calculate what a living wage is in their communities. Across the country councils in Hamilton, Guelph, Kingston, the Waterloo Region, Ottawa, Saskatoon and Calgary are among those that have reportedly considered the idea. When Hamilton was thinking about it, a report by city staff noted:

> *While living wage policies have only been adopted in two Canadian municipalities and there is no comparable research on the impact of such policies in the Canadian context, there has been significant research undertaken in the United States. These studies have found that living wage policies can lead to direct wage gains and tend to benefit those more vulnerable to low wages and poverty, namely adults who work full-time, recent immigrants, visible minorities and lone mothers with children.*

A few private-sector employers have adopted the policy, including the Vancity credit union.

Speaking at the Whistler session, Seth Klein of the CCPA said it is true that there would be resistance in many communities. "It's not for no reason that there's [only] one municipality in Canada that's become a living wage employer." But in New Westminster's case the response has turned out to be positive, he said, with even the corporate press saying nice things about it. Politicians are in a position to build support for it, he added. Klein stressed that he is a policy guy and not a political strategist, but he encouraged attendees to make the idea an election issue in their communities.

According to a 2013 release from the Living Wage Campaign, about 1.8 million people in Canada who work don't earn enough to bring themselves and their families above the poverty line. Some 150,000 Canadians depend on food banks so they can eat, it said. "Unlike provincially mandated minimum wages, a living wage is an evidence-based standard that calculates the costs of living in a given community based on a basket of goods and services," the release said. "Minimum wages do not come close to meeting the actual cost of living for individuals and families, whereas a living wage can make a world of difference in health outcomes and quality of life." Of course it would be entirely possible to improve minimum wages by following the New Westminster lead and tying the wages to what goods actually cost and by reassessing the wages regularly.

But even setting minimum wages at a living level would do nothing for the many working-age people who have left, or been left out of, the labour market. The unemployment rate for BC has tended to be between 5 and 7 percent in recent years, but the unemployed include only those who are actively looking for work. A different picture emerges when the 36 percent, as of this writing, of working-age people who have left the labour market entirely are considered. "Declining unemployment rates in Canada and the United States over the past four years have been largely driven by declines in labour force participation," Statistics Canada observed in 2014. "The participation rate—the percentage of the working-age population that is employed or looking for work—has declined in both countries since the beginning of the last downturn." Canada was experiencing its lowest participation rate since 2001 and the United States since 1978, Statistics Canada observed.

Despite Premier Clark's much-trumpeted BC Jobs Plan, job growth in the province has been no better than the Canadian average. In June 2014, Statistics Canada reported that in the previous year employment in BC had gained 0.4 percent, but the population of people over fifteen years of age had grown even faster at 1.3 percent. The numbers matched the Canadian averages exactly. The other western provinces, Alberta and Saskatchewan, experienced employment growth of 3.7 percent and 1.3 percent respectively over the same period. BC budget documents released in February 2014 showed that even the government doesn't think the BC Jobs Plan is working, pointed out Iglika Ivanova, an economist in the ccpa's BC office. "It's working politically, but it's not working economically," she said. The government's projections showed the unemployment rate staying the same and the labour force participation rate stuck at 64.1 percent for years into the future. The rate of expected new job growth is matched by the anticipated growth in population. Said Ivanova: "That shows me they don't believe the Jobs Plan is working."

Half a year later, in September 2014, when the government released its glossy thirty-two-page 3 *Year Progress Update* on the jobs plan, the numbers suggested the results had been weak. "Since 2001, total employment in the province has increased by 20.2 per cent, adding more than 388,000 new jobs," the document highlighted on page 3. "Since the BC Jobs Plan launch, the province has added more than 50,000 jobs." While it might seem odd to try to demonstrate the plan's success by quoting figures going back a decade before the plan was announced, a detail a spokesperson said was included for context, crunching the numbers shows why the government must have been tempted. Based on the government's figures, some 33,800 jobs were created on average each year between 2001 and 2011. In the three years immediately after the 2011 launch of the BC Jobs Plan, growth in the number of jobs averaged 16,700 a year. In the three years after the plan was launched, the rate of job growth had dropped to half the rate it had been for the preceding decade.

Shirley Bond, minister of jobs, tourism and skills training, released the three-year update while touring a Vancouver salt business. The document argued that job growth needs to be assessed over time, not month to month, and that the government had laid the foundation for economic growth. But Shane Simpson, the New Democratic Party's critic for economic development, jobs, labour and skills, said it showed the Jobs Plan hadn't worked. "It's been a failure no matter how you look at it," he said. Since the launch of the plan, BC had been the second-worst province in the country for job growth in the private sector, and the third worst for wage growth, he said. He noted that in various sections the government's report picks different starting dates, at times measuring from 2001, 2009 or 2011. "You have them putting out a plan that can't pick a date," he said. "I think it's trying to mask the reality this plan has failed."

Several sections of the update cited numbers for economic growth rather than job creation, Simpson noted. "There was a time when they were pretty closely linked," he said. But investment in the province no longer automatically translated into jobs, he said. "We're seeing a whole lot of economic growth now without jobs attached to it."

It's not hard to see that in many areas the BC economy is able to function with fewer and fewer people, often thanks to technological changes. For example, fewer people in large machines now can do—and more quickly—logging that used to require a person on each end of a saw and a team to move logs out of the bush. One afternoon I watched an operation in the West Kootenay where one person in a feller buncher cut several trees a minute and another in a skidder took them down the hillside to be loaded onto a truck. The hill was denuded at a speed that would have been unimaginable for loggers a hundred years ago. Despite our self-image as a resource-based economy, built by fishers, loggers and miners, that's not where most people actually work. While jobs do open up in new sectors of the economy—video-game design, for example—there have been worries for some time that the quality of jobs is changing. The discussion guide for the 2013 Simon Fraser University Public Square on BC's economic future found that as of 2012 roughly four out of five BC workers were employed in the services sector. That kind of change will continue for the foreseeable future. A 2014 study from the Pew Research Center in Washington, D.C. and Elon University in North Carolina suggested that by 2025 driverless vehicles would eliminate professions like truck or taxi driving. An August 2014 *Globe and Mail* article on the study quoted Stowe Boyd, the lead researcher at Gigaom Research in New York, as saying the central question in a few years would be what people were for in an economy where only a small number of humans were needed to guide the robots that actually did the work. A month later the newspaper published an article by Tavia Grant on disappointing private-sector job numbers, in which Greg Wight—CEO of Algoma Central Corp.—was quoted as saying his company was spending money on new ships, but not people, to raise capacity. "We can operate with fewer crew members because of technological improvements," he said.

Many young people are well aware of the reduced promises of the labour market, but not all see it as a problem. Reduced expectations present an opportunity, Jordan Bober, organizer of the Living the New Economy conference, told me. People entering their adult years today are unquestionably going to do worse financially than their parents did, the thirty-year-old from Vancouver said in a 2013 interview. When the older generation were coming of age in the 1960s and '70s they could find jobs whenever they wanted them, he said, making possible the "voluntary poverty" movement of activists opting out of the mainstream economy. Bober, who has a master's degree in economics from a university in Gothenburg, Sweden, said, "It's not voluntary anymore." People don't have the same options today, he said. "Even if people of my age want [to], they won't be able to insert themselves into the dominant economy and get jobs and wages their parents could."

Bober said he frequently meets people who are loaded down with debt from going to school, but who are unable to find meaningful work. It's common in BC to meet someone who has a master's degree and is working at a minimum-wage job in a coffee shop or a hotel. "That's a massive tragedy and a waste of human resources," he said. He gave as an example his girlfriend, who has a master's degree in political science. She was doing demanding work, but making less money than the receptionist at her shared office space. "It's ridiculous," he said. "People are fed up with that. We have aspirations too…People want to be recognized for the value they're creating." As he put it, "Inequality is probably one of the biggest issues with the current economy."

Andy Yan, a researcher and urban planner at Bing Thom Architects, told a Vancouver audience about his research on the median incomes for people between the ages of twenty-five and fifty-five who have bachelor's degrees or higher. Yan found that in Vancouver such incomes trailed far behind those of their peers in the rest of the country's top ten metropolitan areas, according to a 2014 *Vancouver Sun* column by Pete McMartin. "It was the first time in my career of giving lectures…when an audience gasped at the answer," McMartin quoted Yan as saying. "I was so surprised by the numbers myself…that I had to run them three or four times to make sure they were right." The median income for degree holders in Vancouver in 2011 was $41,981, far behind Ottawa at $62,202 and pulling down the national average of $50,981. This was despite the fact—or perhaps because of it—that Vancouverites were more likely than other Canadians to hold a degree.

The idea for holding Living the New Economy conferences— which by the end of 2013 had been held twice in Vancouver and once in Victoria—came from Nicole Moen, a co-founder of the Healing Cities Institute. She told the crowd of a hundred or so in Victoria on the opening evening in a cold (the heating system was broken) former railway roundhouse that she woke up one night wanting to organize an event about money. Formal and informal topics included marketing with integrity, indigenomics, permaculture and alternative currencies. Among the opening-night attendees were several representatives of event sponsor Vancity credit union, people of various ages looking to find their way in the economy, and at least one city councillor.

The conventional economy is about self-interest, while the new economy is about co-operation and gift relationships, explained Charles Eisenstein—a degrowth activist and the author of *Sacred Economics*—in a video address to the conference. With youth unemployment over 50 percent in parts of Europe and pushing 20 percent in the United States, there's incentive for young people to work less, consume less and share more, he said. The youth unemployment rate is not quite so high in BC at 14 percent, but is still more than double the rate for the rest of the province's population. Partly the reduced consumption and increased sharing is about economic necessity, but it's also about building the quality of relationships, Eisenstein said.

In many ways, the idea behind the New Economy movement is to turn the necessity of coping with reduced expectations into a virtue of addressing major environmental and social problems. Conference organizer Bober said he envisions a future where many more people may have less money and fewer possessions, but will be much richer in spirit. "People will be living with a lot less money, but it doesn't mean they're going to be poorer," he said. They may reduce their costs for housing by finding ways to live together in larger groups, he said. Car sharing, where ownership and costs are divided up among many people, will become more common, he said. "It's going to be very rare for people to own their own cars, as it probably should be." Many young people will depend on their parents longer, much the way a generation are in Spain, where about half the population under thirty years of age can't get work, he said.

"The fact is we will never live the way our parents did because we've come up against ecological constraints that are non-negotiable," he said, but he saw that as being for the best. "There's so much more to life than living and consuming the way we have over the last few decades." Part of the solution requires redefining when we think we have enough, he said. "I think we're well under way. People in my circles, and it's not the majority, are very happy even living under the poverty line," he said. "If I have my rent and my food covered, a little bit over that, I'm doing just dandy." Many people live their lives on a "treadmill" where the work itself leads to otherwise unnecessary costs, such as running a car or maintaining a lifestyle, Bober said. "You never feel that you have enough ... I've felt the richest I've ever felt in the last couple years since I abandoned my stable income."

Bober was critical of campaigns that simply call for higher wages. "It's still rooted in the industrial worldview of the economy," he said. "When they're talking about wages it implies there's someone above you who's paying you to do something for them." In the new economy, individuals may be part-owners of their own businesses and there will be changes in where income comes from and how wealth is stored. "Just raising the wages to $20 an hour or something—it's not going to address our relationships with each other or the Earth. That alone will not."

I largely agreed with what he was saying. When my wife, Suzanne, and I think back to our time as students living on minimal amounts of money, we figure we're no more happy now than we were then despite our increased savings, our home and our steady incomes. A friend who makes a quarter of a million a year tells me he's constantly worried about money. Another friend who recently declared bankruptcy strikes me as no worse off emotionally than my wealthier pal. Various people I know who make much more money than the average struggle to be happy.

Bober's ideas are consistent with recent thinking about measuring well-being instead of gross domestic product. Mark Anielski, in the 2007 book *The Economics of Happiness*, argued for redefining economic progress to better align with the things that matter to quality of life, including supportive relationships, environmental health and spiritual well-being. Research quoted in, for example,

The Spirit Level, by Richard Wilkinson and Kate Pickett, suggests that as national income per person begins to rise there are initial gains in both life expectancy and in the portion of people who describe themselves as "very happy" or "quite happy." But as incomes rise further, there is little more gain. People in countries like Tanzania or Indonesia that are relatively poor are just as likely to say they are happy as are people in much richer countries like Norway or the United States.

Interestingly, *The Spirit Level* also argues that greater equality would lead to reduced consumerism and a healthier environment. Consumption, which households frequently fund by taking on debt, is very much about social status and people trying to unsustainably keep up with their neighbours, the authors wrote. Their response is one answer to the common assumption that greater equality would mean helping people have more money that they can spend on more stuff, something critics point out would be environmentally destructive, especially in a province like British Columbia where the average person's ecological footprint is already too large to be sustainable on a finite planet.

Robert Reich, former US secretary of labour, provided another response when he pointed out that economies don't necessarily have to be tied to the consumption of natural resources. He was responding to a question from *Georgia Straight* editor Charlie Smith ahead of a 2013 talk in Vancouver. "That question assumes that the only kind of consumption is of material goods that deplete natural resources," Smith quoted him as saying. "But of course, there are many other kinds of consumption. We could consume education. We can have more and better health care. We can have more and better environmental protection, for example." Rich countries tend to have cleaner environments than poor countries do, he pointed out, arguing the outcome was a result of the greater capacity that comes with economic growth. "We mustn't confuse consumerism—that is, the acquisition of more stuff—with the capacity of an economy to do a whole variety of things, including generating a sustainable environment."

For Bober, the key has been finding ways to make his working life feel meaningful. "I feel like there's not a wasted moment in my life," he said. "When you feel like you have a meaningful existence, you're not really craving for more." That was also a central message of the Living the New Economy conference. "The new economy is essentially about how we relate with each other," he said. "It's about creating a system that will slowly make the old system obsolete over time." The goal is to build an economy that's more interconnected and sustainable, he said, and listed options that are available as including social impact bonds, co-operatives, crowdfunding and building a peer-to-peer economy. "It's really kind of a matter of showing what is being done." At the movement's core are decisions about how we interact with each other and with the environment. "It's creating an economy that's designed with people and the planet as the priority," he said. We can get away from the economy being an end in itself and instead empower people, he said, adding that one of the benefits is people can do it for themselves. "I'm not really keen on waiting for people with the power…to make the changes that are needed."

So there's one possible answer to inequality, at least for those who have already achieved a minimum standard of comfort and aren't living in abject poverty: transcend it by adjusting your expectations, while working to build the economy you want. Personally, I find the idea attractive, particularly from an environmental point of view. I'm not sure, though, that I want to count on whatever social capital I've accumulated in my life to keep food on the table in my senior years. Arriving there with some savings and a pension would be nice too. But perhaps my thinking is too mired in the old economy, the one that seems likely to continue delivering massively unequal outcomes.

CHAPTER 11

SEEKING SOLUTIONS: RAISE THE POOR, STRENGTHEN THE MIDDLE AND CONSTRAIN THE TOP

THE FIRST THING TO KNOW about addressing inequality is that experts who study the issue say it matters much more that it *is* done than *how* it is done. The second is that there are countless public policy options that would make our societies more equal if there were the political will to put them in place.

The authors of *The Spirit Level: Why More Equal Societies Almost Always do Better* observed that countries like Japan—where incomes before taxes are relatively close—do as well on health and social outcomes as nations like Sweden or Norway where incomes are redistributed through taxes that support public programs. "There are many different ways of reaching the same destination," wrote Richard Wilkinson and Kate Pickett. "What matters is the level of inequality you finish up with, not how you get it." Addressing inequality does not necessarily mean increasing the size of the public sector, they wrote, and they warned that even those who cut taxes might unintentionally force an expansion on the government with the need for more prisons, police and care for people with mental illnesses or addictions.

Those with the power to make public policy have numerous options. And while some will tell you that tackling inequality is difficult or complicated, the basics are dead simple: anything that constrains incomes at the top or raises them at the bottom will make people more equal. Often, as Iglika Ivanova in the BC office of the Canadian Centre for Policy Alternatives pointed out to me, the solutions are the flip side of the causes of inequality. If we got to where we are by lowering taxes, stagnating low-income wages, escalating top incomes and shrinking unions, it's easy to see what's needed to change direction.

In his 2012 book *The Price of Inequality,* Joseph Stiglitz—a winner of the Nobel Memorial Prize in Economic Sciences—argued for taking several approaches at once. "Addressing inequality is of necessity multifaceted," he wrote. "We have to rein in the excesses at the top, strengthen the middle, and help those at the bottom. Each goal requires a program of its own." Taking steps to reduce inequality could mean developing a labour market where people at the top no longer receive salaries that are so many times larger than those people at the bottom make. Or it may mean a need for Robin Hood-style public policy that takes from the rich through taxes and gives to those in need through income supports or other programs.

While researching this book I compiled a list of ideas that would reduce inequality (see below). I don't intend them to be prescriptive, or to all be put in place at once. Following some of them, such as implementing a guaranteed livable income, should in fact make others, like raising welfare rates, unnecessary. And for my purposes here I'm not worrying about what other consequences any of these policies might have; anyone actually implementing any of them would of course want to do so with great care. My primary point is simply that countless tools are available if we want to address inequality. Keep in mind too that whatever policies we pursue, including the ones we have in place now, have an impact.

WAYS TO REDUCE INEQUALITY

1. *Create well-paying jobs:* This is the number one solution put forward by the Organization for Economic Co-operation and Development, the Business Council of British Columbia and BC Premier Christy Clark. It is an essential place to start and a big part of the solution, but it is not the end. Consider that inequality in British Columbia has tended to grow when the economy has been strong and that homelessness in the province spiked during the economic boom years of the early 2000s. Consider also the number of people needed in low-paid service jobs so that we can have our grande lattes, double-doubles and fast-food burgers. Remember too the number of people left out of the labour force, either by disability or a lack of work. Getting people working and making sure those jobs pay decent wages is only step one.

2. *Raise the minimum wage:* After 2001 in British Columbia, the hourly pay going to the lowest-paid workers stayed frozen for a decade. Then, after years of labour-backed campaigning and public debate, the minimum wage was raised in May 2012, to $10.25 an hour. Regular increases tied to inflation would be fair to workers and predictable for employers. But first the wage should be matched to what it costs to live in our communities.

3. *Expand living wages:* The BC office of the CCPA calculated the living wage in 2014 at $17.20 an hour in the Fraser Valley, $18.93 in the Victoria region and $20.10 in Metro Vancouver. The wage, as discussed in Chapter 10, reflects what a two-income family would need to pass the poverty line and afford basics like shelter, child care, transportation and food. Some municipalities and employers have started paying living wages in recent years and the idea could spread. Advocates point out there's

something wrong when people who work still have to rely on charities such as food banks to eat.

4. *Eliminate income taxes for low earners:* Sharon Keen, a Victoria researcher who has reached retirement age without significant savings and finds the Canada Pension Plan and Old Age Security pension don't meet her needs, argues that she shouldn't have to pay taxes on income below the poverty line. After allowing for credits, in 2015 a single person with no children or other dependents would owe provincial tax of 15 percent on any income earned above $19,000 and federal tax of 5.06 percent on income starting at about $17,000. "The tax threshold is still not poverty level," Keen said. "Revenue Canada won't even let us earn $20,000 before we pay taxes...What I need is Revenue Canada to have a poverty-level tax threshold." At times Keen has failed to send the government the money they want from her. "I'm still at war with them, they just don't know where I am...I'm in the toilet. I don't know how I'm going to get by."

5. *Provide affordable child care:* Professor Paul Kershaw of the University of British Columbia said it's clear something is wrong when a year of daycare costs some 50-percent more than a year of university tuition. Reducing the cost to $10 a day, as a coalition of groups has been advocating, would help families at a time when they're crunched for cash and would help women's wages keep pace with men's since it would become less attractive to take years out of the labour market. The proposal would fall short of matching Quebec's $7-a-day program, but would be a significant improvement for BC. Paul Summerville, a former political candidate and investment banker, also makes the case for supporting better child care. If making ends meet in Canada requires $85,000, and if that requires two people working, "then you need to be very thoughtful about your

daycare strategy," he said. Supporting better child care would also reduce inequality for women, who after graduating from university earn 25-percent less than their male equivalents, he said. Women also only fill 10 percent of corporate board directorships in Canada. "Women should be able to have children in twenty-first-century Canada without having to leave the workforce to have those kids," he said. There's also much research, including by the late Clyde Hertzman at UBC, showing that spending money to give kids a good start saves all kinds of costs later.

6. *Raise child tax benefits:* Sometimes described as the "baby bonus," this joint federal and provincial transfer to families is aimed at preventing or eliminating child poverty. As of this writing, monthly payments for a family's first two children are $119.41 per child with amounts reduced when family net income exceeds $43,561. That works out to just over $1,400 a year per child. It's significant in many household budgets, but the amount could be raised, particularly for low-income families.

7. *Create cheaper housing:* Reducing the major expense for most BC households would leave money in people's pockets. Solutions could include building more subsidized or non-market housing, controlling rents, expanding programs to subsidize rental payments, and adopting policies that reduce home prices or borrowing costs. Some of these we already do, but we could do them more aggressively. Rents in the province are allowed to increase 2-percent faster than inflation. For several years, with federal funding scarce, few social housing units were created. A consistent and sustained approach is needed.

8. *Encourage unionization:* Jobs where workers are represented by a union tend to pay more and come with better benefits. They

also raise the wages and working conditions in non-unionized workplaces as employers are forced to compete for staff. Unions have been in decline across Canada, particularly in British Columbia, where the portion of the workforce that was unionized dropped from 43 percent in 1981 to 30 percent in 2012, according to Statistics Canada. While many factors influenced the decline, governments set the rules that make it easier or harder for unions to form and to negotiate. As economist Iglika Ivanova of the CCPA put it, "I think we have to do something to shift the power between the concerns of capital and labour." She described the perspective as "very old-school."

9. *Strengthen labour standards:* The CCPA's Ivanova said European economies have done very well over the long term while raising employment standards for workers. Changes in BC could include mandating more vacation time, regulating work hours and setting minimum lengths for shifts. The BC New Democratic government elected in 1991 made major changes to the labour code that were undone shortly after the BC Liberals were elected in 2001. "A lot of things we need to do cost money, but things like strengthening employment standards don't cost anything to government," Ivanova said.

10. *Make part-time work pay the same as full-time:* In an interview published in *The Tyee*, Sylvia Fuller—an associate professor in sociology at UBC—said that paying people who work part-time less than those who work full-time, which is legal throughout Canada, leads to inequality. "In Europe, there's a requirement that employers don't pay different wage rates just by virtue of being full- or part-time status, that they provide workers doing similar jobs the same pay rate." People who are mothers are more likely to be working part-time, she noted.

11. *Spread the work around:* Mexican telecom billionaire Carlos Slim Helú made headlines in 2014 by advocating for a work week of three eleven-hour days followed by four days off, which had Virgin Group billionaire Richard Branson saying it could work. The plan would have average workers on the job for thirty-three hours a week, which would be fine if they were still paid well enough to meet what they felt were their needs, and would have the added benefit of creating an opportunity to share the available work more widely and so grow the participation rate in the labour force. Giving workers European-length holidays of six or more weeks instead of the Canadian standard of two or three weeks would have a similar effect of better sharing the work. Again, making it a success would likely require people to accept slightly lower wages, which in theory should also push down the price of housing and other goods.

12. *Adopt an anti-poverty strategy:* The benefits of a healthy economy are unlikely to reach everybody, especially given the deep, intergenerational nature of much of British Columbia's poverty. Seven out of ten provinces had anti-poverty strategies by September 2014, but despite its higher-than-average poverty levels, BC did not, noted Mary Ellen Turpel-Lafond, the province's Representative for Children and Youth. (By late 2014, according to the BC Poverty Reduction Coalition website, BC was the only Canadian province still without a poverty-reduction strategy.) The provincial government in BC seems to take the attitude that it has a right not to know what's happening, Turpel-Lafond said. Instead the province needs to consistently track key indicators and report on them regularly, she said, arguing for an evidence-based approach that looks at how the province's economic and social policies are turning out, then adjusts accordingly. Without looking, we won't have the information we need to take action, she said.

13. *Raise welfare rates:* "People on welfare are the poorest of the poor," said Bill Hopwood, an organizer of the Raise the Rates Coalition, when I asked him what he would do to reduce inequality. "A first clear action would be to raise welfare." Payments as of December 2014 for single people in BC who were considered employable were $610 a month, which included $375 to cover shelter in a province where there is not much available for that. After rent the amount left little for food, personal care, job-search expenses or anything else.

14. *Provide a guaranteed livable income (GLI):* The idea, which has gone by various names, is to pay every citizen a base amount regardless of what they do. Doing so would keep people from falling below a certain point while eliminating the need for large government bureaucracies that administer social programs, according to advocates. Some anti-poverty activists are skeptical, saying much depends on the rate being set high enough to allow people a comfortable existence, something they don't trust governments to do and maintain. Noting the living wage in Vancouver is about $20 an hour, Hopwood said he could imagine politicians setting a GLI of $10,000 a year, but abolishing all other supplements. "Then actually people would be worse off," he said. Much depends on the intent. "Is it a measure to save money or a measure to tackle poverty? Some of the advocates see it as a way to save money." Others worry about reducing the incentive to work, but when Dauphin, Manitoba tried it, activist Mathew Kagis said, the town found just three groups worked less: new mothers, kids going to school and people going back to school. "Everybody else pretty much kept doing what they were doing," he said.

15. *Give out money:* In a 2014 essay for *Foreign Affairs* magazine, Brown University political scientist Mark Blyth and hedge fund

manager Eric Lonergan argued for central banks stimulating the economy by giving cash to the 80 percent of households earning the lowest incomes, an idea they said had been proposed in different forms by economists as diverse as John Maynard Keynes and Milton Friedman. "In the short term, such cash transfers could jump-start the economy," they said. "Over the long term, they could reduce dependence on the banking system for growth and reverse the trend of rising inequality." The authors argued that such transfers wouldn't cause damaging inflation and would boost the economy. "Lower-income households are more prone to consume, so they would provide a greater boost to spending," they said.

16. *Support immigrants and refugees:* Several sources say that new Canadians are taking longer to integrate into the country's economy than was the case fifteen years ago. In BC, an immigrant with a university degree doesn't make as much money as a non-immigrant who doesn't have a degree. Less-educated female immigrants are among the worst off in our economy. Many of the people I met while volunteering as a tutor with the Victoria Immigrant and Refugee Centre in the years around 2000 came to Canada hoping to give their children the opportunity for a better life. Immigration policies and supports such as language classes can help make those transitions between countries much smoother.

17. *Appoint a national children's commissioner:* The Canadian Council of Child and Youth Advocates has made repeated calls for the appointment of an independent official who would have an "emphasis on Aboriginal children and youth and the national dimension of the work on programs, evaluation and outcomes." The council also wants "a national initiative to measure and report on child welfare, education and health outcomes for

Aboriginal children and youth," moves towards fully implementing the United Nations Convention on the Rights of the
Child, and a national plan to improve outcomes for Aboriginal
children and youth.

18. *Expand the Employment Insurance (EI) system:* Self-employment
    has risen significantly over the past few decades, especially in
    British Columbia. Some 18.5 percent of the workforce in the
    province in 2012 was self-employed, about 3 percent above the
    national average. Sometimes these are highly paid consultants
    who make enough money to prepare for ups and downs in their
    careers, but often the self-employed are working under contracts
    that come without benefits and make them ineligible to partic-
    ipate in the EI system. Finding a way to extend the EI system to
    people who are self-employed would help many people during
    periods of temporary unemployment or after they have babies.

19. *Improve pensions:* The Canadian Labour Congress and others
    have been campaigning for several years to double the size of
    the Canada Pension Plan, partly in response to the decline in
    defined benefit pension plans and the rise of less-predictable
    defined contribution plans. Of course many workers, including
    the growing ranks of the self-employed, have no pension other
    than the CPP at all. Doubling the CPP would do little for those
    at the bottom, but it would do a lot to strengthen the retirement
    incomes of people who made between $50,000 and $100,000 a
    year during their working lives. The proposal has had the sup-
    port of several provinces, including at times BC, but so far has
    been quashed by the federal government.

20. *Make post-secondary education cheaper:* Between 1995 and 2014,
    undergraduate tuition fees in BC more than doubled. Many
    graduating students owe tens of thousands of dollars in an era

when many are finding it hard to land solid jobs, get into the housing market and start families. Professional fields like medicine and engineering pull up the average earnings of graduates, but graduates in many other fields struggle to get established. Canadian researchers have also found that education level was as good a predictor as income level of whether someone would be engaged in their community and active politically. If everyone is to have equal opportunity, either to earn income or have a voice in decisions that affect them, making education available to all at a price that doesn't excessively hamper them financially is key. A student from Denmark who was working with us at *The Tyee* on an internship in 2014 told me that in his country not only is university education free, but students receive a stipend of more than $1,000 a month while they study. For those worried about how to pay for cheaper education, there are progressive income taxes that take more from people who earn more, such as university graduates.

21. *Invest in training:* Many employers, especially in northern BC, say there's a shortage of skilled labour. At the same time there are large numbers of people who are officially unemployed (the official unemployment rate is about 7 percent in BC as of this writing), and even more have given up on finding a job and aren't participating in the labour market (over 35 percent of the working-age population in the province were neither employed nor looking for work). Governments can do more to help people get the skills they need to better participate in the economy.

22. *Support micro-credit programs:* Adopting an idea that's been huge in Asia, the Community Micro Lending group in Victoria has been providing small loans to people who would otherwise be unlikely to be able to get credit. Coordinator Lisa Helps, who a year after our 2013 interview was elected mayor of Victoria,

told me about some of their success stories: Bobby started a business with a snow shovel and a bus pass, then got a larger loan to buy a power washer and a truck; Chelsea needed six months' rent to move her mortgage brokerage into a real estate agency; Gavin, who received about $5,000 for a used pickup truck and a couple of wheelbarrows eighteen months ago, now made $250,000 a year and his stone-mason business had four employees. Investors get a return similar to what they would get from a GIC, while the loan recipients pay an interest rate that reflects the credit risk but is much lower than it would be on a credit card or at a payday lender. Helps called the rates "fair."

23. *Provide interest-free loans:* In 2004, researcher Mark Anielski wrote a report for Vancity credit union on whether it could emulate Sweden's JAK Members Bank by providing interest-free loans. A loan from JAK, which has been active in Sweden since the 1960s, cost about a third as much over its lifetime as one from a conventional bank, Anielski found. On a loan of $20,000, at the interest rates of the day, the bank loan would have cost $9,700 compared to $3,000 at JAK, he calculated. That was enough to cover JAK's expenses, he said. "The JAK banking model demonstrates that charging of interest is not a necessary requirement of running efficient and effective and indeed profitable financial services of a members-owned cooperative enterprise," Anielski wrote. Vancity or another institution could certainly do the same, "and moreover why not?" he said. A decade later, though, the credit union had yet to embrace that change.

24. *Increase financial literacy:* Helps said that although programs that aid people after they've come into financial trouble are essential, it would be wise to put more support into prevention. Education and financial literacy are key, she said. People get

into deeper difficulty with money because they are already having money trouble, she observed. Empowering people around finances and helping them build knowledge of how the financial system works would help them avoid getting into that hole in the first place, she said. Tom Hamza, president of the Investor Education Fund financed by the Ontario Securities Commission, said there needs to be more education in the client's interest "in the last yard before the teller's window" when people need to figure out if what's on offer is in their best interest. With the rise of self-managed private pensions and retirement savings, financial literacy becomes even more essential.

25. *Extend public health care:* Universal health care, paid for collectively through the tax system, already goes a long way to reduce inequality in Canada, ensuring that a medical misfortune won't bankrupt a family the way it can in the United States and many other countries. But some important areas are left out of our system, including eye care and prescription drugs. Providing dental care, particularly to people most in need financially, would also be an equalizer, said Adrian Dix, a former health critic and past leader of the NDP. The health of people's teeth affects their lives in all kinds of ways, including their employment and income prospects, he said.

26. *Adopt a "housing first" policy:* In their 149-page 2008 report *Housing and Support for Adults with Severe Addictions and/or Mental Illness in British Columbia*, Michelle Patterson and Julian Somers of Simon Fraser University, Karen McIntosh and Alan Shiell of the University of Calgary, and Jim Frankish of UBC offered a dozen "key actions" that need to be taken to provide housing and support to people with severe addictions and/or mental illness, starting with a "housing first" policy to provide permanent,

independent homes to people without time limits or requiring residents to get addictions treatment. They also suggested creating more multidisciplinary treatment teams to help people cope with mental illnesses in their homes; taking a "harm reduction" approach at housing facilities and accepting the use of drugs and alcohol on-site; and preventing hospitals and prisons from discharging people with "no fixed address" without knowing where they will go. "Without adequate housing and support, people with [severe addictions and/or mental illness] who are homeless often cycle through the streets, prisons and jails, and high-cost health care settings such as emergency rooms and psychiatric inpatient units," said the 2008 report, which was written for the health ministry. "This is ineffective and costly in both human and financial terms." With help, the report added, the people in question could stay in stable housing. "It is time to implement these evidence-based solutions for British Columbians in need."

* * *

THERE ARE IDEAS above, such as improving employment standards or raising minimum wages, that governments can put in place without directly affecting their own revenues. Others, such as extending the health system or increasing funding for education and welfare, would clearly require an investment of public dollars. Raising that money would bring the added benefit of constraining incomes at the top, something advocates for greater equality say is key. "It's not just raising the poorest," said Hopwood at Raise the Rates. "It's reversing the differential between the very rich and the rest of us. It's reversing neo-liberalism, really."

In our democracy, raising taxes might not be popular, even among those likely to benefit. I was reminded of this one summer day as I was riding my bicycle on the Galloping Goose Trail in Victoria. Someone had written Tax Is Theft in chalk on the asphalt, and another message a little farther along read Not My

Debt. I found it ironic that the anonymous author of the slogans had chosen a trail built and maintained with tax dollars from three levels of government as the venue for the message. The author might not feel ownership of the public debt, but he or she quite possibly learned to spell in a publicly funded school (even the private schools in BC receive public funding), travels on publicly funded roads and may well have been born in a publicly funded hospital. It's easy to hate taxes if you ignore or take for granted the things they finance.

Nonetheless, politicians know that tax cuts almost always offer the path of least resistance. It's much more difficult to explain why a tax is a good thing than it is to call for tax cuts. For at least thirty years cutting taxes has dominated North American politics—including policies of Ronald Reagan and Gordon Campbell—and has accelerated growing inequality. Public support for those policies, championed by well-funded think tanks and academics, have made it difficult for politicians to criticize them.

Journalist Linda McQuaig and tax expert Neil Brooks observed in *The Trouble with Billionaires* that even left-wing political forces have been reluctant to advocate taking money from the rich. "By declining to protest the concentration of wealth, progressives have conceded important ground," they wrote. "At the centre of their case should be a strong moral argument about the illegitimacy of a small number of people gaining control over too large a share of society's resources, and with it, undue control over society." McQuaig has since run as the candidate in a losing campaign for the federal NDP in the 2014 Toronto-Centre by-election, where inequality was an issue but her party declined to take a strong tax-the-rich position. The New Democrats' position, while entirely in line with the other mainstream Canadian political parties, was far removed from the conclusions McQuaig and Brooks reached in their 2010 book. "We...believe that the key to any solution involves making our tax system considerably more progressive," they wrote. "While reforms in education, child care, housing, and other areas would all contribute to the overall quest for a more equal society, their impact is likely to be gradual and slow-moving at best." The more efficient route to equality is through improving how people are taxed, they argued. "The tax system, with its huge and comprehensive reach, has the capacity to reduce inequality much more quickly and decisively."

With that in mind—and given the luxury afforded to writers who don't need to count on anyone's vote, or for that matter campaign funding—here are a few ways to constrain incomes and wealth at the top and keep the rich from getting richer so much quicker than everyone else, continuing my list of ideas for reducing inequality:

WAYS TO REDUCE INEQUALITY (CONTINUED)

27. *Introduce a maximum wage:* We've had minimum wage laws in much of the developed world for ages, so why not set a maximum? People in Switzerland voted on a proposal in 2013 that would have capped the pay of the top earner in any place of employment at twelve times what the lowest-paid person receives. The idea was that nobody should make more in a month than someone else working in the same place makes in a year. Such a cap would also create an incentive for those in charge to raise salaries at the bottom; for every $1 raise given to someone in an entry-level position, the people at the top could still get $12. The Swiss proposal found support from 35 percent of voters, but not nearly enough to pass.

28. *Make the tax system fairer:* Progressive taxes that take more from the wealthy fight inequality while flatter taxes tend to do the opposite. In *The Trouble with Billionaires*, Linda McQuaig and Neil Brooks advocate taxes of 60 percent on earnings over $500,000 and 70 percent on earnings over $2.5 million. Federally,

in 2014 the top income tax bracket started at $136,270, while provinces varied on where they set the level. Anyone making over $150,000 in BC was paying the province's top tax rate, which amounted to 45.8 percent when combined with federal taxes. Relatively flat taxes like the province's Medical Services Plan, which charges the same amount to anyone who makes over $30,000 a year, are even worse. While the province has bragged about keeping income taxes low, MSP premiums have soared, making the overall system less fair. In 2013, for the first time, BC collected more revenue from MSP than it did from corporate taxes.

29. *Tax 100 percent of capital gains:* In 2000, under prime minister Jean Chrétien, Canada changed how it taxes the money people make when they sell their shares in publicly traded companies that have grown in value. Instead of taxing the full amount, Canada began taxing just half. This, of course, benefits people who own stocks, generally the better off among us and about 8.5 percent of the population in 2012. Returning to a policy where all money made by selling stocks is counted as income would reduce the unfairness.

30. *Cap the contributions allowed to a Tax Free Savings Account (TFSA):* The federal government introduced TFSAs—which allow money to accumulate tax-free—in 2008. For the first couple of years Canadians could put in $5,000 a year, which was later raised to $5,500. Prime Minister Stephen Harper has talked about raising the annual contribution to $10,000. In 2013 a Bank of Montreal report said that about 48 percent of Canadians had TFSAs. It seems obvious that the most likely to use them are people who make enough money that they have some to save. Economics Professor Kevin Milligan of UBC argued in a paper for the *Canadian Tax Journal* that TFSAs could eventually seriously

hamper the government's ability to raise revenue. "Because unused contribution amounts accumulate over time, the TFSA will have much larger consequences when it becomes a mature system," he wrote. An eighteen-year-old who opened a TFSA in 2012 would have about $110,000 in contribution room by the time she or he was forty, assuming annual limits of $5,000 per year, Milligan wrote. "This means that the TFSA will affect coming generations much more than we have observed in its first few years." Multiplied across the population, that would lead to "a noticeable decline in the federal tax base and an even bigger impact on federal revenues." One possible solution would be to cap the lifetime contribution allowed to a TFSA, perhaps at $50,000 as the CCPA's Armine Yalnizyan has suggested.

31. *Adopt an inheritance tax:* One of the main arguments in favour of a system that allows unequal outcomes is that merit can be rewarded. People can get ahead by working harder, being smarter and taking some risks with their investments. What then about people who have made no greater contribution than to have had the good fortune to be born to wealthy parents? Through no effort or ability of their own, they've been given a lead in the rat race, one they are statistically likely to keep. The United States taxes inheritances and McQuaig and Brooks argue for introducing a small levy on large estates in Canada as well.

32. *Introduce a Tobin tax:* Named after James Tobin, the American economist and Nobel Memorial Prize in Economics winner who first suggested the idea, the proposal is to tax financial transactions. If the tax were set at a level small enough, wrote McQuaig and Brooks, "it would have no impact on serious investors making long-term investments, but would amount to a million pinpricks in the flesh of those engaging in high-volume,

quick-turnover, speculative activities." If adopted on a global scale, it could also raise billions.

33. *Hike taxes on consumption and carbon:* The classic tax-shift argument is that we should charge more on the things we want less of and less on the things we want more of. Carbon and consumption taxes target people who burn more fuel and consume more goods, activities with a detrimental impact on the environment. In general, the people consuming more are the wealthy, but a caveat is necessary. One of the criticisms of BC's carbon tax is that it punishes people living in rural places who have few options to get around other than driving, and that the level of taxation is the same regardless of how much money they make. One way to offset this regressiveness is to redistribute some or all of the money in ways that reach people in need, either through programs or directly like we do now with the general sales tax credit. Such taxes would have the added benefit of reducing the damage to the environment that future generations will inherit.

34. *Raise corporate taxes, restore bank taxes:* After a decade of cutting corporate taxes, the BC government took a page from the NDP's platform and in February 2013, a few months before a provincial election, announced a small increase. There has also been pressure to re-instate a tax on financial institutions that the government axed when Carole Taylor was finance minister, but so far the government has appeared uninterested.

35. *Introduce a wealth tax:* French economist Thomas Piketty in his book *Capital in the Twenty-First Century* argues for a global wealth tax that would prevent the 0.1 percent of top earners from building up dynasties, passing their riches on from generation to generation. Taxes are the best way to reduce extreme wealth

inequality, he wrote. "Without taxes, society has no common destiny, and collective action is impossible."

36. *Let inflation rise:* Central banks have in recent years been trying to keep inflation low without slipping into deflation. The effects of inflation are complicated. On one hand rising prices make it an even greater stretch for people with low or fixed incomes to afford what they need. On the other, inflation makes it cheaper for debtors, whether they are homeowners or governments, to pay back what they owe and it erodes the value of accumulated capital.

* * *

WHEN I WROTE a story in *The Tyee* with several ideas for reducing inequality, readers weighed in with their preferences. There was no obvious consensus. If it were up to me, I would take a varied approach. I worry more about the effects of abject poverty than I do about the lifestyles of the rich, so I would start by developing an anti-poverty strategy that would focus on raising children who are free of need, particularly for food and shelter, and thus able to fully participate in education and their communities. I would look for ways to strengthen families, both through direct financial transfers and through programs such as improved child care. The Scandinavian countries, France, the United Kingdom, Belgium, Hungary and Austria each spend at least 3 percent of their GDP supporting families, according to OECD figures from 2007, which is more than double what we spend in Canada. I'd also advocate steps to make housing more affordable, including through the creation of non-market housing. In Singapore, which has a small land base, more than 80 percent of the population live in public housing that's designed to be affordable and of decent quality. We could do the same. I don't particularly care how we pay for these things, though I'd support generating revenue in ways that take money from those who are most able to pay. Progressive taxes strike me as fairer than taxes that are flatter. Making a difference will require taking a long-term view. Much of the poverty and many of the social issues we face are intergenerational in nature, so we should expect improvements to also take generations before we see results.

Some readers may feel that in outlining possible ways to address inequality, I've left out charity. There are many good organizations doing important, even essential, work in BC and around the world. This includes things like feeding people who are hungry, providing shelter to people who are homeless and helping people navigate the overly bureaucratic welfare system. But I agree with Bill Hopwood from Raise the Rates when he points out there's a big difference between charity and justice. He gave the example of Carrie Gelson, a Grade 2–3 teacher from a Vancouver elementary school who wrote a letter that got published widely about the number of children who were coming to school hungry. The response from the community was to raise money for the school. While the action was in some ways admirable, something is lost when charity is provided to one school rather than finding a response that works on the wider problem. Hopwood said, "In a sense it's absolving government from taking responsibility."

Pediatrician Barbara Fitzgerald, who teaches at UBC, mentioned the same letter from Gelson in a 2014 opinion piece in the *Vancouver Sun*. "Here we are, three years later, and children are still arriving at school not having slept in a bed, or eaten anything for supper the night before," she wrote. Parents are stressed trying to pay their hydro bills, buy groceries and explain to their children why they have no money to do anything fun, she said. "More donated spaghetti won't solve the problem." Her experience as a doctor allowed her to see how life would be for these children, she wrote. "Without adequate support for learning, healthy food to eat and safe places to sleep and play, the odds are they won't finish school, and won't be employable in a job that lifts them out of poverty." Fitzgerald predicted that when they grow up, they will "have more unplanned children, commit more crimes and spend more (expensive) time in our criminal justice system."

Fitzgerald is president of the Mom to Mom Child Poverty Initiative Society, but doesn't think charity is the answer. "When I see a young child in my clinic who is living in a situation of poverty and neglect, I ask myself how I, as a voting citizen, am responsible for this," she wrote. "I have contributed to this state of affairs by allowing governments to be elected with policies that condone and contribute to these limiting and heartless conditions."

While there are steps individuals and others can take, there's no question that governments are best placed to make a difference. It's a point that Joseph Stiglitz stressed in his 2012 book *The Price of Inequality*. "By understanding the origins of inequality, we can better grasp the costs and benefits of reducing it," he wrote. "Much of the inequality that exists today is a result of government policy, both what the government does and what it does not do." Governments have the power to move money from the top to the bottom and the middle, or vice versa, making inequality and politics closely intertwined, he wrote. "Inequality is, to a very large extent, the result of government policies that shape and direct the forces of technology and markets and broader societal forces." That leaves government in the position of being both the source of the problem and the most able to solve it. "There is in this a note of both hope and despair," wrote Stiglitz. "Hope because it means that this inequality is not inevitable, and that by changing policies we can achieve a more efficient and a more egalitarian society." But also despair, since it is so hard to change the political processes that shape the government's policies, Stiglitz wrote.

In *The Trouble with Billionaires*, Linda McQuaig and Neil Brooks made a similar point, spending some time looking at how Bill Gates's success depended on strong public supports. Microsoft founder Gates regained his status as the world's richest person in 2014, according to *Forbes* magazine, by the way. The winners in our economy—from billionaire Jim Pattison on down to people who make salaries of just under seven figures—succeed just fine under the current rules. Some would argue they succeed because of them. Pattison's car businesses would be worthless without publicly funded roads and he'd have a tough time finding 39,000 people to hire if it weren't for public funding for education. If the rules favour some people over others, those rules can be changed so that the end result is fairer, McQuaig and Brooks wrote. That, unfortunately, is easier said than done.

CHAPTER 12

POLITICAL CONSTRAINTS: CYNICISM, COMPROMISE AND WHO VOTES

WHEN ENGLISH ACTOR, COMEDIAN AND activist Russell Brand called in late 2013 for revolution and dismissed the possibilities of democracy, the response of huge numbers of people sharing the news on social media made it clear he had expressed something many were feeling. The system we have today is delivering widening disparity and creating an exploited underclass that has few prospects for a better life, Brand had said in his *New Statesman* essay and a BBC interview. He called for a revolution to overturn the current structure, saying there was no point voting because it wouldn't make a difference.

Talking about inequality with people in British Columbia, I repeatedly heard similar sentiments expressed about the state of politics. One articulate young person—who told me the province's disability support system has made it harder for him to get an education, find a job and move forward—said, "I don't even vote at this point because I don't think it does any good." He pointed out that in the 2013 provincial election even the New Democratic Party, which talks about fighting poverty and reducing inequality, proposed a hike in disability payments of just $20 a month, an amount so small compared to the need that it was "laughable." That is, even when the parties were talking about policies that would affect him directly, they weren't saying anything he could support. Jessica Sothcott, quoted in Chapter 1 on how BC government policies were making it hard to provide for her family, told me she never voted because the debate seemed to have nothing to do with her, though she had recently changed her mind and planned to participate in the next election.

"The impoverished policy and political culture is a challenge," said Mary Ellen Turpel-Lafond, the Representative for Children and Youth in BC. "Personally I feel like we haven't had much success." Her mandate restricts her to assessing government programs, rather than turning her attention to unaddressed needs. Instead she's found ways to make points about the structural nature of poverty in the province by working around the edges. For the report *Fragile Lives, Fragmented Systems,* put out by her office in 2011, for example, she said she connected sudden infant death syndrome to deep intergenerational poverty, parental abuse, substance abuse and substandard housing. On another topic, the government was preparing a push to end domestic violence, but Turpel-Lafond pointed out that it wouldn't succeed without working on root causes. Domestic violence is linked to poverty, addictions and mental illness, she said.

Politics is about winning elections, not solving problems, Turpel-Lafond said in an interview, and the politicians, understandably, focus on engaging the people who are most likely to vote. "The political culture is [that] *poverty* is a swear word." In BC there isn't even agreement within the government about what poverty means and what standard of living should be considered necessary, she said. "Do you need to have a mattress in a room to raise a child? Simple question." It's tough, however, to even have those discussions, she said. Christy Clark came into office talking about "Families First," but the concept got killed at her first cabinet meeting, said Turpel-Lafond. She said she had been advised in her work as the

Representative for Children and Youth not to use the word *poverty* in seeking action from the province. "It is equivalent to a swear word," she said, adding she had been told, "Use a Gini coefficient, not the *p*-word." The Gini coefficient is a measure used to determine how equally wealth and income are distributed and Turpel-Lafond said she finds using it to be sterile. "The Gini coefficient doesn't seem to reflect to me the straitened circumstances of many in BC," she said. "There's no concept of the people behind this."

Chris Shaw is an author, scientist and activist who volunteered as a medic at the Occupy protest in Vancouver but stresses he is speaking for himself and is not a spokesperson for the movement. Shaw wrote the 2008 book *Five Ring Circus: Myths and Realities of the Olympic Games* and was a leading opponent of hosting the 2010 Olympic and Paralympic Winter Games in BC. There's a reason Russell Brand's comments about people not voting resonated, he told me over Skype one day. "I think the vast bulk of people who don't vote think there's no purpose. Nothing changes." At the municipal level, for example, it matters little in Vancouver whether the city elects the right-wing Non Partisan Association, moderate Larry Campbell, or left-wing Vision Vancouver, said Shaw. "Why get up and go do that?" The same could be said federally in Canada or nationally in the United States, he said. "People who are at the disadvantaged end of that inequality ladder [realize voting] is not going to make any difference," he said. "We don't really live in a democracy... We elect constitutional dictatorships in Canada."

The mainstream media plays a role too, said Shaw, observing that social issues and poverty get little attention. "It's not like they don't know it exists. You'd have to be deaf, dumb and blind not to know the Downtown Eastside exists." There's little interest in the media in ideas that challenge the status quo, he said. "The coverage on Occupy was pretty routinely negative." Few mainstream reporters made any attempt to figure out what the movement was about, he said. "We all know news can be slanted…When the *Sun* wants economic data, they go to the Fraser Institute, not the CCPA [Canadian Centre for Policy Alternatives]."

Jim Sinclair, while president of the BC Federation of Labour, also noted that most of the provincial media are owned by just a few large companies headed by millionaires. They tend to hire reporters, editors and columnists who share their view of the world and purge those who do not. Sinclair himself worked as a reporter at the *Nelson Daily News* until it was bought by Conrad Black.

Plummeting numbers for voter turnout may well reflect the fact that many are opting out, and tuning out, of a discussion that seems to have nothing to do with them. In the May 2013 provincial election, about 58 percent of people who were eligible to vote cast a ballot, according to figures from Elections BC. The number was up from the 51 percent who voted in 2009, but was still far below the 71 percent who participated as recently as 1983. Covering the 2013 campaign in Victoria, Vancouver, Prince George, Quesnel and Williams Lake, I met many people who told me that they disliked all the politicians, that the candidates all seemed to be in it for themselves and were all out of touch with ordinary people's concerns. (See Figure 12.1.)

The problem with opting out, though, is that governments and politicians still have the power to set the rules that shape how our society turns out, whether it will be more equal or less, even if you haven't encouraged them by voting. If you're opposed to what Christy Clark and Stephen Harper are doing, it works out just fine for them to have you stay home on voting day.

Part of the problem, I suspect, is that politics involve compromise. It's a point well illustrated by Linda McQuaig's attempt to get elected to the House of Commons in Ottawa for the NDP in a November 2013 by-election in Toronto-Centre. As noted previously, writers and academics are unconstrained by a need to find public support for their ideas, unlike politicians. McQuaig, who had

**FIGURE 12.1: BC VOTER TURNOUT, BY PERCENTAGE OF
ELIGIBLE VOTERS, 1983–2013**

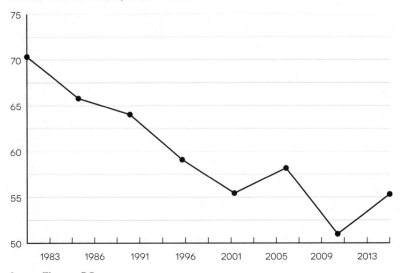

Source: Elections BC

previously written several excellent books on inequality in Canada, in a co-authored book published in 2010 proposed raising the country's marginal tax rates to 60 percent on income over $500,000 a year and to 70 percent on income over $2.5 million. She and her tax lawyer co-author Neil Brooks also advocated introducing an inheritance tax in Canada, similar to what the United States has now. In the US the threshold is set high enough that it applies only to 2 percent of estates, but it raises $25 billion a year. "The tax has little negative effect on economic activity in the country, and is considered largely benign by public finance economists. In other words, it is a levy that appears to do little damage while doing much good," Brooks and McQuaig wrote. The Broadbent Institute, the think tank led by former NDP leader Ed Broadbent, also favours an inheritance tax.

While the by-election campaign was on in Toronto, federal NDP leader Tom Mulcair made a visit to Victoria to participate in a townhall meeting on pensions for seniors. I took the opportunity to ask him what he thought about McQuaig's support for an inheritance tax. His first response was to say that McQuaig is an "extraordinary public intellectual" and an "extraordinary candidate" who is now part of the NDP team and supportive of NDP policy.

So what does Mulcair think about instating an inheritance tax? "Categorically no," he said. When I asked why not, he said, "It's a bad idea." Now feeling that it was taking more questions than I had expected to get a full answer, I asked why it was a bad idea. Mulcair responded, "First of all, it would be contrary to [the planning] done for decades and decades by individuals and families. It wouldn't produce much of a result and it would be a bureaucratic nightmare." He paused, then asked, "Those enough in the way of answers for you?" Earlier, during the townhall question-and-answer session, Mulcair had talked about raising taxes on corporations, but dismissed higher rates for individual high-income earners. Instead he focused on cracking down on tax evaders. "With regards to individuals, the most important thing to do is make sure people are actually paying their taxes," he said. "The constant recourse to tax havens, tax shelters in other countries, moving money offshore and then not paying your taxes as that money grows, that's what we're going to go after."

The NDP's failure to support an inheritance tax can't have been a surprise to McQuaig, who in her book noted that the party previously floated such a policy under late leader Jack Layton, but made a hasty retreat after receiving criticism from the media. It's also worth noting that none of the other mainstream Canadian parties support an inheritance tax or significantly raising income taxes either. The issue is, in effect, non-partisan. In fact, there appears to be political appetite to do things that would actually make inequality worse. At the federal Conservative Party's 2013 convention, delegates debated resolutions that supported tax cuts for the rich, restrictions on unions, curtailment of collective bargaining rights and cuts to public pensions. McQuaig ultimately lost to Liberal Chrystia Freeland, a journalist who herself had written a much less strident book than McQuaig's about growing inequality.

Adrian Dix has had some time to reflect on the opportunities and the challenges that growing inequality presents for leaders of progressive parties. We spoke one day in his office while he was still leader of the BC New Democrats, but after he had announced his resignation following the unexpected defeat in the 2013 provincial election. "Growing inequality is an argument for social democratic policies, but also a political challenge for social democrats," said Dix. "We're seeing this in election results around the world—that as inequality grows, people's desire to participate in the political process, those that aren't benefiting from it, is less and their cynicism is more." As inequality wins at the voting booth and grows unchecked, so does cynicism, Dix said. "Convincing people change is possible in a society that's heading in that direction is a difficult thing."

When Dix campaigned for the leadership of the NDP in 2011, he did so on a platform that put addressing inequality at the forefront. Ahead of the 2013 election, when polls showed his party with a solid lead over the governing BC Liberals and that he was likely to be the next premier, he still named addressing inequality as his number one priority. The party's policies—perhaps somewhat obscured behind a slogan of "Change for the Better, One Practical Step at a Time"—included raising corporate taxes, increasing income taxes for high earners, and spending more on training opportunities.

To illustrate the challenge, Dix explained an example from the provincial election. The BC Liberals offered voters a one-time $1,200 grant for a family's Registered Education Savings Plan account when a child turned six. Dix and the NDP argued the grants would help people who were least in need, people with the wherewithal to open an RESP for their kids. Few children of the wealthy would miss out on the grants, but many in low-income households would. The NDP instead proposed using the money to support early childhood education for everyone. The spending would be no greater, but the help would make it to even the children in the deepest need. Six months after losing the election, Dix observed that the people who were most likely to benefit from the Liberals' approach turned out to vote for them. The people who would have done better under the NDP plan, he said, either didn't pay close enough attention to realize that they would do better; didn't turn out to vote; or were cynical about government's ability to make a difference. Put simply, well-off people who are benefiting from inequality are much more likely to vote than are those who are struggling to get by with low incomes.

Dix did acknowledge he had some success with other policies that addressed inequality, even without winning the election to see them fulfilled. His proposals to raise taxes on corporations and high-income earners were initially dismissed by his opponents and the media, he said, but "two years later they essentially adopted my position." Hiking those taxes was a reversal of twelve years of public policy in BC that had been maintained through good and bad economic times, he said. "I campaigned on it, engaged on it, and won the debate."

The provincial and federal New Democratic parties set their policies separately, but out of interest I asked Dix for his perspective on inheritance taxes and the federal party's decision to avoid the topic. He figured the party was responding to real concerns from voters. For one thing, even if a government says it will only introduce such a tax on very large estates of more than say $10 million, people will suspect that the threshold will be lowered over time, he said. Second, there's an "aspirational" element to it where many people who don't have estates that large imagine that one day they will, he said.

Compromise—aiming to meet the wishes of the people who are actually likely to vote—is just one of many factors affecting the positions politicians take. The influence of money is another. Policies can be reversed, or tweaked in ways to make their outcomes fairer, but as author Joseph Stiglitz and others point out, as the rich get richer they have more money to spend influencing politics, either directly through political donations or indirectly by funding the advocacy groups that promote their interests. "People with the income get to change the rules of the game so they can keep it," said Iglika Ivanova, an economist with the BC office of the Canadian Centre for Policy Alternatives. You see it in the funding for non-governmental organizations, she said. "Someone pays for this stuff. It's not a coincidence that the people who defend the rights of poor people work on shoestring budgets and those who defend the wealthy have huge budgets."

Money also plays a big role in who gets to run. I'd known Briony Penn, a colleague of mine at Victoria's *Monday Magazine* for several years before she got into politics. She was a Liberal candidate in a Capital Regional District riding at a time when the Conservatives held a minority government and a new election could be called at any time. But the government survived much longer than expected. By the time the election was called, Penn—a long-time environmental activist and writer—had been the Liberal candidate for some eighteen months, during which, she said, her long-time employers, including the federal and provincial environment ministries and *Monday*, were uncomfortable employing her. "I can't earn a living when I'm a candidate." Eventually Penn stepped out of the process. "If you want to have people running who aren't rich, we have to find a different system," she told me. "Look around. Look at the people who run. They're rich or they have someone supporting them." The challenges are particularly hard on people like her who are single, female and self-employed, she said. "I don't have any financial buffers now," she said. "The elephant in the room for women in politics is money. It's got to be named. It's got to be addressed."

In interviews, several suggestions came up that aimed at reducing the influence of money, addressing the crisis in democracy and making politics more responsive to average people:

- *Get big money out of politics.* "You get as much democracy as you can buy these days," said Mathew Kagis, who was forty-five when I interviewed him in 2013. He had volunteered as a medic in the protest camp during Occupy Vancouver and had run for office for the Work Less Party. "I mind them buying my government," he said. The federal government has put caps on donations in recent years, though there's debate about whether or not the move has made much of a difference. There are, however, no such restrictions at the provincial and municipal levels in British Columbia, allowing companies and people to give hundreds of thousands of dollars to politicians. The perception is politicians are bought and owned by big donors. Kagis said the best approach would be to get private money out of politics completely.

- *Fund campaigns publicly.* One way to compensate for getting big donation money out of politics—whether it's from corporations, unions or individuals—is to provide public funding for campaigns, said Kagis. Rather than fund every candidate who comes forward, he suggested making it more difficult to run by requiring candidates to collect many more signatures on their nomination papers than they now need, giving them a much stronger show of community support before they could get on the ballot. Once they achieved that bar, though, they would receive enough public money to run a campaign. You could also make public funding dependent on receiving a certain portion of the vote so that the public wouldn't be asked to fund countless fringe candidates. Kagis said he thought such a system would encourage more independents to run and would result in more minority governments, which would be a good thing. "To me that's one way you get democracy."

- *Introduce proportional representation.* Several sources argued for moving to a system that better reflects the wishes of the electorate. In BC we've twice voted on adopting a single transferable vote (STV) system, though we've failed to pass it, and several jurisdictions use mixed-member proportional (MMP) representation, both of which aim to create houses of representatives with numbers from individual parties matching their respective share of the popular vote. Supporters of the current winner-takes-all voting system have said it forces politicians who want longevity to adopt more moderate positions than they otherwise would and that STV and MMP would encourage representatives to cater to small numbers of voters on the fringes. Proponents of a proportional system argue, however, that people could vote for politicians who better match their beliefs and parties could no longer form the government with 40 percent of the votes, a figure that gets even worse when eligible voters who choose not to cast a ballot are considered. In the 2009 BC election, for example, Gordon Campbell's Liberals formed the government with the support of about one out of five of the people in the province who were eligible to vote. A proportional system, therefore, runs the risk of creating messy parliaments, but it would be much more democratic.

- *Pay politicians the median income.* In British Columbia the median market income for households is around $45,000. Half of British Columbia families make less than that, half make more. MLAs, on the other hand, make more than twice that much, putting them and their families securely in the top half of earners, as long as they hold their jobs. Cabinet ministers, the premier, the Opposition leader, committee heads, party whips and caucus chairs make even more, compensating them for the extra work. "If politicians represented BC demographically, quite a few of them would be on welfare at any given time," observed Bill Hopwood at Raise the Rates. And as an official working with one of the parties told me, it is hard for people who are doing so much better than most to identify with the needs of poor, or even average, people. This could be fixed by tying pay for politicians to the median, giving them an incentive to encourage higher wages for all. Think politicians would never do that? In Alabama they adopted such a system, with representatives voting to start tying their pay in 2014 to the median household income for the state. The vote meant a pay cut of thousands of dollars and no more automatic cost-of-living increases. Mike Ball, a Republican who sponsored the bill, was quoted as saying that tying pay for representatives to the median is fair. "If our people prosper, we will prosper," he said.

There's no question that our democracy is far from perfect and it's intriguing to think about ways to improve it. The lumbering political machine is often slow to respond to emerging issues like climate change and inequality, or to do so in a meaningful way. The system skews towards the middle ground, which can be limiting in a province that by 2014 had grown to 4.6 million people in a country of 35.2 million where opinions are diverse. Established interests, who often are the sponsors of parties and political events, wield more influence than is healthy. For the meantime, however, it is the system we have and it's not nearly as monolithic as it sometimes appears. We do have choices, and there are many ways to influence policies, both directly and indirectly.

CHAPTER 13

OCCUPYING CHANGE: BC POLITICS AND PUBLIC DEMAND

O N A RAINY FEBRUARY 2014 evening in Victoria, I joined an audience of forty or so people in the Salvation Army Citadel for a debate between candidates wanting to lead the British Columbia Conservative Party. The job had come open after the 2013 election, when under the leadership of former MP John Cummins the party failed to capitalize on disarray among the BC Liberals. Despite having polled high enough at times in the two years before the vote to appear a serious threat to the government, the Conservatives had failed to elect even a single MLA.

During the debate, the two candidates agreed on much, including the need to heal the wounds from the party's recent history, that the government was doing a horrible job and that the New Democratic Party would be worse. A telling moment came up, however, when Daniel Brooks criticized his opponent Rick Peterson's involvement in a charitable effort to provide breakfasts to children in schools. Brooks, who eventually won the top job, was a rural tourism operator from Vanderhoof, and Peterson an urban business guy from Vancouver. "I'm sorry, I disagree with breakfast programs for kids," said Brooks, a then thirty-eight-year-old parent of seven. "I feed my kids breakfast every morning... That is taking care of your child, that's my individual responsibility to do as a parent. As soon as we expect the government to take those responsibilities for us, we go down a very slippery slope towards socialism."

The party members, 1,165 of whom voted a couple of months later in the contest, chose Brooks over Peterson by a margin of almost two to one. In an interview after becoming leader, Brooks told me the Conservatives would form a government that would never be beholden to either the Chamber of Commerce or unions. The party under him would stand for low taxes, small government, a diverse economy and sustainable development. As for inequality, he recognized it was an issue but said it was difficult to solve. "I guess I believe that God made us equal," he said, adding that at least we're born that way. "Somehow we separate ourselves after that." One of Brooks' seven daughters is an indigenous girl his wife and he adopted, and he said he fears she will be mistreated because of her background. "I think it's a very legitimate fear," he said. He said he feels compassion for those who experience discrimination, but, "if there were easy solutions we would have done them long ago."

To address poverty, the key is to get people into jobs and to make sure they can get ahead by working, Brooks said. "Nothing fixes poverty faster than a job, but just because you've got a job doesn't mean you're no longer in poverty." There's a need for big tax reforms, he said. It's not a matter of taxing the rich to give to the poor, he clarified, but of making sure the working people aren't carrying too much of the burden.

The Conservatives, who consistently get a significant number of votes despite the failure in recent decades to elect any MLAs, are on what I'd call the near fringes of BC politics. Also on the near fringes is the BC Green Party, which in 2013 had its first win with climate scientist Andrew Weaver becoming the MLA for the Victoria-area constituency of Oak Bay-Gordon Head. The party, which has supported moving to a steady state economy that eschews economic growth as a goal, included in the ten core principles listed on its website (as of early 2015) that "the worldwide increase in poverty and inequity is unacceptable." The party's social services platform in 2013 included the commitment that it would start by "replacing all existing income assistance programs" with a guaranteed livable income. The party would also exempt anyone living below the poverty line from paying provincial income tax.*

To get a sense of the further fringes, Elections BC's list of political party names used in the province in the past ten years runs to nine pages. Among many others, it includes the BC Vision Party, BC First Party, BC Marijuana Party, BC Unity Party, Christian Heritage Party of BC, Communist Party of BC, Feminist Institute of BC, Work Less Party, None of the Above Party of BC and the Sex Party. There's something, it would seem, for everyone.

Even between the two parties that have dominated the province's politics—the BC Liberals and the BC NDP—there are many points of difference and voters are offered a choice. Yes, most voters will find supporting any party is a compromise, but that's to be expected when winning requires the support of more than a million people, each with individual perspectives and desires. As Dave Zirnhelt, a former NDP cabinet minister, put it to me one day in Williams Lake during the 2013 BC election, the parties have a role to play aggregating positions and presenting the public with packages of policies from which to choose. The parties pick positions on complex issues and put them together so voters can tick a box on a ballot that best approximates their ideals.

Premier Christy Clark's perspective, and how her party functions, were very much on display at the BC Liberal Party's 2014 convention in Kelowna, a city with preppy clothing stores, marinas full of shiny boats and a surprising number of homeless people

---

* Activist and author Chris Shaw observed that in BC the Greens tend to worry about offending people, then end up with policies that are inoffensive but uninspiring. "The dominant idea out there is elections are won in the middle of the road," he said, adding that's only true as long as large numbers of people fail to vote. "In other countries the Greens do a lot better by offending a lot of people."

walking the streets with their belongings heaped in shopping carts. Delegates defeated resolutions related to mental health care, child care and housing affordability. Motions that didn't even make it to the floor for debate included proposals on ending the clawback of child-support payments from single parents' disability cheques, writing a poverty-reduction strategy, and reducing ferry fares.

It was a convention at which delegates and guests could unwind by riding a mechanical bull and sipping complementary Okanagan wine at a Saturday-night party. The few of us reporting on the convention asked Clark about the appetite for change in the party and the failure of those motions to find support. "We're not the party of tax more, spend more," she told us following her keynote address to the convention, where lunch was sponsored by oil and gas companies Suncor, Cenovus Energy and MEG Energy. "We're the party of grow the economy so that we have more resources so people can have more money in their own pockets to spend and so we have more money to look after people."

Of the eighty resolutions constituency associations and party committees submitted, just eighteen were debated in the two hours scheduled for the policy session. Ahead of the session, delegates could each pick their top five priorities to debate, with the order that issues would be addressed to be based on the rankings. Motions on balancing the budget and limiting taxes led the way. Several times a party spokesperson promised me he would provide the full rankings of motions, but he never delivered.

"We are engaging in more debate over more issues than I think we did over the last ten years," said Clark, whose leadership received a 98.8-percent vote of approval. "That reflects my view that political parties are a place for debate." People should have a right to bring forward their views, even if they're controversial, she said, adding, "People can belong to our party even if they don't agree with 100 percent of what we're doing."

The other dominant party, the BC New Democratic Party, was reduced to two MLAs in 2001 after a decade in government, but has rebuilt to the point where many observers were surprised it didn't win in the 2013 election. Issues of poverty and equality have consistently been part of the party's platform, although with greater or lesser emphasis at different times. Former leader Adrian Dix, who won the job saying the party couldn't win an election by cozying up to the BC Liberals and needed to work to appeal to non-voters, talked frequently as leader about inequality and took a chance in promoting policies like raising taxes on high-income earners and corporations.

But there is only so far the party has been willing to go. While many NDP MLAs will say welfare rates are too low, for example, the party has generally avoided discussion of raising the rates or specifying how much they should go up. In 2014 a single person in the expected-to-work category received $610 a month, the same level as in 2007. During the 2013 campaign, the NDP proposed raising the income-assistance rates by $20 a month, with further increases to be tied to the rate of inflation, along with several other measures the party said would alleviate poverty. Advocates like Bill Hopwood of Raise the Rates said the proposed increase would do little to help. "Twenty dollars a month, it's just going to vanish," Hopwood said, adding that most of the extra cash would go to higher rents, amounting to a subsidy for landowners. "It won't tackle poverty one iota." Hopwood said adjustments to the welfare system should be made as part of a broader poverty-reduction strategy that also includes such issues as support for social housing. Hopwood later noted that, although Dix had emphasized addressing inequality during the leadership campaign, in his view the topic had disappeared from the agenda after Dix won the job. "When he became leader that seemed to be forgotten."

The rest of the NDP's plan included strengthening Community Living BC and spending $210 million a year on a BC family bonus to provide up to $829 a year for each child under eighteen years of age. The full amount would have gone to families where the annual income was under $25,000 and would have been phased out for households with higher incomes, ending at $66,000. Hopwood said the steps were positive but it was telling that the bulk of the help would go to families with children. "There's an element of the deserving poor and undeserving poor, (the) old Victorian argument, in there probably," he said. Raise the Rates had been campaigning to get all the parties to commit to raising welfare rates. "I think it's fair to say the welfare increase is a disappointment, to put it mildly," he said, noting $20 works out to well under $1 a day. "It almost needs doubling. To bring it up to the government's poverty line would mean doubling welfare." He mentioned studies, such as one from the Canadian Centre for Policy Alternatives, that point out that any money saved in denying support to people in poverty leads to more strain on other parts of the budget, such as health, education and the justice system. "Fixing it is cheaper than leaving the problem," Hopwood said. "You need to argue that broader picture, rather than a tweak here or a tweak there."

The NDP's commitments in 2013 also included strengthening the enforcement of employment standards, ending child poverty and respecting the union movement. "We need to do a better job of enforcing basic employment standards," Dix told a BC Federation of Labour telephone townhall meeting. "Some people say it's union members that have got it on the chin from the current government over ten years, but really it's non-union members, it's non-union workers who've taken repeatedly cuts to their supports and a failure of the current government to support basic employment standards." He listed ending child poverty, helping young people gain skills for the jobs of the future, investing in the land base and funding "basic health care and education" as key ways to support communities. "These are the priorities for our time, and it means we may not be able to do other things until more resources become available," Dix said. "I think that practical approach is what people want right now."

Then BC Fed president Jim Sinclair closed the townhall telling participants a BC Liberal re-election would be "an absolute disaster" for working people in the province. "No one's going to do this for us as working people," Sinclair said. "This is our moment after twelve years. It would be a shame if we were to lose it, and it would be an absolute positive step for the province if we win it." He added, "If the NDP are successful, our job won't be over, we'll still have to fight for everything we get. The only difference is we'll have a government that respects us."

Certainly there were other indications that in some ways it would have been business as usual under the NDP, perhaps with new actors filling old roles. Ahead of the 2013 election, for example, when it looked like the NDP would win, business boomed for a couple of lobbyists with strong connections to the party: Jim Rutkowski at Hill+Knowlton Strategies and Marcella Munro with Earnscliffe Strategy Group. Some of the high-profile companies Rutkowski registered to lobby on behalf of were the China National Offshore Oil Corporation subsidiary CNOOC International Ltd., the German drug company Bayer Inc., and Gateway Casinos and Entertainment Inc. His clients have also included the accounting firm Deloitte, the Vancouver Airport Authority, Port Metro Vancouver, Loblaw Companies Ltd., and the Association of Professional Engineers and Geoscientists of BC. Munro's clients have included, according to the province's registry of lobbyists, drug makers Eli Lilly and Company, GlaxoSmithKline Inc., and Novartis Pharmaceuticals Canada Inc., as well as LifeLabs, McDonald's restaurants and the company that owned the Tim Hortons doughnut shop brand.

Between May 1, 1996 and April 1, 2000—years when the NDP formed the government—Rutkowski's lobbying filings note he was "Special Assistant to the Minister of Health, Ministerial Assistant to the Minister of Small Business Tourism and Culture, and Ministerial Assistant to the Minister of Finance and Attorney General." He was also one of the few NDP staffers left in the legislature when the party was reduced to two seats in the 2001 election and was central to the party with Carole James as leader, serving as communications director and chief of staff. Munro's biography page at

Earnscliffe, which she joined in 2009, said she "served as a communications strategist in federal and provincial NDP war rooms, and
municipally as communications chair for Mayor Gregor Robertson
and Vision Vancouver's successful 2008 campaign."

Major lobbying firms tend to hire people who are associated with
the various parties, said Dermod Travis, executive director of the
advocacy group Integrity BC, in a 2013 interview. "I don't foresee a
change in the names of the firms, just who's front and centre with
those firms if the government changes," he said. It was natural that
businesses would pay attention to the NDP and want to make sure
they had good relationships with all the parties likely to form the
government, even if it was disturbing that that was what it took
to open doors, he said. "Regrettably it's become part of the way
government works today. That in itself is nefarious."

The Office of the Registrar of Lobbyists for British Columbia
takes a different tack, by the way, arguing in its 2012–13 annual
report: "Lobbying is a valuable component of modern democratic
processes, but its value is not always recognized...It can be mis-
understood and subject to excessive and unwarranted criticism."
Lobbyists make an important contribution by helping decision
makers understand the possible effects of their decisions, it said,
arguing the role has become more necessary as government has
become more complicated.

Of course the election win didn't materialize for the NDP the way
Dix, Sinclair and just about everybody else expected. The New
Democrats lost the election and Dix staying as leader was unten-
able. Within a year, Juan de Fuca MLA John Horgan was acclaimed
to replace Dix, with nobody else competing for the job. The early
indications were that poverty and inequality would remain central
focuses under Horgan's leadership, and that for him it was personal.
When Horgan stood in the legislature to ask his first question of
the government as leader of the official Opposition, the subject he
raised was familiar NDP fare: temporary foreign workers and jobs

for British Columbians. "Today in British Columbia 142,000 people are looking for work, and thousands more are living hand-to-mouth in part-time jobs," said Horgan. "Youth unemployment, honourable speaker, is at 12 percent and we're going into the summer season where students are going to be looking for work," he said. "Yet we've learned here in Victoria fifty applicants for entry-level jobs at McDonald's were turned down and ignored, and instead temporary foreign workers' applications were applied for and granted."

Over the following weeks Horgan repeatedly told the story of his life: he was raised by a single mother after his father died; went "off the rails" in Grade 9; with help he found focus through sports; he became student council president in his last year of high school; he earned a master's degree at university; he worked at various jobs; with hard work he became leader of the BC New Democratic Party; and one day he would like to be the premier of British Columbia. "I'm the product of a single-parent family," Horgan said at a press conference on one of his first days in the job. "I'm the product of being raised in poverty as a young child, and I now stand before you because of the opportunity that was given to me by faith communities, by neighbours, by community and by government, to say that I want to be the next premier of British Columbia. That speaks to giving opportunity and hope to people who are living in poverty and mired, in some cases, in cyclical poverty."

It's a rags-to-respectability story that made a couple of points. One is that from experience Horgan knew the positive effect public services like education can have on individuals. Another is that he intended to define himself and connect to the public in ways that avoid the labels his opponents would try to stick on him. "There was a discussion about who am I, how did I come to be," Horgan told me in his office one afternoon. "We talked about it—mostly [MLAs] Maurine [Karagianis] and Carole [James], my biggest backers—about the fact that I have a very soft side to my being that does not come through in the work that I do," he said. "They felt that was important for the public to have a view of. That I do come from very modest means and difficult times, and I had a couple of off-the-rails experiences as a teenager that I was able to recover from. Not everybody gets that chance."

On various issues, he holds positions that would work towards reducing inequality in the province. "I think you start by doing something simple, like doing away with the clawback for child-support payments for single parents," he said. "That's a good start. [It would cost] $17 million, which conveniently coincides with the exact amount of money the Liberals blew on partisan ads before the last election. That could have gone into kids' mouths. I think that's a better expenditure of money." He's also open to making the tax system fairer, something he's broached in the past by saying we need to have a commission that reviews the province's entire tax regime. "I'm increasingly of the view that we have to get a handle on things like Medical Services [Plan] premiums," he said. "They're a regressive tax. Everybody pays the same amount regardless of your income, regardless of your family circumstance, and I just think we need to reduce those examples whenever we can."

Successful politicians tend to tell people what they want to hear. Sometimes they lead, but more than one politician has candidly said that success in their job depends on figuring out which way the parade is going, then zipping to the front. There's no doubt we're swayed by the prevailing trends elsewhere. In 2001, two decades after the era of Ronald Reagan and Margaret Thatcher, BC voters elected a government that adopted their policies here. Our greatest hope for a new deal on equality may well be that the United States and other governments lead the way, making more space for our federal and provincial leaders to follow.

When it comes to finding policies to address inequality, governments have been able to put solutions in place when they have wanted to, argue Richard Wilkinson and Kate Pickett in *The Spirit Level*. That change doesn't come unless people demand it, however, they wrote. "Rather than greater equality waiting till well-meaning governments think they can afford to make societies more equal, governments have usually not pursued more egalitarian policies until they thought their survival depended on it."

Most change comes from outside politics, said Raise the Rates coordinator Bill Hopwood. "It would be nice if we had politicians who had more confidence and vision," he said, but added: "Change doesn't primarily come from politicians." Social change will only come from advocates and ordinary people demanding it, he said. "It's not going to be easy... There's that bigger ideological battle to be fought." But the debate is winnable, he said. Most people understand that nobody can live on a $10-an-hour minimum wage or a $610 welfare payment. "I think there's an opportunity for a wave of change to build up in society."

In recent years, one of the greatest sources of pressure to act on inequality in North America came from the Occupy movement, which organizers have said was inspired by a poster published in a summer 2011 issue of *Adbusters*, the anti-corporate Vancouver magazine. As Occupy protests spread from New York that fall, The Canadian Press quoted *Adbusters* co-founder Kalle Lasn: "I kept on wanting to go to New York, and now instead of me coming to the occupation, the occupation is coming to me."

Many people felt the movement expressed something and stood for something that was missing in politics, activist and author Chris Shaw said. He volunteered as a medic in the Vancouver camp, but stressed he doesn't speak for the movement. "Occupy did, for a while, provide a very broad tent for a lot of alternative political and social movements," he said. "They were right. Something is wrong."

The movement was incredibly successful at raising awareness of inequality, said Shaw. "I think it captured the imagination of a lot of people, especially a lot of young people," he said, describing it as a Maple Spring. "The fact it happened at all, even with negative reporting, identified for a lot of people there's inequality." It was also a resurgence of what could be called the left, he said, with groups that often disagree, or work in their own silos, teaming up for a while.

However, the movement failed to sell a positive vision, said Shaw. "That was never really articulated anywhere, what the world looks like when we win," he said. "It's good to be outraged and strike out against what's wrong, but where's your positive vision?" A clear media strategy was lacking, outreach was not nearly as slick as it could have been, and the movement did a poor job of appointing people to leadership roles. There was no strategic plan for where the movement should go. The general assemblies got smaller and smaller, eventually petering out and vanishing. "When it didn't emerge and it got wetter and colder out there, it just kind of vanished and it hasn't re-emerged."

The need for change is huge, said Shaw. It's obvious that much more is needed than a small shift in the current system, he said. "We've been tweaking things for a long time and if the inequalities are growing, as I believe they are, tweaking is not an option."

Inequality will not be solved by growing the economy, Shaw continued. "The problem is not just redistributing the stuff so more people have more trash." What's needed is a rational approach to limit growth and stop consumer culture, he said, adding that leaders need to be looking at ways to make communities as resilient against possible future disasters as possible. That included focusing on food security, building systems from the grassroots, and strengthening local economies. Shaw was not exactly hopeful, however: "I think we're going to thunder in really hard and society as we know it will take a big turn." The collapse is coming, but if we're smart about it we may be able to delay it, he said. "If you don't start employing these things intentionally early on, you're going to have a worse outcome."

It's worth noting that some of the other people interviewed for this book, whose comments are included in other chapters, thought it was important to recognize what we've got right in BC and in Canada generally—including relatively high social mobility, generally equal opportunities and a strong education system. For example, Paul Summerville, a former investment banker who has run for office with the NDP provincially and the Liberals federally, said: "I'm not a revolutionary. Smart tweaking is the way to go."

Jordan Bober, the Living the New Economy conference organizer, in a 2013 interview said he had visited the Occupy camp often. "I would call it a formative experience to be there and witness that." The way things work now, he said, growing inequality is closely linked to environmental destruction. "If the system is stacked in such a way that [it] diverts wealth into the hands of a few, you have to grow the entire pie." That's not sustainable, he said. Many of the people he met at Occupy had absorbed the ideas from the movement and were actively living them, he said. They were working on building a more decentralized, less capital-intensive, economy on a *Small Is Beautiful* model, he said, referencing the 1973 book of essays by British economist E.F. Schumacher.

An unfair system will ultimately be unsustainable, and that's not good for anyone. It's an observation made by many, including Liberal MP Chrystia Freeland in her book *Plutocrats* and former US secretary of labour Robert Reich in *Aftershock*. "It's not whether America will continue to reward risk taking," Reich wrote about the long-term effects of the 2008 financial crisis in a passage that could equally apply in Canada and other countries. "It's whether an economic system can survive when those at the top get giant rewards no matter how badly they screw up while the rest of us get screwed no matter how hard we work."

And as Reich told the *Georgia Straight* newspaper ahead of a visit to Vancouver, despite our differences there seems to be much agreement on the kind of societies in which we want to live. "I certainly would argue for a decent society, a humane society," he said. "I think we want to be having many more discussions than we do about what is the nature of a good society." It's pleasantly surprising to discover how many people share a set of basic principles, no matter what political label they put on themselves, Reich said. Most people in North America think that anyone who works full-time should be able to escape poverty, he said. At the same time, he added, they dislike the idea that wealth, and thus opportunity, get passed down from generation to generation within families. "Most people feel that perpetuation of family dynasties is wrong," he said. "We ought to have a lot more mobility. People ought to have equal opportunity and not necessarily be consigned to a certain place on the economic ladder simply because of their parents." The point of the examples, Reich said, is that once you get rid of political labels, "there is a huge amount of consensus about what a good society means."

You can look around the world at the level of equality in societies ranging from Nigeria to Scandinavia, said then BC Federation of Labour president Jim Sinclair. "We know what inequality looks like, and we know what equality looks like," said Sinclair, who noted that even in the most equal countries the rich can afford nice homes and fancy cars. "The question is which do you want to live in." Canada and BC have enjoyed a relatively strong system of social supports in the past, he acknowledged, but added, "I think more and more Canadians are realizing that if we love this country and we like what we've done, we're going to have to fight for it."

In British Columbia, as the Business Council of British Columbia and others have demonstrated, there is a consensus that growing inequality is a threat to the well-being of individuals in the province and to economic development. There is less agreement on what to do to reverse the trend. The options, however, are many, wanting only for the political leadership that will come when the public support for change solidifies. With a wealth of land and natural resources, as well as a diverse, well-educated population, BC is well placed to take the lead and do things differently. There is no better place on Earth to try.

APPENDIX 1

INEQUALITY BY THE NUMBERS

All figures are the most recently available at the time this book was being written in 2014.

- Percentage of Canada's population living in BC in 2013: 13.2
- Percentage of Canadian poor people who lived in the province that year: 14.6
- Jim Pattison's estimated net worth in 2013: $7,390,000,000
- Amount his net worth had increased from a year earlier: $1,250,000,000
- Pattison's rank on list of wealthiest Canadians: 5
- Number of people employed by the Jim Pattison Group in 2014, according to the company's website: 39,000
- Share of income going to top 1 percent of earners in BC in 2011: 9.7 percent
- Factor in 2011 by which income to top 10 percent exceeded income to bottom 10 percent: 12.6
- Number of children living in poverty in BC in 2012: 169,420
- Increase from 2010: 50,460
- Percentage of children in families headed by a single parent in BC in 2012 living in poverty: 50

- Non-mortgage debt per British Columbian in 2013: $39,000
- Rank of this amount among Canadian provinces and territories: 1
- Percentage of retired people in BC carrying debt in 2012, according to CIBC poll: 59
- Percentage of British Columbians in their fifties in 2012 who'd saved less than $100,000 for retirement: 42
- Rank of Vancouver, BC on list comparing 55 cities in 2012 for lowest business taxes: 2
- Rank of Chennai, India: 1
- Portion of the BC labour force that worked in unionized jobs in 1981: 43 percent
- In 2012: 30 percent
- Among provinces, rank of BC's level of taxation on incomes up to $120,000 in 2014–15: 10
- Year BC's revenue from Medical Services Plan premiums surpassed revenue from corporate taxes: 2013
- Percentage of people in Kaslo, BC in 2010 with after-tax incomes below the low-income cut-off: 41.7
- Percentage living on Lasqueti Island, BC below the LICO: 68.2
- In New Denver, BC: 8.7
- In Elkford, BC: 6.9
- In Belcarra, BC: 3.1
- Percentage tax rate author Linda McQuaig advocated in 2010 on incomes over $2.5 million: 70
- Amount by which the NDP, which she ran for in a 2013 by-election, promised to raise those taxes: $0
- Percentage of Canada's income taxes paid in 2011 by richest 20 percent: 75
- Median net worth in 2012 of the richest 10 percent of British Columbians: $2,020,600
- Median net worth for poorest 10 percent in 1999: −$1,400
- In 2005: −$4,800

- In 2012: -$10,700
- Percentage in 2012 of wealth in BC held by richest 10 percent: 56.2
- By bottom 50 percent: 3.1
- Estimated net assets required to be in wealthiest half of world citizens in 2014: $3,650 (US)
- Amount to be in top 10 percent: $77,000 (US)
- Amount to be in top 1 percent: $798,000 (US)
- Percentage of world's total wealth owned by bottom half of global population: 1
- Percentage held by the richest 10 percent: 87
- Percentage held by the richest 1 percent: 48.2

Sources: Statistics Canada, BC Stats, Canadian Business *magazine, First Call, TransUnion, Canadian Imperial Bank of Commerce (CIBC), KPMG, Business Council of British Columbia, Broadbent Institute, Credit Suisse AG and BC Budget and Fiscal Plan 2013/14–2015/16.*

APPENDIX 2

STATE OF THE DEBATE

The following exchange between BC Premier Christy Clark and Nelson-Creston MLA *Michelle Mungall, as recorded in Hansard, took place during the provincial Question Period on April 9, 2014:*

Michelle Mungall: Single-parent families in British Columbia who receive income supports, like disability, have their child support payments clawed back, dollar for dollar, every single month by this government. Last year the total amount taken from BC's poorest kids was $17 million. That's the same amount that the Premier spent on self-promoting ads in the last election.

So my question is to the Premier. How is this putting families first?

Hon. Christy Clark: We have to in this province, do everything that we can to give every child, every young person and every adult all of the opportunities that they would wish for themselves. We have to make sure that we're growing the economy. We have to make sure that people have the skills that they need to participate fully in the economy.

I was very proud today to be part of the signing, the historic signing, with the Lax Kw'alaams and the Metlakatla First Nations on agreements that are going to ensure economic development, economic growth, comes to their region of the province.

In those cases those leaders have a vision for their communities. They have a vision for people in those communities, some of whom haven't been attached to the workforce for a long time. Healthy, wealthy, thriving communities where every young person gets a shot at a great job—that's what we are working toward.

M. Mungall: Rachel Goodine, Diane Taralon, Jennifer Bryce [sic], Crystal Panagard and Tabatha Naysmith [sic] are all single moms with disabilities that prevent them from working full-time outside the home. They receive income supports, and as we all know, the levels of support from this BC Liberal government keep them struggling to put food on the table.

If they could keep their child support payments, the struggle of feeding and clothing their kids would be reduced. That would reduce child poverty in their homes. Those moms are in the gallery today.

My question, again to the Premier: can she explain to the mothers here today how taking child support payments away from their kids is putting their families first?

Hon. C. Clark: As I said a little bit—in my previous answer—we are very much focused on growing the economy as a way to make sure that we look after people in the province for the long term, to make sure that communities are sustainable, that families are sustainable, ensuring that people can look after themselves and each other in the way that they expect to and the way that they should.

While we do that, we also have to maintain a strong social safety net, and we are doing that in British Columbia. Since I became Premier, we have raised the minimum wage three times in our province.* We are proud to be able to say that we have one of the lowest overall tax levels, keeping more money in people's pockets.

We have child care—$135 million invested in child care subsidies this year. And 800,000 people in the province who pay no MSP premiums. Some $3.6 billion since 2001 invested in affordable housing and 98,000 households that benefit from provincial social housing programs and services. And of course, the introduction of the early childhood tax benefit, starting in 2015, to make child care more affordable for 180,000 families. And that's just the beginning.

M. Mungall: The Premier needs to stop brushing these families off with all of her rhetoric and empty slogans and the various numbers that she likes to point out. Why doesn't she ever talk about the fact that BC has had the highest child poverty in this country for ten years running? That's happening under her watch.

Here's another stat for the Premier. Half of BC's single mothers are living in poverty with their kids right now—mothers like Tabitha Naismith, a Surrey mom who's struggling to raise her one-year-old daughter on $642 a month after rent. The BC Liberals are clawing the $100 that her daughter is supposed to be getting in child support payments. They are clawing that back every month. And it is wrong.

Instead of doing the wrong thing, will the Premier do the right thing? End the clawback of child support payments, and give BC's poorest kids their money back.

Hon. C. Clark: We live in a rich country; we live in a rich province. And the fact, the sad fact, is that many people still do not fully participate in that wealth.

We have an obligation as a generation to ensure that everyone across the province has an equal opportunity to take part in the

---

* Clark's government made just one announcement about raising the minimum wage, but phased in the increase over three hikes.

economic growth that is coming in our province. We believe that the best way out of poverty is to make sure that people are participating in the economic growth and that they have the skills that they need to take those jobs. In the meantime, we also have to make sure that that social safety net is there to protect people who need that protection when they are enduring poverty in our province.

I went through quite a number of the investments that our province has made in supporting people who live in poverty. We need to continue to do that, and at the same time, we need to give everyone a hand up. We need to give everyone the help that they need to acquire the skills and the education that they're going to need to create a sustainable future for themselves and their families through employment.

SELECT BIBLIOGRAPHY

The following list includes works that are quoted from or referred to in the chapters of this book. It is by no means a full list of all the reference material consulted.

2001 Census Fast Facts: BC Aboriginal Identity Population—Income and Low Income. Victoria: BC Stats, August 2004. Accessed at www.bcstats.gov.bc.ca

2013 Child Poverty Report Card. Vancouver: First Call: BC Child and Youth Advocacy Coalition, November 2013.

2014 Child Poverty Report Card. Vancouver: First Call: BC Child and Youth Advocacy Coalition, November 2014.

2014 Metro Vancouver Homeless Count: Preliminary Report. Vancouver: Greater Vancouver Regional Steering Committee on Homelessness, April 2014. Accessed at www.stophomelessness.ca

Alexander, Craig, Derek Burleton and Diana Petramala. *Special Report: Assessing the Financial Vulnerability of Households Across Canadian Regions.* Toronto: TD Economics, Feb. 9, 2011. Accessed at www.td.com/economics

Anielski, Mark. *The Economics of Happiness: Building Genuine Wealth.* Gabriola Island, BC: New Society Publishers, 2007.

———. *The JAK Members Bank: Sweden.* Edmonton: Anielski Management Inc., Jan. 16, 2004.

Annual Report 2012/2013. Victoria: Office of the Ombudsperson, June 2013.

Annual Report 2012–2013. Victoria: Office of the Registrar of Lobbyists for British Columbia, 2013.

Ball, David. "'Don't Blame Foreign Workers,' Says Fast Food Employee." *The Tyee*, May 3, 2014. Accessed at www.thetyee.ca

———. "Are Stats Glossing over Vancouver's Housing Crisis?" *The Tyee*, Sept. 24, 2013. Accessed at www.thetyee.ca

Barman, Jean. *The West beyond the West: A History of British Columbia.* 3rd ed. Toronto: University of Toronto Press, 2007.

The BC Agenda for Shared Prosperity. Vancouver: Business Council of British Columbia and BC Chamber of Commerce, Sept. 2013. Accessed at www.bcbc.com

Beddoes, Zanny Minton. "For Richer, for Poorer: Growing Inequality Is One of the Biggest Social, Economic and Political Challenges of Our Time. But It Is Not Inevitable, Says Zanny Minton Beddoes." *Economist*, Oct. 13, 2012. Accessed at www.economist.com

Blyth, Mark, and Eric Lonergan. "Print Less but Transfer More: Why Central Banks Should Give Money Directly to People." *Foreign Affairs*, Sept./Oct. 2014.

Canadian Business staff. "Richest People in Canada 2014." *Canadian Business*, Nov. 26, 2013. Accessed at www.canadianbusiness.com

Canadian Press. "Adbusters Founders Cheer Their Occupy Idea." Oct. 14, 2011. Accessed at www.cbc.ca

Carlyle, Erin. "9.7 Million Americans Still Have Underwater Homes, Zillow Says." *Forbes*, May 20, 2014. Accessed at www.forbes.com

Carrick, Rob. "Gen Y's Pain Is Real: Paycheques Tell the Tale." *The Globe and Mail*, Nov. 28, 2013: B14.

"CEO Compensation." Table, with data prepared by Global Governance Advisors. *The Globe and Mail*, June 2, 2014: B4.

Chandler, Kim. "Alabama House Votes to Tie Legislators' Pay to Alabamians' Income." *Alabama Media Group*, Apr. 5, 2012. Accessed at www.AL.com

Cohen, Marjorie Griffin. *BC Disadvantage for Women: Earnings Compared with Other Women in Canada.* Vancouver: Canadian Centre for Policy Alternatives BC Office, 2012.

Cooper, Sam. "Open Farmland for Homes, Study Says." *Province*, June 4, 2014: A6.

Corak, Miles. "Inequality from Generation to Generation: The United States in Comparison." *The Economics of Inequality, Poverty, and Discrimination in the 21st Century*, ABC-CLIO.

Dahlby, Bev, and Ergete Ferede. "Income Inequality, Redistribution and Economic Growth." University of Calgary, School of Public Policy, *SPP Research Papers*, 6.25 (2013).

Disability Assistance: An Audit of Program Access, Integrity and Results. Victoria: Office of the Auditor General of British Columbia, May 2014.

Dix, Adrian. "B.C. Must Reconcile with Its Past Official Racism against Chinese Canadians." *Georgia Straight*, Jan. 5, 2014. Accessed at www.straight.com

"Education and Occupation of High-Income Canadians." *National Household Survey.* Statistics Canada. Accessed at www12.statcan.gc.ca on Jan. 2, 2014.

"Financial Security—Low Income Incidence." *Indicators of Well-Being in Canada.* On Employment and Social Development Canada website. Accessed at www4.hrsdc.gc.ca on Dec. 20, 2014.

Fister, Emily. "What Makes Us Unequal? Precarious Jobs." *The Tyee*, Aug. 30, 2014. Accessed at www.thetyee.ca

———. "What Makes Us Unequal? Being a Mom." *The Tyee*, Sept. 6, 2014. Accessed at www.thetyee.ca

Fitzgerald, Barbara. "Opinion: Children Need and Deserve Our Help." *Vancouver Sun*, Sept. 16, 2014. Accessed at blogs.vancouversun.com

Freeland, Chrystia. *Plutocrats: The Rise of the New Global Super-Rich and the Fall of Everyone Else.* Toronto: Doubleday Canada, 2012.

Frenette, Marc, and René Morissette. *Wages and Full-Time Employment Rates of Young High School Graduates and Bachelor's Degree Holders, 1997 to 2012.* Statistics Canada, 11F0019M, no. 360, April 2014.

Gladwell, Malcolm. "Million-Dollar Murray." *New Yorker*, Feb. 13, 2006: 96–107.

Global Wealth Report 2014. Zurich: Credit Suisse AG, October 2014.

Goar, Carol. "Parliament's Gift to the Poor: A Lump of Coal." *Waterloo Region Record*, Dec. 14, 2013. Accessed at www.therecord.com

Gold, Kerry. "With Prices Up, a Call for Curbs." *The Globe and Mail*, Dec. 14, 2013: S5.

Grant, Tavia. "The 15-Hour Workweek: Canada's Part-Time Problem." *The Globe and Mail*, Oct. 4, 2014: B6.

Green, David A., and Jonathan R. Kesselman eds. *Dimensions of Inequality in Canada.* Vancouver: UBC Press, 2006.

Hogue, Robert, and Craig Wright. *Housing Trends and Affordability.* Toronto: RBC Economics, Nov. 2013. Accessed at www.rbc.com

Homelessness: Clear Focus Needed. Victoria: Office of the Auditor General of British Columbia, March 2009.

Hunter, Justine. "Ex-Judge Seeks National Plan to Support First Nations Children." *The Globe and Mail*, June 6, 2014: S1.

Income Composition in Canada: National Household Survey, 2011. Statistics Canada, 99-014-X2011001. Accessed at www12.statcan.gc.ca on Aug. 10, 2014.

Income Inequality in Canada: An Overview. Ottawa: Standing Committee on Finance, Dec. 2013. Accessed at www.parl.gc.ca

Income Levels of BCEA Clients after They Leave Income Assistance. British Columbia: Ministry of Employment and Income Assistance, Strategic Policy and Research Branch, LAD Series, 2009.

Ipsos-Reid Corporation. *Public Experience with Financial Services and Awareness of the FCAC.* Financial Consumer Agency of Canada, March 24, 2005.

Ivanova, Iglika. *The Cost of Poverty in BC*. Vancouver: Canadian Centre for Policy Alternatives BC Office, 2011.

Jackson, Emily. "Street Homelessness Doubles in Vancouver." *Metro*, April 23, 2014. Accessed at www.metronews.ca

The Journey Begins: Together, We Can Do Better. Victoria: British Columbia Office of the Seniors Advocate, 2014.

Kelly, Russell. *Pattison: Portrait of a Capitalist Superstar*. Vancouver: New Star Books, 1986.

Kitching, Andrew, and Sheena Starky. *Payday Loan Companies in Canada: Determining the Public Interest*. Library of Parliament of Canada, Jan. 26, 2006. Accessed at www.parl.gc.ca

Klein, Seth, Jane Pulkingham, Sylvia Parusel, Kathryn Plancke, Jewelles Smith, Dixon Sookraj, Thi Vu, Bruce Wallace and Jane Worton. *Living on Welfare in BC: Experiences of Longer-Term 'Expected to Work' Recipients*. Vancouver: Canadian Centre for Policy Alternatives BC Office, 2008.

Law, Michael R., Lucy Cheng, Irfan A. Dhalla, Deborah Heard and Steven G. Morgan. "The Effect of Cost on Adherence to Prescription Medications in Canada." *Canadian Medical Association Journal*, 184.3 (2012): 297–302.

Lee, Marc, Iglika Ivanova and Seth Klein. *BC's Regressive Tax Shift: A Decade of Diminishing Tax Fairness, 2000 to 2010*. Vancouver: Canadian Centre for Policy Alternatives BC Office, 2011.

MacLeod, Andrew. *Super Unequal BC*. Series in *The Tyee*, Jan. 27, 2014 to Feb. 6, 2014. Accessed at www.thetyee.ca

———. *Welfare's New Era in BC*. Series in *The Tyee*, July 9, 2004 to July 14, 2004. Accessed at www.thetyee.ca

McKenna, Barrie. "Driverless Cars on a Jobless Road? The Downside of a Robotic Future." *The Globe and Mail*, Aug. 6, 2014: B1.

McMartin, Pete. "Vancouver—Lotus Land or Lowest Land?" *Vancouver Sun*, Oct. 1, 2014. Accessed at www.vancouversun.com

McMartin, Will. "Taylor Hired by Bank after Killing BC's Bank Tax." *The Tyee*, Sept. 14, 2009. Accessed at www.thetyee.ca

McQuaig, Linda, and Neil Brooks. *The Trouble with Billionaires: How the Super-Rich Hijacked the World and How We Can Take It Back.* Toronto: Viking Canada, 2010.

Milligan, Kevin. "Policy Forum: The Tax-Free Savings Account—Introduction and Simulations of Potential Revenue Costs." *Canadian Tax Journal/Revue Fiscale Canadienne,* 60:2 (2012): 355–60.

Montani, Adrienne, and John Millar. "Adrienne Montani and Dr. John Millar: How Long Must Poor Kids in B.C. Wait for Government to Act?" *Province,* Nov. 26, 2013. Accessed at blogs.theprovince.com

OECD. *Divided We Stand: Why Inequality Keeps Rising.* OECD Publishing, 2011.

———. "Families are Changing." *Doing Better for Families,* Chapter 1. OECD, 2011. 17–53.

Oppal, Wally. *Forsaken: The Report of the Missing Women Commission of Inquiry.* Victoria: Missing Women Commission of Inquiry, 2012.

Osberg, Lars. "Can More Education Solve Canada's Income Inequality Problem?" *Broadbent Blog,* Sept. 18, 2014. Accessed at www.broadbentinstitute.ca

Overdue: The Case for Increasing the Persons With Disabilities Benefit in BC. Disability Without Poverty Network, July 2012. Accessed at www.cmha.bc.ca

Patterson, Michelle, Julian Somers, Karen McIntosh, Alan Shiell and Charles James Frankish. *Housing and Support for Adults with Severe Addictions and/or Mental Illness in British Columbia.* Vancouver: Simon Fraser University, Faculty of Health Sciences, Centre For Applied Research in Mental Health and Addiction, 2007.

Pattison, Jimmy, and Paul Grescoe. *Jimmy: An Autobiography.* Toronto: Seal Books of McClelland-Bantam Inc., 1987.

Piketty, Thomas. *Capital in the Twenty-First Century.* Trans. Arthur Goldhammer. Cambridge, MA: The Belknap Press of Harvard University Press, 2014. Kindle edition.

Pitts, Gordon. "Lunch with the Irreplaceable Canadian Billionaire Jimmy Pattison." *The Globe and Mail,* Jan. 18, 2013. Accessed at www.theglobeandmail.com

Prentiss, Anna, Thomas Foor, Guy Cross, Lucille Harris and Michael Wanzenried. "The Cultural Evolution of Material Wealth-Based Inequality at Bridge River, British Columbia." *American Antiquity*, 77.3 (2012): 542–64.

Pringle, Heather. "The Ancient Roots of the 1%." *Science*, 344.6186 (2014): 22–24.

Reich, Robert B. *Beyond Outrage: What Has Gone Wrong With Our Economy and Our Democracy, and How to Fix It.* New York: Vintage Books, 2012.

———. *Aftershock: The Next Economy and America's Future.* New York: Alfred A. Knopf, 2010.

Report of the Royal Commission on Aboriginal Peoples. Ottawa: Royal Commission on Aboriginal Peoples, 1996.

Schrier, Dan. "Mind the Gap: Income Inequality Growing." *Infoline Report*, 12.04 BC Stats, Jan. 27, 2012.

Shaw, Chris. *Five Ring Circus: Myths and Realities of the Olympic Games.* Gabriola Island, BC: New Society Publishers, 2008.

Smith, Charlie. "Robert Reich Predicts Obama Will Unilaterally Lift Debt Ceiling Rather Than Allow a U.S. Default." *Georgia Straight*, Oct. 4, 2013. Accessed at www.straight.com

Stiglitz, Joseph E. *The Price of Inequality: How Today's Divided Society Endangers Our Future.* New York: W.W. Norton & Co., 2012.

Stilwell, Moira. *Action Plan for Repatriating BC Medical Students Studying Abroad.* 2011. Accessed at www.socasma.com on Jan. 14, 2015.

"Study: Long-Term Trends in Unionization, 1981 to 2012." *The Daily.* Statistics Canada, Nov. 26, 2013. Accessed at www.statcan.gc.ca

"Study: The Labour Market in Canada and the United States since the Last Recession, 2007 to 2014." *The Daily.* Statistics Canada, July 30, 2014. Accessed at www.statcan.gc.ca

"Study: The Ups and Downs of Minimum Wage, 1975 to 2013." *The Daily.* Statistics Canada, July 16, 2014. Accessed at www.statcan.gc.ca

Summerville, Paul. "The Twin Virtues: Inequality of Outcome and Equality of Opportunity." *Canada's Excellent Future*. Accessed at www.excellentfuture.ca on Jan. 2, 2015.

Swift, Richard, ed. *The Great Revenue Robbery: How to Stop the Tax Cut Scam and Save Canada*. Toronto: Between the Lines, 2013.

Sylvester, Shauna, Daniel Savas and Jackie Pichette. *Charting BC's Economic Future: 100 Community Conversations Discussion Guide*. Vancouver: Simon Fraser University, 2013.

"Top 10: Richest Neighbourhoods." *Ask Men*. Accessed at www.askmen.com on July 30, 2014.

"True Progressivism: A New Form of Radical Centrist Politics Is Needed to Tackle Inequality without Hurting Economic Growth." *Economist*, Oct. 13, 2012. Accessed at www.economist.com

Wallace, Bruce, Seth Klein and Marge Reitsma-Street. *Denied Assistance: Closing the Front Door on Welfare in BC*. Vancouver: Canadian Centre for Policy Alternatives BC Office, 2006.

Weinstein, Edwin L. *The Canadian Money State of Mind Risk Survey 2014: Investor Risk, Behaviour & Beliefs*. The Brondesbury Group, 2014.

Wilkinson, Richard G., and Kate Pickett. *The Spirit Level: Why Equality Is Better for Everyone*. New York: Penguin Books, 2010.

Wilson, Daniel, and David Macdonald. *The Income Gap Between Aboriginal Peoples and the Rest of Canada*. Ottawa: Canadian Centre for Policy Alternatives, 2010.

Woo, Andrea. "Mining, Forestry Tied to Domestic Violence." *The Globe and Mail*, July 24, 2014: S1.

Yaffe, Barbara. "Vancouver Investors Engage in Risky Business." *Vancouver Sun*, Nov. 4, 2014. Accessed at www.vancouversun.com

Yalnizyan, Armine. "Who Benefits from the TFSA?" *Progressive Economics Forum*, April 8, 2011. Accessed at www.progressive-economics.ca

Yew, Madhavi Acharya-Tom. "Growing Inequality in Society a Corrosive Thing: TD Chief." *Toronto Star*, Sept. 16, 2014. Accessed at www.thestar.com

ACKNOWLEDGMENTS

THIS BOOK WOULDN'T exist without David Beers, founding editor at *The Tyee*, the online BC magazine where I've worked since 2007. He called me one day to say he had funding from Tides Canada Initiatives for me to take two or three months away from covering politics to write about inequality in British Columbia, giving me an opportunity to look at one of the defining global issues of our time, one that involves everyone on Earth, and examine how it plays out locally. David also deserves credit for having the vision to found *The Tyee* at a time when digital publications, especially serving a relatively small jurisdiction, were marginal. He's made it work while taking a solutions-oriented approach and encouraging a focus on social and environmental issues. A portion of the content of this book has been adapted from stories I originally researched and wrote for *The Tyee*.

Howard White, co-owner of Harbour Publishing, saw the *Super Unequal BC* series in *The Tyee* and was eager to see the themes expanded into a book. I'm thankful to him for making it easy for me to say yes. Thanks also to the team at Harbour, including managing editor Anna Comfort O'Keeffe, for helping make it happen.

I'm grateful to editor Cheryl Cohen for the careful attention and wise guidance that has improved the text greatly throughout. Any remaining errors or omissions are of course solely mine.

John McLeod, Carra Simpson, Bob Mackin and Pete Quily provided timely advice that I very much appreciated. Thank you as well to the many sources—too many to name everyone individually—who shared their thoughts, research and perspective with me over the years, not all of whom appear in the text. Sharon Keen though deserves to be singled out; besides telling me about her personal experience, she provided a steady stream of clippings and other research that was frequently useful. Staff at the BC Legislative Library also deserve credit for efficient and patient help with elements of the research.

Thank you for the encouragement to the lunch gang of writers Frances Backhouse, Jude Isabella, Peter Fairley and Erica Gies; supportive writing friends including Alan Cassels, Alisa Gordaneer, David Leach, Jenny Manzer, Will McMartin and Sean Holman; *Tyee* managing editor Robyn Smith, editor Jane Armstrong and the rest of the *Tyee* team; the ad hoc group of Victoria environmental reporters; and colleagues in the BC legislature press gallery. I have much gratitude to the hosts and producers at CFAX, CKNW and CBC who have given me frequent opportunities to talk publicly about this topic and others, and to the Voice of BC team, Vaughn Palmer, Kristina Verruyt and (recently retired) John Richardson.

Thanks as well to the many friends and family members who suggested and discussed ideas, and otherwise supported this endeavour, particularly Stephen Winn, Foster Griezic, Bill Eisenhauer, Gabriela Hirt, Greg Lawrance, Kari Hewett, Oren Lupo, Chip Johnston, Brett Harrison, the Darrochs, the McLeods, Patricia MacLeod, Stuart MacLeod, Nancy McCullough, Virginia MacLeod, Jeremiah Warren, Judy and Don Coxe, Marianne and John Hodges, and Nell Hodges and John Balogh.

And finally, I owe a very special thank you to Suzanne MacLeod and our daughters, who provided feedback, moral support and much-needed distraction throughout this project. Thanks for sharing the journey.

INDEX

ABOUT THE AUTHOR

ANDREW MACLEOD IS the legislative bureau chief for *The Tyee* independent online magazine (thetyee.ca). His work has been referred to in the BC legislature and the Canadian House of Commons and Senate. He won a 2006 Association of Alternative Newsweeklies award for news writing and was a finalist for a 2007 Western Magazine Award for best article in BC and the Yukon. His reporting has appeared in *Monday Magazine*, the *Georgia Straight*, *BC Business*, *24 Hours*, the *San Francisco Bay Guardian*, Detroit's *Metro Times*, Portland's *Willamette Week* and elsewhere. He lives with his family in Victoria and is learning to play the Scottish small pipes.